BARTLETT'S POEMS FOR OCCASIONS

BARTLETT'S POEMS FOR OCCASIONS

Geoffrey O'Brien, General Editor

Foreword by Billy Collins

Little, Brown and Company

NEW YORK · BOSTON · LONDON

Little, Brown and Company
Hachette Book Group
237 Park Avenue, New York, NY 10017
Visit our Web site at www.HachetteBookGroupUSA.com
.

Little, Brown and Company is a division of Hachette Book Group, Inc. The Little, Brown name and logo are trademarks of Hachette Book Group, Inc.

Copyright acknowledgments follow the index.

The editor would like to thank Deborah Baker for her encouragement on this project. A portion of the work was completed during a residency at the Bellagio Study and Conference Center of the Rockefeller Foundation.

This 2008 edition published for Barnes and Noble, Inc., by arrangement with Hachette Book Group, Inc.
ISBN 978-0-316-04234-5

10 9 8 7 6 5 4 3 2 1

HML

Design & Typography: Interrobang Design Studio

Printed in the United States of America

Contents

———— - ————

THE HUMAN CONDITION   251

Foreword

———————

ONE EVENING IN LONDON LAST
YEAR, SOMEONE HAD THE IDEA OF BRINGING TOGETHER THE VISITING
UNITED STATES POET LAUREATE — ME — AND THE CURRENT BRITISH
poet laureate, Andrew Motion. Over dinner at a small restaurant, we speculated
ignorantly as to whether this was the first ever face-to-face meeting of the two
nation's laureates. Did Rita Dove ever have a drink with Ted Hughes? we wondered. And then we decided to agree that our meeting was unprecedented, if only
to bring a bit of historical weight to the table. Though separated by a common language, we managed to talk easily about this and that, and when the subject of our
positions came up, we began to compare laureate notes. Motion, it seemed, was a
functionary of the royal household; I was an employee of the Library of Congress.
He was presented by the Queen with a cask of dry wine; I was paid an annual
stipend out of a private fund. But the difference that truly defined our roles and
most clearly revealed national character was that only the British laureate was
obliged to write poems commemorating public events, ranging from the death of
the Queen Mother, which came on the heels of Motion's appointment, to perhaps
the marriage of a disreputable viscount. The American laureate was under no such
obligation. In short, the British laureate was required to write occasional poems,
whereas the American laureate only had to write poems occasionally.

The occasional poem, that is, a poem commemorating some event of widely
recognized importance, has a deep history. From the odes of Pindar celebrating ath-
letic victories to Tennyson's ultimate laureate poem, "Ode on the Death of the Duke
of Wellington," to Miller Williams's poem on Bill Clinton's second presidential inau-
guration, poems have served as literary tributes meant to add a bit of gravitas and
possibly confer the touch of immortality to certain public occasions. Before such

modern means of recording as cameras and audio devices, occasional poems also served the real function of preserving events in the national memory by producing a lasting historical record in rhyme and meter. Poems were the videotape and the still cameras of the past. They extended the original mnemonic purpose of poetry to act as a stay against the gradual amnesiac effects of time. Today, when all manner of earthly life is being digitally captured, these poems are generally thought to have become as ceremonial as the ceremonies to which they attempt to add verbal luster.

Bartlett's Poems for Occasions is an extremely generous collection that extends the meaning of *occasion* beyond the publicly significant to include personal occasions, the vast spectrum of large and small circumstances that make up human life. The immensity of the range of occasions is apparent from just a glimpse at the table of contents, which shows that poetry has a way of getting into every corner of experience. The book uses as its organizational principles the habitual ways we tend to organize life. Poems connected to the natural cycle of the seasons are followed by ones marking the social calendar we fit over the seasonal one featuring such mythic and historic dates as Halloween, Independence Day, and the birth of Christ. Then we are carried, poem by poem, through the cycle of human life, from cradle to coffin, from Blake's "Infant Joy" to Chidiock Tichborne's "Elegy for Himself," with stops along the way to hear the songs of exuberant youth, emergent adulthood, sober midlife, retirement, and often complaining old age. We then are given a tour of the mansion of human experience including the rooms of friendship, love, work, disappointment, contentment (a shortish section), sorrow (noticeably longer), valediction, separation, bravery, and epiphany. Poems touching on the ultimate topics of God and immortality exist side by side with occasional poems in the traditional sense, those provoked by national events, particularly war. Here, a dissonant chorus of voices both idealizes and condemns such conflicts.

The notion of occasional poetry can be extended further insofar as every moment of perception is in itself an occasion. Since the English Romantics, poetry has been seen as a means of preserving discrete glimpses into the world around us, refined ways of seeing. Some poems simply want to rescue a single moment from the burning building of time. Here is A. R. Ammons's "Winter Scene":

> There is now not a single
> leaf on the cherry tree:

except when the jay
plummets in, lights, and,

in pure clarity, squalls:
then every branch

quivers and
breaks out in blue leaves.

This impressionist vision of sound turning into sight, noise into color, is a true occasion, a private one which suddenly radiates outward to include all readers. Or take the chill conveyed by this untitled little poem by Buson:

What piercing cold I feel:
      my dead wife's comb, in our bedroom,
         under my heel . . .

How could any formal elegy on, say, the Duke of Bedford, do more to convey the shock of grief than these three modest lines? Besides recording private epiphanies, every poem can be said to commemorate the occasion of its being written, the singular event of its composition. Every poem is finally its own birth announcement.

It is typical for people — especially people who are not habitual readers of poetry — to turn to verse in times of stress and uncertainty. The aftermath of 9/11 witnessed a sudden surge of interest in poetry, a search for words that could provide stability and consolation. Oddly, the poem that emerged as the popular favorite was Auden's "September 1, 1939," a poem written in a New York bar by a man who had just fled the impending war in Europe. In their haste to make the poem relevant, readers italicized certain lines (". . . the lie of Authority / Whose buildings grope the sky") and largely ignored the poem's final salute to irony: "Ironic points of light / Flash out wherever the Just / Exchange their messages." But the general call for poems revealed an ancient dependence on formalized language as a way of bracing ourselves in wobbly times.

Engagements, anniversaries, birthdays, commencements, inaugurations, and especially weddings and funerals are often in need of a poem that will add stability to the occasion and connect it to a tradition of similar events. After all, poetry is the deepest history of human emotion that we have, and its formal arrangements — particularly its patterns of rhyme and meter — have the power to embody and ritualize feeling. The right poem can bring the balm of structure to the griefstricken and provide the joyous with a pattern of choric dance. I might add that a truly fitting wedding poem is not an easy thing to find, even in a recently published anthology devoted to wedding poems. It is no accident that in Bartlett's, as in life, marriage poems are greatly outnumbered by love poems — here by a margin of nearly 5 to 1.

This capacious anthology has an obvious social usefulness. Just as one might thumb through the more familiar *Bartlett's Familiar Quotations* in search of relevant bon mots to spice up an address or add wit to a speech, so, too, one may look here for a poem whose recitation might enhance and possibly dignify any number of public gatherings. But because the range of poems gathered here is so broad, extending well beyond the conventional definition of occasional poetry, readers can also browse within for poems to suit any mood, time of year, or predicament — poems to augment personal moments, to pluck them from the rush of time. Plus, poems are always offering the reader the opportunity to memorize them and, therefore, take advantage of poetry's ultimate portability. "I never heard anyone humming a building," Sammy Cahn once snapped in defense of his decision to be a lyricist and not an architect. Nor can you memorize a statue or recite a painting. But a poem you can easily carry with you in one of the inside pockets of memory, and you can pull it out anytime at all, even if the occasion is nothing more than a rainy day, and a sunny one will do just as well.

Introduction

***

THIS IS A BOOK OF POEMS AR-
RANGED IN RELATION TO THE CIRCUMSTANCES AND SEASONS OF HUMAN
LIFE. I HAVE DIVIDED THE POEMS INTO FIVE PARTS. THE FIRST PART,
"The Cycles of Nature," has a selection of poems arranged by season. The poems
in the second part, "The Round of the Year," are ones that celebrate the rituals of
seasonal holidays, including New Year's, Mother's and Father's Days, the Fourth of
July, and Thanksgiving. The third part, "The Cycles of Life," includes poems tracing our earliest explorations of infancy, the pleasures and anxieties of youth, the
challenge of entering adulthood, the peaks of marriage and midlife, the approach
of retirement, aging, and death. The fourth part, "The Human Condition," maps
our social and emotional lives: the torments and fulfillments of love; friendship
and contentment; the working life; farewells; sufferings shared or undergone in
solitude; and endurance. Finally, the last part, "Public Moments and Ultimate
Matters," includes poems that address our public lives in the wider arena of history, the cataclysms of war, and the death of kings and confront life's ultimate
questions. In all five sections I cast a wide net, considering poems from over a
dozen different languages and historical epochs dating from ancient Egypt to the
present day to find those that might serve as companion, guide, or source of
knowledge about human ways of coping with the unforeseeable, inescapable, and
immeasurable vicissitudes of existence. Much of this work can be considered as
part of a deep and ancient wisdom literature, to be shared with others to commemorate a special occasion, or to mark that same occasion privately, in quiet self-
reflection. But I have made room as well for poems that have been so often recited
or memorized that they have in effect become part of the language. The surprise of
meeting up with a phrase such as "into each life some rain must fall" in Henry

Wadsworth Longfellow's "The Rainy Day" or "all that Heav'n allows" in the earl of Rochester's "All my past life is mine no more" is not so minor a pleasure as it might seem. The most overfamiliar of poems can spring unexpectedly into new life, not only for their own merits but for the freight of feeling that so many earlier readers have in a sense imparted to them. On the other hand, I have allowed ample space to the less familiar — to poets both recent and ancient whose names are not so frequently mentioned, to translations that can only begin to represent the scope of such treasuries as the Sanskrit or the Japanese traditions, to lesser-known poems by well-known poets (such as Rudyard Kipling's indelible protest "To a Dead Statesman") that turned out to be perfectly apt for one or another of the book's occasions.

Does a book of poems for occasions require a user's manual? To apply a poem to your own life is in itself a creative act. The categories into which this book is divided are intended to suggest directions, coordinates, possible routes. They can only hint at the occasions when a reader might turn to them, occasions that seem to call for words beyond what we can ourselves easily articulate: a family gathering at Thanksgiving (the Iroquois prayer "The Thanksgivings"), the birth of a baby (Walter De La Mare's "The Birthnight"), a graduation (Langston Hughes's "Dreams"), a funeral (Alfred, Lord Tennyson's "Crossing the Bar"), a wedding ceremony (William Shakespeare's sonnet "Let me not to the marriage of true minds"). A poem of winter might, recited under different circumstances, evoke a festive mood, or a grief-struck one. The poems grouped here under the rubric "Retirement from Work and from the World" are hardly limited to readers of retirement age (any hard-pressed student might find equal solace in Andrew Marvell's garden). The poems gathered under the heading "Separations and Farewells" encompass a range of moods as varied as there are kinds of separations; Michael Drayton's famous "Since there's no help, come let us kiss and part" — almost the archetype of breakup poems — does end, after all, on a note of lingering hope for reconciliation.

It may take an imaginative leap to recognize a treasured friend in a poem about a veteran of the Roman imperial army (by Horace) or a courtier of ancient China (by Ezra Pound). The pleasures of a midwinter dinner party might be marked by the late medieval trappings of Thomas Campion's "Now winter nights enlarge." A great passion might be shared with John Donne in a world where, only recently, "sea-discoverers to new worlds have gone." The faith of poetry is that inner truths, the hard-won structures of thought and feeling, prevail over the accidentals of time and circumstance.

Readers of poetry perform a similar operation. No two people will find the same things in the same poems, or for the same reasons. The categories here are rough signposts, but it is for the reader to decide when it is an appropriate moment to go to a particular place. The spring poem contemplated in the depths of winter, the poem of war read in time of provisional peace, the evocation of departed grandparents juxtaposed with the immediacy of childbirth, the meditation on loss read amid seeming plenitude — these are the readings that can provoke and disarm, pitting the reality of the poem against the reality of the reader's state of being. Similarly, this book's categories are not separate enclosures but interconnected rooms, with their fair share of secret passageways and unexpected panoramic views of the surrounding hills.

This approach to anthologizing poetry might seem quaintly old-fashioned, a throwback to those thematically arranged multivolume treasuries assembled by American fireside poets of the nineteenth century such as Henry Wadsworth Longfellow and William Cullen Bryant. Alongside the Bible and Shakespeare, these were copious collections designed to form part of the standard household library. For Longfellow and Bryant it went without saying that poems could appropriately be grouped according to the moods and occasions for which they were best suited.

This was not a sentimental fancy but a thoroughly pragmatic recognition of the proven *utility* of poetry as instructor, entertainer, healing agent, aid to meditation, and liberator of the imagination. Even Francis Palgrave's *The Golden Treasury* — the most widely disseminated of Victorian poetry anthologies, and still one of the best of any era — avoided a strictly chronological arrangement. An arrangement purely by chronology would have, in Palgrave's words, "rather fit a collection aiming at instruction than at pleasure, and the wisdom which comes through pleasure"; he preferred to group its poems according to "gradations of feeling or subject."

As Palgrave noted, a chronological arrangement is more obviously suited to the serious student. But only in more recent times — in America, since the mid-twentieth century — has the assumption taken hold that poetry is something to be relegated to the classroom. In any case, historically minded anthologies exist, in profusion, enabling anyone who likes to examine in close detail the precise moment, for instance, when early English Drab of Edward Dyer or George Gascoigne gives way to the Italianate flourishes of the Tudor Renaissance in the work of Sir Philip Sidney or Edmund Spenser. For earlier readers, poetry had a private, domestic aspect; poems were sung or recited in intimate circumstances and carried with them a reminder of emotions and associations that might otherwise be lost to memory. The power of such associations became all the greater when the poem was committed to memory, thereby becoming in some sense part of the body of the reader, to be evoked at will whenever needed.

In classrooms poems become objects to be dissected according to whatever rules of analysis prevail at a given moment. In our own day, when the emphasis of academic study tends to be historical and ideological, the danger is that a given poem can end up figuring as a mere illustration of larger tendencies, a "for instance" to be slotted into a grid of social circumstance.

This is not to deny the potential value of such analysis. It is naive or simplistic to take refuge in the notion of aesthetic timelessness. No poem can be read eternally in precisely the way the poet intended. Poetry is one kind of map and history another; to bring them together (as we do, however inadequately, anytime we read) is to be continually startled out of complacency by unanticipated disconnects and equally unanticipated connections. When we read a Shakespeare sonnet or a Robert Burns ballad we measure simultaneously our closeness to and our distance from the moment in which they wrote, not unlike the experience of looking at an old photograph of a long-dead relative.

The present volume has another goal. By bringing together very different poems, from very different times and places, that address themselves to aspects of human life, it tries to uncover likenesses and correspondences to the times we live in. In the reign of James I, Ben Jonson invited a friend to supper while assuring him that there would be no government spies among the guests to eavesdrop on their conversation. During the draft riots of 1863 Herman Melville contemplated the breakdown of law and order from a rooftop in lower Manhattan and wondered about the future of democracy if it could be protected only by martial force. On the eve of World War I, Thomas Hardy imagined the dead of England woken by artillery barrages fired in preparation for war. Any of these poems might be read with resonance today. And then there are the more intimate correspondences. For an ancient Egyptian poet passion is evoked by water mixed with flour, for a seventeenth-century poet as fire encountering flax. The love consummated by an anonymous medieval writer "under the greenwood tree" is celebrated by Edith Wharton in the early twentieth century in imagery of a railroad station where trains are forever arriving and departing.

Percy Bysshe Shelley — quoted approvingly by Palgrave — thought of the individual poems of different poets as "episodes to that great Poem which all poets, like the cooperating thoughts of one great mind, have built up since the beginning of the world." This grand Romantic notion actually comes rather close to describing the effect of any anthology, if it is read straight through as if it were the work of a single author.

Connections among poems are to some extent familial. They speak not only to us but among themselves, agreeing or arguing, bring up new instances to confirm or contradict an elder's formulation, sending messages calm or agitated to those already gone or yet to come. When William Blake wrote that "the poets are in eternity" he was not, I think, alluding to the immortality bestowed by fame. All poems in some sense are written in the same instant. To read them is to enter an unending moment, the distended moment of their conception and composition.

Most poets, like other artists, make an effort to be original. In a culture addicted to novelty, it seems almost a confession of failure not to offer a product that isn't thoroughly up to the minute, "branded" by a new design concept, a new message, new subject matter. But the fashions of poetry are measured in millennia, not months. The modern English poet Basil Bunting wrote, "Poets are well advised to stick to commonplaces," and added only half ironically, "which is what most of them do." In Bunting's view, poets, even the greatest of them, rarely had anything truly unprecedented to add to the store of human thought and knowledge; their role was rather to seek new ways to conceptualize and express what amounted to the Same Old Thing. A few thousand years earlier, the biblical voice of the Ecclesiast affirmed something similar: "There is no new thing under the sun."

Similar sentiments have been expressed in most times, in most places. Yet human experience stubbornly resists the notion that it can be reduced to a repetition of what has been already done and already said. The unfolding moment promises a singularity, a uniqueness of fate, an emerging possibility of something altogether untried. That possibility may, as in the budding of friendship or passionate desire, be of a splendid fulfillment; it may equally be of personal disaster, or, in the face of global chaos and environmental degradation, of a catastrophe apocalyptic in scale. In any event the individual is inclined to wonder if anyone could conceivably have witnessed or undergone such things before.

In the collision between a past containing all that was ever thought or spoken and a future not yet imaginable, the poem finds its uneasy birth, looking for a new way to use a language that comes heavy with accumulated associations. The poem just born takes its place among the poems already emerged, each registering the shock of a particular moment. If poetry, in Ezra Pound's definition, is "news that stays news," then there is no time limit on its power to illuminate or inform. What the best poems offer is pertinent information about the fact of being alive. They respond to situations that, however remote in space or time, are in some form always going on. The sun that rises to interrupt the lovers in John Donne's poem is rising right now; the twig broken off by Walt Whitman in Louisiana snaps in our own hand; the slant of winter light to which, in Emily Dickinson's paradoxical description, "the Landscape listens" lights up the page where we read of it. The poets are in eternity; the poems are here, in the air, in the room, in the world.

Any poem exists not at one point in time but at an infinite number of points, as many as there are readers and occasions to read it, and as many times as a single reader will return to a particular poem, always finding the experience a little bit different each time. Within the singular and finite terms of a human life the poem makes possible a manifold perspective where voices are enabled to converse together. This is a conversation that takes place within the reader, and it is in the act of reading poetry as much as in the act of writing it that the form finds its most perfect fulfillment. It is our hope, in fact, in the interests of expanding that conversation, that readers of this volume will write to the publisher with suggestions for future editions.

BARTLETT'S POEMS FOR OCCASIONS

The Cycles of Nature

THIS ANTHOLOGY BEGINS, LITER-
ALLY ENOUGH, WITH THE FOUR SEASONS THEMSELVES. IN WEATHER, AS
IN HABITAT, POETS FIND A MIRROR OF THEIR OWN BEING IN THE VERY
otherness of what is outside them, and in cyclical seasonal alteration they have
often found a model of poetic form itself. It is a model based on metamorphosis,
of forms changing into their opposites and then changing back, in a fixed order
and rhythm that is the world's meter: what is most fixed is a process of continuous
change. The evocation of season may be literal or may have the deepest metaphorical intentions; but in this area, the literal and the metaphorical have a way of coin-
ciding. The seasons are both the symbols and the very substance of our lives.

SPRING

Loveless hearts shall love tomorrow, hearts that have loved shall love anew

From *The Vigil of Venus (Pervigilium Veneris)*

> Loveless hearts shall love tomorrow, hearts that have loved
> shall love anew,
> > Spring is young now, spring is singing, in the spring
> > the world first grew;
> > In the spring the birds are wedded, in the springtime
> > true hearts pair,
> > Under the rain of her lover's kisses loose the forest
> > flings her hair.
> > Now in shadows of the woodland She that binds all
> > true loves' vows,
> > She shall build them bowers tomorrow of Her own green
> > myrtle-boughs.
> > There Dione high enthronèd on her lovers lays
> > her law —
> Loveless hearts shall love tomorrow, hearts that have loved
> shall love once more.

ANONYMOUS
LATIN (3RD CENTURY)
TRANSLATED BY F. L. LUCAS

Spring, the sweet spring, is the year's pleasant king

> Spring, the sweet spring, is the year's pleasant king;
> Then blooms each thing, then maids dance in a ring,
> Cold doth not sting, the pretty birds do sing:
> > Cuckoo, jug-jug, pu-we, to-witta-woo!
>
> The palm and may make country houses gay,
> Lambs frisk and play, the shepherds pipe all day,

And we hear aye birds tune this merry lay:
    Cuckoo, jug-jug, pu-we, to-witta-woo!

The fields breathe sweet, the daisies kiss our feet,
Young lovers meet, old wives a-sunning sit;
In every street these tunes our ears do greet:
    Cuckoo, jug-jug, pu-we, to-witta-woo!
     Spring, the sweet spring!

THOMAS NASHE
ENGLISH (1567–1601?)

When daisies pied, and violets blue

When daisies pied, and violets blue,
  And lady-smocks all silver-white,
And cuckoo-buds of yellow hue
  Do paint the meadows with delight,
The cuckoo then, on every tree,
Mocks married men, for thus sings he,
    Cuckoo, cuckoo!
   O word of fear,

Unpleasing to a married ear!
When shepherds pipe on oaten straws,
  And merry larks are ploughmen's clocks,
When turtles tread, and rooks, and daws,
  And maidens bleach their summer smocks,
The cuckoo then, on every tree,
Mocks married men, for thus sings he,
    Cuckoo, cuckoo!
   O word of fear,
Unpleasing to a married ear!

WILLIAM SHAKESPEARE
ENGLISH (1564–1616)

Get up, get up for shame! the blooming morn
Upon her wings presents the god unshorn.
    See how Aurora throws her fair
      Fresh-quilted colours through the air:
    Get up, sweet slug-a-bed, and see
    The dew-bespangling herb and tree.
Each flower has wept, and bowed toward the east,
Above an hour since; yet you not drest,
    Nay! not so much as out of bed?
    When all the birds have matins said,
    And sung their thankful hymns; 'tis sin,
    Nay, profanation to keep in,
Whenas a thousand virgins on this day
Spring sooner than the lark to fetch in May.

Rise and put on your foliage, and be seen
To come forth, like the spring-time, fresh and green,
    And sweet as Flora. Take no care
    For jewels for your gown or hair:
    Fear not; the leaves will strew
    Gems in abundance upon you:
Besides, the childhood of the day has kept,
Against you come, some orient pearls unwept.
    Come, and receive them while the light
    Hangs on the dew-locks of the night:
    And Titan on the eastern hill
    Retires himself, or else stands still
Till you come forth. Wash, dress, be brief in praying:
Few beads are best when once we go a-Maying.

Come, my Corinna, come; and coming, mark
How each field turns a street, each street a park
    Made green and trimmed with trees: see how
    Devotion gives each house a bough
    Or branch; each porch, each door, ere this,
    An ark, a tabernacle is,
Made up of white-thorn neatly interwove,

As if here were those cooler shades of love.
　　Can such delights be in the street
　　And open fields, and we not see't?
　　Come, we'll abroad: and let's obey
　　The proclamation made for May,
And sin no more, as we have done, by staying;
But, my Corinna, come, let's go a-Maying.

There's not a budding boy or girl this day
But is got up and gone to bring in May.
　　A deal of youth ere this is come
　　Back, and with white-thorn laden home.
　　Some have dispatched their cakes and cream,
　　Before that we have left to dream:
And some have wept and wooed, and plighted troth,
And chose their priest, ere we can cast off sloth:
　　Many a green-gown has been given;
　　Many a kiss, both odd and even;
　　Many a glance too has been sent
　　From out the eye, love's firmament:
Many a jest told of the keys betraying
This night, and locks picked: yet we're not a-Maying!

Come, let us go, while we are in our prime,
And take the harmless folly of the time!
　　We shall grow old apace, and die
　　Before we know our liberty.
　　Our life is short, and our days run
　　As fast away as does the sun.
And as a vapour or a drop of rain,
Once lost, can ne'er be found again:
　　So when or you or I are made
　　A fable, song, or fleeting shade,
　　All love, all liking, all delight
　　Lies drowned with us in endless night.
Then, while time serves, and we are but decaying,
Come, my Corinna, come, let's go a-Maying.

ROBERT HERRICK
ENGLISH (1591–1674)

To Daffodils

Fair daffodils, we weep to see
   You haste away so soon:
As yet the early-rising sun
   Has not attained his noon.
     Stay, stay,
    Until the hasting day
      Has run
   But to the evensong;
And, having prayed together, we
   Will go with you along.

We have short time to stay, as you,
   We have as short a spring;
As quick a growth to meet decay,
   As you, or anything.
     We die,
   As your hours do, and dry
      Away,
   Like to the summer's rain;
Or as the pearls of morning's dew
   Ne'er to be found again.

ROBERT HERRICK
ENGLISH (1591–1674)

The Spring

Now that the Winter's gone, the earth hath lost
Her snow-white robes; and now no more the frost
Candies the grass, or casts an icy cream
Upon the silver lake or crystal stream:
But the warm sun thaws the benumbed earth,
And makes it tender; gives a sacred birth
To the dead swallow; wakes in hollow tree
The drowsy cuckoo and the humble-bee.
Now do a choir of chirping minstrels bring
In triumph to the world the youthful Spring:
The valleys, hills, and woods in rich array

Welcome the coming of the long'd-for May.
Now all things smile: only my love doth lour,
Nor hath the scalding noonday sun the power
To melt that marble ice which still doth hold
Her heart congeal'd, and makes her pity cold.
The ox, which lately did for shelter fly
Into the stall, doth now securely lie
In open fields; and love no more is made
By the fireside, but in the cooler shade
Amyntas now doth with his Chloris sleep
Under a sycamore, and all things keep
    Time with the season: only she doth carry
    June in her eyes, in her heart January.

THOMAS CAREW
ENGLISH (1595?–1639?)

To Spring

O thou with dewy locks, who lookest down
Thro' the clear windows of the morning, turn
Thine angel eyes upon our western isle,
Which in full choir hails thy approach, O Spring!

The hills tell each other, and the list'ning
Vallies hear; all our longing eyes are turned
Up to thy bright pavillions: issue forth,
And let thy holy feet visit our clime.

Come o'er the eastern hills, and let our winds
Kiss thy perfumèd garments; let us taste
Thy morn and evening breath; scatter thy pearls
Upon our love-sick land that mourns for thee.

O deck her forth with thy fair fingers; pour
Thy soft kisses on her bosom; and put
Thy golden crown upon her languish'd head,
Whose modest tresses were bound up for thee!

WILLIAM BLAKE
ENGLISH (1757–1827)

Lines Written in Early Spring

I heard a thousand blended notes,
While in a grove I sate reclined,
In that sweet mood when pleasant thoughts
Bring sad thoughts to the mind.

To her fair works did Nature link
The human soul that through me ran;
And much it grieved my heart to think
What man has made of man.

Through primrose tufts, in that green bower,
The periwinkle trailed its wreaths;
And 'tis my faith that every flower
Enjoys the air it breathes.

The birds around me hopped and played,
Their thoughts I cannot measure: —
But the least motion which they made,
It seemed a thrill of pleasure.

The budding twigs spread out their fan,
To catch the breezy air;
And I must think, do all I can,
That there was pleasure there.

If this belief from heaven be sent,
If such be Nature's holy plan,
Have I not reason to lament
What man has made of man?

WILLIAM WORDSWORTH
ENGLISH (1770–1850)

Home-Thoughts, from Abroad

Oh, to be in England
Now that April's there,
And whoever wakes in England
Sees, some morning, unaware,
That the lowest boughs and the brushwood sheaf
Round the elm-tree bole are in tiny leaf,
While the chaffinch sings on the orchard bough
In England — now!

And after April, when May follows,
And the whitethroat builds, and all the swallows!
Hark, where my blossomed pear-tree in the hedge
Leans to the field and scatters on the clover
Blossoms and dewdrops — at the bent spray's edge —
That's the wise thrush; he sings each song twice over,
Lest you should think he never could recapture
The first fine careless rapture!
And though the fields look rough with hoary dew,
All will be gay when noontide wakes anew
The buttercups, the little children's dower
— Far brighter than this gaudy melon-flower!

ROBERT BROWNING
ENGLISH (1812–1889)

When the hounds of spring are on winter's traces

Chorus from *Atalanta in Calydon*

When the hounds of spring are on winter's traces,
The mother of months in meadow or plain
Fills the shadows and windy places
With lisp of leaves and ripple of rain;
And the brown bright nightingale amorous
Is half assuaged for Itylus,
For the Thracian ships and the foreign faces,
The tongueless vigil, and all the pain.

Come with bows bent and with emptying of quivers,
Maiden most perfect, lady of light,

With a noise of winds and many rivers,
   With a clamour of waters, and with might;
Bind on thy sandals, O thou most fleet,
Over the splendour and speed of thy feet;
For the faint east quickens, the wan west shivers,
   Round the feet of the day and the feet of the night.

Where shall we find her, how shall we sing to her,
   Fold our hands round her knees, and cling?
O that man's heart were as fire and could spring to her,
   Fire, or the strength of the streams that spring!
For the stars and the winds are unto her
As raiment, as songs of the harp-player;
For the risen stars and the fallen cling to her,
   And the southwest-wind and the west-wind sing.

For winter's rains and ruins are over,
   And all the season of snows and sins;
The days dividing lover and lover,
   The light that loses, the night that wins;
And time remembered is grief forgotten,
And frosts are slain and flowers begotten,
And in green underwood and cover
   Blossom by blossom the spring begins.

The full streams feed on flower of rushes,
   Ripe grasses trammel a travelling foot,
The faint fresh flame of the young year flushes
   From leaf to flower and flower to fruit;
And fruit and leaf are as gold and fire,
And the oat is heard above the lyre,
And the hoofèd heel of a satyr crushes
   The chestnut-husk at the chestnut-root.

And Pan by noon and Bacchus by night,
   Fleeter of foot than the fleet-foot kid,
Follows with dancing and fills with delight
   The Mænad and the Bassarid;
And soft as lips that laugh and hide

The laughing leaves of the trees divide,
And screen from seeing and leave in sight
    The god pursuing, the maiden hid.

The ivy falls with the Bacchanal's hair
    Over her eyebrows hiding her eyes;
The wild vine slipping down leaves bare
    Her bright breast shortening into sighs;
The wild vine slips with the weight of its leaves,
But the berried ivy catches and cleaves
To the limbs that glitter, the feet that scare
    The wolf that follows, the fawn that flies.

ALGERNON CHARLES SWINBURNE
ENGLISH (1837–1909)

Spring

Nothing is so beautiful as Spring —
    When weeds, in wheels, shoot long and lovely and lush;
    Thrush's eggs look little low heavens, and thrush
Through the echoing timber does so rinse and wring
The ear, it strikes like lightnings to hear him sing;
    The glassy peartree leaves and blooms, they brush
    The descending blue; that blue is all in a rush
With richness; the racing lambs too have fair their fling.

What is all this juice and all this joy?
    A strain of the earth's sweet being in the beginning
In Eden garden. — Have, get, before it cloy,

Before it cloud, Christ, lord, and sour with sinning,
Innocent mind and Mayday in girl and boy,
    Most, O maid's child, thy choice and worthy the winning.

GERARD MANLEY HOPKINS
ENGLISH (1844–1889)

Spring Pools

These pools that, though in forests, still reflect
The total sky almost without defect,
And like the flowers beside them, chill and shiver,
Will like the flowers beside them soon be gone,
And yet not out by any brook or river,
But up by roots to bring dark foliage on.

The trees that have it in their pent-up buds
To darken nature and be summer woods —
Let them think twice before they use their powers
To blot out and drink up and sweep away
These flowery waters and these watery flowers
From snow that melted only yesterday.

ROBERT FROST
AMERICAN (1874–1963)

Spring

To what purpose, April, do you return again?
Beauty is not enough.
You can no longer quiet me with the redness
Of little leaves opening stickily.
I know what I know.
The sun is hot on my neck as I observe
The spikes of the crocus.
The smell of the earth is good.
It is apparent that there is no death.
But what does that signify?
Not only under ground are the brains of men
Eaten by maggots.
Life in itself
Is nothing,
An empty cup, a flight of uncarpeted stairs.
It is not enough that yearly, down this hill,
April
Comes like an idiot, babbling and strewing flowers.

EDNA ST. VINCENT MILLAY
AMERICAN (1892–1950)

O sweet spontaneous

O sweet spontaneous
earth how often have
the
doting

     fingers of
prurient philosophers pinched
and
poked

thee
,has the naughty thumb
of science prodded
thy

    beauty   . how
often have religions taken
thee upon their scraggy knees
squeezing and

buffeting thee that thou mightest conceive
gods
     (but
true

to the incomparable
couch of death thy
rhythmic
lover

    thou answerest

them only with

        spring)

E. E. CUMMINGS
AMERICAN (1894–1962)

The White Fury of the Spring

Oh, now, now the white fury of the spring
Whirls at each door, and on each flowering plot —
The pear, the cherry, the grave apricot!
The lane's held in a storm, and is a thing
To take into a grave, a lantern-light
To fasten there, by which to stumble out,
And race in the new grass, and hear about
The crash of bough with bough, of white with white.
Were I to run, I could not run so fast,
But that the spring would overtake me still;
Halfway I go to meet it on the stair.
For certainly it will rush in at last,
And in my own house seize me at its will,
And drag me out to the white fury there.

LIZETTE WOODWORTH REESE
AMERICAN (1856–1935)

SUMMER

Summer is y-comen in

Summer is y-comen in,
Loud sing cuckoo!
Groweth seed and bloweth meed
And springeth the wood now —
Sing cuckoo!
Ewe bleateth after lamb,
Loweth after calf cow;
Bullock starteth, buck farteth.
Merry sing cuckoo!
Cuckoo! Cuckoo!
Well singest thou cuckoo:
Nor cease thou never now.
Sing cuckoo, now, sing cuckoo!
Sing cuckoo! sing cuckoo, now!

ANONYMOUS
ENGLISH (13TH CENTURY)

Now welcome, somer, with thy sonne softe

Now welcome, somer, with thy sonne softe,
That hast thise wintres wedres overshake,
And driven away the large nightes blake.

Saint Valentin, that art ful heigh on lofte,
Thus singen smale fowles for thy sake:
Now welcome, somer, with thy sonne softe.

Wel han they cause forto gladen ofte,
Sith eech of hem recovered hath his make;
Ful blisful mowe they singe whan they wake:
Now welcome, somer, with thy sonne softe.

GEOFFREY CHAUCER
ENGLISH (C. 1342–1400)

Why are our summer sports so brittle?

Why are our summer sports so brittle?
The leaves already fall,
The meads are drownèd all;
Alas, that summer lasts so little.
No pleasure could be tasted
If flowery summer always lasted.

ANONYMOUS
ENGLISH (MEDIEVAL)

Summer Moods

I love at eventide to walk alone
Down narrow lanes o'erhung with dewy thorn
Where from the long grass underneath the snail
Jet black creeps out and sprouts his timid horn.
I love to muse o'er meadows newly mown
Where withering grass perfumes the sultry air
Where bees search round with sad and weary drone
In vain for flowers that bloomed but newly there,

While in the juicy corn the hidden quail
Cries "wet my foot" and hid as thoughts unborn
The fairy-like and seldom-seen land rail
Utters "craik craik" like voices underground
Right glad to meet the evening's dewy veil
And see the light fade into glooms around.

JOHN CLARE
ENGLISH (1793–1864)

Summer Wind

It is a sultry day; the sun has drunk
The dew that lay upon the morning grass;
There is no rustling in the lofty elm
That canopies my dwelling, and its shade
Scarce cools me. All is silent, save the faint
And interrupted murmur of the bee,
Settling on the sick flowers, and then again
Instantly on the wing. The plants around
Feel the too potent fervors: the tall maize
Rolls up its long green leaves; the clover droops
Its tender foliage, and declines its blooms.
But far in the fierce sunshine tower the hills,
With all their growth of woods, silent and stern,
As if the scorching heat and dazzling light
Were but an element they loved. Bright clouds,
Motionless pillars of the brazen heaven —
Their bases on the mountains — their white tops
Shining in the far ether — fire the air
With a reflected radiance, and make turn
The gazer's eye away. For me, I lie
Languidly in the shade, where the thick turf,
Yet virgin from the kisses of the sun,
Retains some freshness, and I woo the wind
That still delays his coming. Why so slow,
Gentle and voluble spirit of the air?
Oh, come and breathe upon the fainting earth
Coolness and life. Is it that in his caves

He hears me? See, on yonder woody ridge,
The pine is bending his proud top, and now
Among the nearer groves, chestnut and oak
Are tossing their green boughs about. He comes;
Lo, where the grassy meadow runs in waves!
The deep distressful silence of the scene
Breaks up with mingling of unnumbered sounds
And universal motion. He is come,
Shaking a shower of blossoms from the shrubs,
And bearing on their fragrance; and he brings
Music of birds, and rustling of young boughs,
And sound of swaying branches, and the voice
Of distant waterfalls. All the green herbs
Are stirring in his breath; a thousand flowers,
By the road-side and the borders of the brook,
Nod gayly to each other; glossy leaves
Are twinkling in the sun, as if the dew
Were on them yet, and silver waters break
Into small waves and sparkle as he comes.

WILLIAM CULLEN BRYANT
AMERICAN (1794–1878)

I hear a river thro' the valley wander

I hear a river thro' the valley wander
Whose water runs, the song alone remaining.
A rainbow stands and summer passes under.

TRUMBULL STICKNEY
AMERICAN (1874–1904)

The Oven Bird

There is a singer everyone has heard,
Loud, a mid-summer and a mid-wood bird,
Who makes the solid tree trunks sound again.
He says that leaves are old and that for flowers
Mid-summer is to spring as one to ten.
He says the early petal-fall is past
When pear and cherry bloom went down in showers

On sunny days a moment overcast;
And comes that other fall we name the fall.
He says the highway dust is over all.
The bird would cease and be as other birds
But that he knows in singing not to sing.
The question that he frames in all but words
Is what to make of a diminished thing.

ROBERT FROST
AMERICAN (1874–1963)

Heat

O wind, rend open the heat,
cut apart the heat,
rend it to tatters.

Fruit cannot drop
through this thick air —
fruit cannot fall into heat
that presses up and blunts
the points of pears
and rounds the grapes.

Cut the heat —
plough through it,
turning it on either side
of your path.

H.D.
AMERICAN (1886–1961)

Eel-Grass

No matter what I say,
  All that I really love
Is the rain that flattens on the bay,
  And the eel-grass in the cove;
The jingle-shells that lie and bleach
  At the tide-line, and the trace
Of higher tides along the beach:
  Nothing in this place.

EDNA ST. VINCENT MILLAY
AMERICAN (1892–1950)

Summer Night

The sounds
Of the Harlem night
Drop one by one into stillness.
The last player-piano is closed.
The last victrola ceases with the
"Jazz Boy Blues."
The last crying baby sleeps
And the night becomes
Still as a whispering heartbeat.
I toss
Without rest in the darkness,
Weary as the tired night,
My soul
Empty as the silence,
Empty with a vague,
Aching emptiness,
Desiring,
Needing someone,
Something.

I toss without rest
In the darkness
Until the new dawn,
Wan and pale,
Descends like a white mist
Into the court-yard.

LANGSTON HUGHES
AMERICAN (1902–1967)

The House Was Quiet and the World Was Calm

The house was quiet and the world was calm.
The reader became the book; and summer night

Was like the conscious being of the book.
The house was quiet and the world was calm.

The words were spoken as if there was no book,
Except that the reader leaned above the page,

Wanted to lean, wanted much most to be
The scholar to whom his book is true, to whom

The summer night is like a perfection of thought.
The house was quiet because it had to be.

The quiet was part of the meaning, part of the mind:
The access of perfection to the page.

And the world was calm. The truth in a calm world,
In which there is no other meaning, itself

Is calm, itself is summer and night, itself
Is the reader leaning late and reading there.

WALLACE STEVENS
AMERICAN (1879-1955)

Summer

There is that sound like the wind
Forgetting in the branches that means something
Nobody can translate. And there is the sobering "later on,"
When you consider what a thing meant, and put it down.

For the time being the shadow is ample
And hardly seen, divided among the twigs of a tree,
The trees of a forest, just as life is divided up
Between you and me, and among all the others out there.

And the thinning-out phase follows
The period of reflection. And suddenly, to be dying
Is not a little or mean or cheap thing,
Only wearying, the heat unbearable,

And also the little mindless constructions put upon
Our fantasies of what we did: summer, the ball of pine needles,
The loose fates serving our acts, with token smiles,
Carrying out their instructions too accurately —

Too late to cancel them now — and winter, the twitter
Of cold stars at the pane, that describes with broad gestures
This state of being that is not so big after all.
Summer involves going down as a steep flight of steps

To a narrow ledge over the water. Is this it, then,
This iron comfort, these reasonable taboos,
Or did you mean it when you stopped? And the face
Resembles yours, the one reflected in the water.

JOHN ASHBERY
AMERICAN (B. 1927)

To Autumn

O Autumn, laden with fruit, and stained
With the blood of the grape, pass not, but sit
Beneath my shady roof; there thou mayest rest,
And tune thy jolly voice to my fresh pipe;
And all the daughters of the year shall dance!
Sing now the lusty song of fruits and flowers.

"The narrow bud opens her beauties to
The sun, and love runs in her thrilling veins;
Blossoms hang round the brows of morning, and
Flourish down the bright cheek of modest eve,
Till clust'ring Summer breaks forth into singing,
And feather'd clouds strew flowers round her head.

"The spirits of the air live on the smells
Of fruit; and joy, with pinions light, roves round
The gardens, or sits singing in the trees."
Thus sang the jolly Autumn as he sat;
Then rose, girded himself, and o'er the bleak
Hills fled from our sight; but left his golden load.

WILLIAM BLAKE
ENGLISH (1757–1827)

To Autumn

Season of mists and mellow fruitfulness!
  Close bosom-friend of the maturing sun;
Conspiring with him how to load and bless
  With fruit the vines that round the thatch-eaves run;
To bend with apples the mossed cottage-trees,
  And fill all fruit with ripeness to the core;
    To swell the gourd, and plump the hazel shells
  With a sweet kernel; to set budding more,
And still more, later flowers for the bees,

Until they think warm days will never cease,
　　For Summer has o'er-brimmed their clammy cells.

Who hath not seen thee oft amid thy store?
　　Sometimes whoever seeks abroad may find
Thee sitting careless on a granary floor,
　　Thy hair soft-lifted by the winnowing wind;
Or on a self-reaped furrow sound asleep,
　　Drowsed with the fume of poppies, while thy hook
　　Spares the next swath and all its twinéd flowers;
And sometimes like a gleaner thou dost keep
　　Steady thy laden head across a brook;
　　Or by a cider-press, with patient look,
　　Thou watchest the last oozings, hours by hours.

Where are the songs of Spring? Ay, where are they?
　　Think not of them, thou hast thy music too,
　　While barréd clouds bloom the soft-dying day,
And touch the stubble-plains with rosy hue;
　　Then in a wailful choir, the small gnats mourn
　　Among the river sallows, borne aloft
　　Or sinking as the light wind lives or dies;
And full-grown lambs loud bleat from hilly bourn;
　　Hedge-crickets sing; and now with treble soft
　　The red-breast whistles from a garden-croft,
　　And gathering swallows twitter in the skies.

JOHN KEATS
ENGLISH (1795–1821)

No!

　　No sun — no moon!
　　No morn — no noon —
No dawn — no dusk — no proper time of day —
　　No sky — no earthly view —
　　No distance looking blue —
No road — no street — no "t'other side the way" —
　　No end to any Row —

No indications where the Crescents go —
    No top to any steeple —
No recognitions of familiar people —
    No courtesies for showing 'em —
    No knowing 'em —
No travelling at all — no locomotion,
No inkling of the way — no notion —
    "No go" — by land or ocean —
    No mail — no post —
No news from any foreign coast —
No Park — no Ring — no afternoon gentility —
    No company — no nobility —
No warmth, no cheerfulness, no healthful ease,
  No comfortable feel in any member —
No shade, no shine, no butterflies, no bees,
  No fruits, no flowers, no leaves, no birds, —
    November!

THOMAS HOOD
ENGLISH (1799–1845)

The Harvest Moon

It is the Harvest Moon! On gilded vanes
  And roofs of villages, on woodland crests
  And their aerial neighborhoods of nests
  Deserted, on the curtained window-panes
Of rooms where children sleep, on country lanes
  And harvest-fields, its mystic splendor rests!
    Gone are the birds that were our summer guests,
    With the last sheaves return the laboring wains!
All things are symbols: the external shows
  Of Nature have their image in the mind,
  As flowers and fruits and falling of the leaves;
The song-birds leave us at the summer's close,
  Only the empty nests are left behind,
  And pipings of the quail among the sheaves.

HENRY WADSWORTH LONGFELLOW
AMERICAN (1807–1882)

The Latter Rain

The latter rain, it falls in anxious haste
Upon the sun-dried fields and branches bare,
Loosening with searching drops the rigid waste
As if it would each root's lost strength repair;
But not a blade grows green as in the spring,
No swelling twig puts forth its thickening leaves;
The robins only mid the harvests sing
Pecking the grain that scatters from the sheaves;
The rain falls still — the fruit all ripened drops,
It pierces chestnut burr and walnut shell,
The furrowed fields disclose the yellow crops,
Each bursting pod of talents used can tell,
And all that once received the early rain
Declare to man it was not sent in vain.

JONES VERY
AMERICAN (1813–1880)

Mnemosyne

It's autumn in the country I remember.

How warm a wind blew here about the ways!
And shadows on the hillside lay to slumber
During the long sun-sweetened summer-days.

It's cold abroad the country I remember.

The swallows veering skimmed the golden grain
At midday with a wing aslant and limber;
And yellow cattle browsed upon the plain.

It's empty down the country I remember.

I had a sister lovely in my sight:
Her hair was dark, her eyes were very sombre;
We sang together in the woods at night.

It's lonely in the country I remember.

The babble of our children fills my ears,
And on our hearth I stare the perished ember
To flames that show all starry thro' my tears.

It's dark about the country I remember.

There are the mountains where I lived. The path
Is slushed with cattle-tracks and fallen timber,
The stumps are twisted by the tempests' wrath.

But that I knew these places are my own,
I'd ask how came such wretchedness to cumber
The earth, and I to people it alone.

It rains across the country I remember.

TRUMBULL STICKNEY
AMERICAN (1874–1904)

November Night

Listen . .
With faint dry sound,
Like steps of passing ghosts,
The leaves, frost-crisp'd, break from the trees
And fall.

ADELAIDE CRAPSEY
AMERICAN (1878–1914)

Heart of Autumn

Wind finds the northwest gap, fall comes.
Today, under gray cloud-scud and over gray
Wind-flicker of forest, in perfect formation, wild geese
Head for a land of warm water, the *boom,* the lead pellet.

Some crumple in air, fall. Some stagger, recover control,
Then take the last glide for a far glint of water. None

Knows what has happened. Now, today, watching
How tirelessly *V* upon *V* arrows the season's logic,

Do I know my own story? At least, they know
When the hour comes for the great wing-beat. Sky-strider,
Star-strider — they rise, and the imperial utterance,
Which cries out for distance, quivers in the wheeling sky.

That much they know, and in their nature know
The path of pathlessness, with all the joy
Of destiny fulfilling its own name.
I have known time and distance, but not why I am here.

Path of logic, path of folly, all
The same — and I stand, my face lifted now skyward,
Hearing the high beat, my arms outstretched in the tingling
Process of transformation, and soon tough legs,

With folded feet, trail in the sounding vacuum of passage,
And my heart is impacted with a fierce impulse
To unwordable utterance —
Toward sunset, at a great height.

ROBERT PENN WARREN
AMERICAN (1905–1989)

My November Guest

My sorrow, when she's here with me,
  Thinks these dark days of autumn rain
Are beautiful as days can be;
She loves the bare, the withered tree;
  She walks the sodden pasture lane.

Her pleasure will not let me stay.
  She talks and I am fain to list:
She's glad the birds are gone away,
She's glad her simple worsted grey
  Is silver now with clinging mist.

The desolate, deserted trees,
   The faded earth, the heavy sky,
The beauties she so truly sees,
She thinks I have no eye for these,
   And vexes me for reason why.

Not yesterday I learned to know
   The love of bare November days
Before the coming of the snow;
But it were vain to tell her so,
   And they are better for her praise.

ROBERT FROST
AMERICAN (1874–1963)

WINTER

When icicles hang by the wall

From *Love's Labour's Lost*
   When icicles hang by the wall,
     And Dick the shepherd blows his nail,
   And Tom bears logs into the hall,
     And milk comes frozen home in pail,
   When blood is nipped, and ways be foul,
   Then nightly sings the staring owl,
       Tu-wit to-who!
       A merry note,
While greasy Joan doth keel the pot.

When all around the wind doth blow,
   And coughing drowns the parson's saw,
And birds sit brooding in the snow,

And Marian's nose looks red and raw,
When roasted crabs hiss in the bowl,
Then nightly sings the staring owl,
    Tu-wit to-who!
    A merry note,
While greasy Joan doth keel the pot.

WILLIAM SHAKESPEARE
ENGLISH (1564–1616)

Blow, blow, thou winter wind

From *As You Like It*

    Blow, blow, thou winter wind,
    Thou art not so unkind
      As man's ingratitude;
    Thy tooth is not so keen,
    Because thou art not seen,
      Although thy breath be rude.
Heigh-ho! sing, heigh-ho! unto the green holly:
Most friendship is feigning, most loving mere folly:
    Then, heigh-ho, the holly!
    This life is most jolly.

    Freeze, freeze, thou bitter sky,
    That dost not bite so nigh
      As benefits forgot:
    Though thou the waters warp,
    Thy sting is not so sharp
      As friends remember'd not.
Heigh-ho! sing, heigh-ho! unto the green holly:
Most friendship is feigning, most loving mere folly:
    Then, heigh-ho, the holly!
    This life is most jolly.

WILLIAM SHAKESPEARE
ENGLISH (1564–1616)

Now winter nights enlarge

Now winter nights enlarge
The number of their hours,
And clouds their storms discharge
Upon the airy towers.
Let now the chimneys blaze,
And cups o'erflow with wine;
Let well-tuned words amaze
With harmony divine.
Now yellow waxen lights
Shall wait on honey love,
While youthful revels, masques, and courtly sights
Sleep's leaden spells remove.

This time doth well dispense
With lovers' long discourse;
Much speech hath some defence,
Though beauty no remorse.
All do not all things well;
Some measures comely tread,
Some knotted riddles tell,
Some poems smoothly read.
The summer hath his joys
And winter his delights;
Though love and all his pleasures are but toys,
They shorten tedious nights.

THOMAS CAMPION
ENGLISH (1567–1620)

Snow-Flakes

Out of the bosom of the Air,
   Out of the cloud-folds of her garments shaken,
Over the woodlands brown and bare,
   Over the harvest-fields forsaken,
      Silent, and soft, and slow
      Descends the snow.

Even as our cloudy fancies take
  Suddenly shape in some divine expression,
Even as the troubled heart doth make
  In the white countenance confession,
    The troubled sky reveals
    The grief it feels.

This is the poem of the air,
  Slowly in silent syllables recorded;
This is the secret of despair,
  Long in its cloudy bosom hoarded,
    Now whispered and revealed
    To wood and field.

              HENRY WADSWORTH LONGFELLOW
                    AMERICAN (1807–1882)

The Snow-Storm

    Announced by all the trumpets of the sky,
Arrives the snow, and, driving o'er the fields,
Seems nowhere to alight: the whited air
Hides hills and woods, the river, and the heaven,
And veils the farm-house at the garden's end.
The sled and traveller stopped, the courier's feet
Delayed, all friends shut out, the housemates sit
Around the radiant fireplace, enclosed
In a tumultuous privacy of storm.

    Come see the north wind's masonry.
Out of an unseen quarry evermore
Furnished with tile, the fierce artificer
Curves his white bastions with projected roof
Round every windward stake, or tree, or door.
Speeding, the myriad-handed, his wild work
So fanciful, so savage, nought cares he
For number or proportion. Mockingly,
On coop or kennel he hangs Parian wreaths;
A swan-like form invests the hidden thorn;
Fills up the farmer's lane from wall to wall,

Maugre the farmer's sighs; and, at the gate,
A tapering turret overtops the work.
And when his hours are numbered, and the world
Is all his own, retiring, as he were not,
Leaves, when the sun appears, astonished Art
To mimic in slow structures, stone by stone,
Built in an age, the mad wind's night-work,
The frolic architecture of the snow.

RALPH WALDO EMERSON
AMERICAN (1803–1882)

The night is darkening round me

The night is darkening round me,
The wild winds coldly blow;
But a tyrant spell has bound me
And I cannot, cannot go.

The giant trees are bending
Their bare boughs weighed with snow.
And the storm is fast descending,
And yet I cannot go.

Clouds beyond clouds above me,
Wastes beyond wastes below;
But nothing drear can move me;
I will not, cannot go.

EMILY BRONTË
ENGLISH (1818–1848)

The Sky is low — the Clouds are mean

The Sky is low — the Clouds are mean.
A Travelling Flake of Snow
Across a Barn or through a Rut
Debates if it will go —
A Narrow Wind complains all Day
How some one treated him
Nature, like Us is sometimes caught
Without her Diadem —

EMILY DICKINSON
AMERICAN (1830–1886)

January

Again I reply to the triple winds
running chromatic fifths of derision
outside my window:
                    Play louder.
You will not succeed. I am
bound more to my sentences
the more you batter at me
to follow you.
                    And the wind,
as before, fingers perfectly
its derisive music.

WILLIAM CARLOS WILLIAMS
AMERICAN (1883–1963)

Winter Scene

There is now not a single
leaf on the cherry tree:

except when the jay
plummets in, lights, and,

in pure clarity, squalls:
then every branch

quivers and
breaks out in blue leaves.

A. R. AMMONS
AMERICAN (1926–2001)

Ancient Music

Winter is icummen in,
Lhude sing Goddamm,
Raineth drop and staineth slop,
And how the wind doth ramm!
  Sing: Goddamm.
Skiddeth bus and sloppeth us,
An ague hath my ham.
Freezeth river, turneth liver,
  Damn you, sing: Goddamm.
Goddamm, Goddamm, 'tis why I am, Goddamm,
  So 'gainst the winter's balm.
Sing goddamm, damm, sing Goddamm,
Sing goddamm, sing goddamm, DAMM.

EZRA POUND
AMERICAN (1885–1972)

Dust of Snow

The way a crow
Shook down on me
The dust of snow
From a hemlock tree

Has given my heart
A change of mood
And saved some part
Of a day I had rued.

ROBERT FROST
AMERICAN (1874–1963)

Stopping by Woods on a Snowy Evening

Whose woods these are I think I know.
His house is in the village though;
He will not see me stopping here
To watch his woods fill up with snow.

My little horse must think it queer
To stop without a farmhouse near
Between the woods and frozen lake
The darkest evening of the year.

He gives his harness bells a shake
To ask if there is some mistake.
The only other sound's the sweep
Of easy wind and downy flake.

The woods are lovely, dark and deep.
But I have promises to keep,
And miles to go before I sleep,
And miles to go before I sleep.

ROBERT FROST
AMERICAN (1874–1963)

The days are short,
  The sun a spark
Hung thin between
  The dark and dark.

Fat snowy footsteps
  Track the floor,
And parkas pile up
  Near the door.

The river is
  A frozen place
Held still beneath
  The trees' black lace.

The sky is low.
  The wind is gray.
The radiator
  Purrs all day.

JOHN UPDIKE
AMERICAN (B. 1932)

The Round of the Year

———————

WITHIN THE LARGER CYCLES OF NATURE ARE THOSE CYCLES OF HUMAN CONSTRUCTION, THE HOLIDAYS AND FESTIVALS THAT ELICIT, AMONG OTHER DECORATIONS, THE WORK of poets. The range of feeling is as wide as the intent of these various occasions, from the bittersweet reflections of the New Year through the intimate merriment of Valentine's Day, to the uplifting exhortation suited to the Fourth of July, the dark imaginations of Halloween, the celebratory mode of Thanksgiving, and — in the tradition most widely rooted in Europe and America — the jubilant tones of the Christmas season. Somewhat apart from these are those poems that pay tribute to parents and grandparents — whether in the context of Mother's and Father's Days or any other family anniversary — as thoroughly unpredictable and varied in their nuances as the relationships they reflect.

Seeing the Year Out

Want to know what the passing year is like?
A snake slithering down a hole.
Half his long scales already hidden,
How to stop him from getting away?
Grab his tail and pull, you say?
Pull all you like — it does no good.
The children try hard not to doze,
Chatter back and forth to stay awake,
But I say let dawn cocks keep still!
I fear the noise of watch drums pounding.
We've sat so long the lamp's burned out.
I get up and look at the slanting Dipper.
How could I hope next year won't come?
My mind shrinks from the failures it may bring.
I work to hold on to the night
While I can still brag I'm young.

SU TUNG-P'O
CHINESE (1036–1101)
TRANSLATED BY BURTON WATSON

The Old Year

1

The Old Year's gone away
To nothingness and night
We cannot find him all the day
Nor hear him in the night
He left no footstep mark or place
In either shade or sun
Tho' last year he'd a neighbours face
In this he's known by none

2

All nothing every where
Mists we on mornings see

They have more substance when they're here
And more of form than he
He was a friend by every fire
In every cot and hall
A guest to every hearts desire
And now he's nought at all

3

Old papers thrown away
Or garments cast aside
E'en the talk of yesterday
Are things identified
But time once torn away
No voices can recall
The eve of new years day
Left the old one lost to all

JOHN CLARE
ENGLISH (1793–1864)

Auld Lang Syne

Should auld acquaintance be forgot
And never brought to mind?
Should auld acquaintance be forgot,
And auld lang syne!

For auld lang syne my jo,
For auld lang syne,
We'll tak a cup o' kindness yet,
For auld lang syne.

And surely ye'll be your pint stowp!
And surely I'll be mine!
And we'll tak a cup o' kindness yet,
For auld lang syne.
For auld &c.

We twa hae run about the braes,
And pou'd the gowans fine;
But we've wander'd mony a weary fitt,

Sin auld lang syne.
            For auld &c.

We twa hae paidl'd in the burn,
    Frae morning sun till dine;
But seas between us braid hae roar'd,
    Sin auld lang syne.
            For auld &c.

And there's a hand, my trusty fiere!
    And gie's a hand o' thine!
And we'll tak a right gude-willie-waught,
    For auld lang syne.
            For auld &c.

ROBERT BURNS
SCOTTISH (1759–1796)

Ring out, wild bells, to the wild sky

From *In Memoriam*

Ring out, wild bells, to the wild sky,
    The flying cloud, the frosty light:
    The year is dying in the night;
Ring out, wild bells, and let him die.

Ring out the old, ring in the new,
    Ring, happy bells, across the snow:
    The year is going, let him go;
Ring out the false, ring in the true.

Ring out the grief that saps the mind,
    For those that here we see no more;
    Ring out the feud of rich and poor,
Ring in redress to all mankind.

Ring out a slowly dying cause,
    And ancient forms of party strife;
    Ring in the nobler modes of life,
With sweeter manners, purer laws.

Ring out the want, the care, the sin,
    The faithless coldness of the times;
    Ring out, ring out my mournful rhymes,
But ring the fuller minstrel in.

Ring out false pride in place and blood,
    The civic slander and the spite;
    Ring in the love of truth and right,
Ring in the common love of good.

Ring out old shapes of foul disease;
    Ring out the narrowing lust of gold;
    Ring out the thousand wars of old,
Ring in the thousand years of peace.

Ring in the valiant man and free,
    The larger heart, the kindlier hand;
    Ring out the darkness of the land,
Ring in the Christ that is to be.

                    ALFRED, LORD TENNYSON
                        ENGLISH (1809–1892)

A Song for New Year's Eve

Stay yet, my friends, a moment stay —
    Stay till the good old year,
So long companion of our way,
    Shakes hands, and leaves us here.
        Oh stay, oh stay,
One little hour, and then away.

The year, whose hopes were high and strong,
    Has now no hopes to wake;
Yet one hour more of jest and song
    For his familiar sake.
        Oh stay, oh stay,
One mirthful hour, and then away.

The kindly year, his liberal hands
    Have lavished all his store.
And shall we turn from where he stands,
    Because he gives no more?
      Oh stay, oh stay,
One grateful hour, and then away.

Days brightly came and calmly went,
    While yet he was our guest;
How cheerfully the week was spent!
    How sweet the seventh day's rest!
      Oh stay, oh stay,
One golden hour, and then away.

Dear friends were with us, some who sleep
    Beneath the coffin-lid:
What pleasant memories we keep
    Of all they said and did!
      Oh stay, oh stay,
One tender hour, and then away.

Even while we sing, he smiles his last,
    And leaves our sphere behind.
The good old year is with the past;
    Oh be the new as kind!
      Oh stay, oh stay,
One parting strain, and then away.

WILLIAM CULLEN BRYANT
AMERICAN (1794–1878)

VALENTINE'S DAY

Saint Valentine's Day

Well dost thou, Love, thy solemn Feast to hold
In vestal February;
Not rather choosing out some rosy day
From the rich coronet of the coming May,
When all things meet to marry!
   O, quick, prævernal Power
That signall'st punctual through the sleepy mould
The Snowdrop's time to flower,
Fair as the rash oath of virginity
Which is first-love's first cry;
O, Baby Spring,
That flutter'st sudden 'neath the breast of Earth
A month before the birth;
Whence is the peaceful poignancy,
The joy contrite,
Sadder than sorrow, sweeter than delight,
That burthens now the breath of everything,
Though each one sighs as if to each alone
The cherish'd pang were known?
At dusk of dawn, on his dark spray apart,
With it the Blackbird breaks the young Day's heart;
In evening's hush
About it talks the heavenly-minded Thrush;
The hill with like remorse
Smiles to the Sun's smile in his westering course;
The fisher's drooping skiff
In yonder sheltering bay;
The choughs that call about the shining cliff;
The children, noisy in the setting ray;
Own the sweet season, each thing as it may;
Thoughts of strange kindness and forgotten peace
In me increase;
And tears arise

Within my happy, happy Mistress' eyes,
And, lo, her lips, averted from my kiss,
Ask from Love's bounty, ah, much more than bliss!
    Is't the sequester'd and exceeding sweet
Of dear Desire electing his defeat?
Is't the waked Earth now to yon purpling cope
Uttering first-love's first cry,
Vainly renouncing, with a Seraph's sigh,
Love's natural hope?
Fair-meaning Earth, foredoom'd to perjury!
Behold, all amorous May,
With roses heap'd upon her laughing brows,
Avoids thee of thy vows!
Were it for thee, with her warm bosom near,
To abide the sharpness of the Seraph's sphere?
Forget thy foolish words;
Go to her summons gay,
Thy heart with dead, wing'd Innocencies fill'd,
Ev'n as a nest with birds
After the old ones by the hawk are kill'd.
    Well dost thou, Love, to celebrate
The noon of thy soft ecstasy,
Or e'er it be too late,
Or e'er the Snowdrop die!

COVENTRY PATMORE
ENGLISH (1846–1865)

St. Valentine's Day

To-day, all day, I rode upon the Down,
With hounds and horsemen, a brave company.
On this side in its glory lay the sea,
On that the Sussex Weald, a sea of brown.
The wind was light, and brightly the sun shone,
And still we galloped on from gorse to gorse.
And once, when checked, a thrush sang, and my horse
Pricked his quick ears as to a sound unknown.
I knew the Spring was come. I knew it even
Better than all by this, that through my chase
In bush and stone and hill and sea and heaven
I seemed to see and follow still your face.
Your face my quarry was. For it I rode,
My horse a thing of wings, myself a god.

WILFRID SCAWEN BLUNT
ENGLISH (1840–1922)

A Very Valentine

Very fine is my valentine.
Very fine and very mine.
Very mine is my valentine very mine and very fine.
Very fine is my valentine and mine, very fine very mine and
mine is my valentine.

GERTRUDE STEIN
AMERICAN (1874–1946)

Happiest February

> Many more happy Valentines.
> How many?
> As the last
>   makes no sense.
> As many as many.
> As more rolls out the vines
> Which shade green in the snow
> Of a cold fourteenth
> Of their happiest February.

LOUIS ZUKOFSKY
AMERICAN (1904–1978)

CELEBRATING FAMILY

With my father

> With my father
> I would watch dawn
> over green fields.

KOBAYASHI ISSA
JAPANESE (1763–1827)
TRANSLATED BY ROBERT HASS

To Her Father with Some Verses

> Most truly honoured, and as truly dear,
> If worth in me or ought I do appear,
> Who can of right better demand the same
> Than may your worthy self from whom it came?
> The principal might yield a greater sum,
> Yet handled ill, amounts but to this crumb;
> My stock's so small I know not how to pay,
> My bond remains in force unto this day;

Yet for part payment take this simple mite,
Where nothing's to be had, kings loose their right.
Such is my debt I may not say forgive,
But as I can, I'll pay it while I live;
Such is my bond, none can discharge but I,
Yet paying is not paid until I die.

ANNE BRADSTREET
AMERICAN (1612–1672)

A Birthday

My heart is like a singing bird
   Whose nest is in a watered shoot;
My heart is like an apple-tree
   Whose boughs are bent with thickset fruit;
My heart is like a rainbow shell
   That paddles in a halcyon sea;
My heart is gladder than all these
   Because my love is come to me.

Raise me a dais of silk and down;
   Hang it with vair and purple dyes;
Carve it in doves and pomegranates,
   And peacocks with a hundred eyes;
Work it in gold and silver grapes,
   In leaves and silver fleurs-de-lys;
Because the birthday of my life
   Is come, my love is come to me.

CHRISTINA ROSSETTI
ENGLISH (1830–1894)

To My Mother

To-day's your natal day;
    Sweet flowers I bring:
Mother, accept I pray
    My offering.

And may you happy live,
    And long us bless;
Receiving as you give
    Great happiness.

CHRISTINA ROSSETTI
ENGLISH (1830–1894)

To My Mother

You too, my mother, read my rhymes
For love of unforgotten times,
And you may chance to hear once more
The little feet along the floor.

ROBERT LOUIS STEVENSON
SCOTTISH (1850–1894)

My grandfather, dead long before I was born

My grandfather, dead long before I was born,
died among strangers; and all the verse he wrote
was lost —
except for what
still speaks through me
as mine.

CHARLES REZNIKOFF
AMERICAN (1894–1976)

Those Winter Sundays

Sundays too my father got up early
and put his clothes on in the blueblack cold,
then with cracked hands that ached
from labor in the weekday weather made
banked fires blaze. No one ever thanked him.

I'd wake and hear the cold splintering, breaking.
When the rooms were warm, he'd call,
and slowly I would rise and dress,
fearing the chronic angers of that house,

Speaking indifferently to him,
who had driven out the cold
and polished my good shoes as well.
What did I know, what did I know
of love's austere and lonely offices?

ROBERT HAYDEN
AMERICAN (1913–1980)

Lineage

My grandmothers were strong.
They followed plows and bent to toil.
They moved through fields sowing seed.
They touched earth and grain grew.
They were full of sturdiness and singing.
My grandmothers were strong.

My grandmothers are full of memories
Smelling of soap and onions and wet clay
With veins rolling roughly over quick hands
They have many clean words to say.
My grandmothers were strong.
Why am I not as they?

MARGARET WALKER
AMERICAN (1915–1998)

Mother to Son

Well, son, I'll tell you:
Life for me ain't been no crystal stair.
It's had tacks in it,
And splinters,
And boards torn up,
And places with no carpet on the floor —
Bare.
But all the time
I'se been a-climbin' on,
And reachin' landin's,
And turnin' corners,
And sometimes goin' in the dark
Where there ain't been no light.
So boy, don't you turn back.
Don't you set down on the steps
'Cause you finds it's kinder hard.
Don't you fall now —
For I'se still goin', honey,
I'se still climbin',
And life for me ain't been no crystal stair.

LANGSTON HUGHES
AMERICAN (1902–1967)

my father moved through dooms of love

my father moved through dooms of love
through sames of am through haves of give,
singing each morning out of each night
my father moved through depths of height

this motionless forgetful where
turned at his glance to shining here;
that if(so timid air is firm)
under his eyes would stir and squirm

newly as from unburied which
floats the first who,his april touch

drove sleeping selves to swarm their fates
woke dreamers to their ghostly roots

and should some why completely weep
my father's fingers brought her sleep:
vainly no smallest voice might cry
for he could feel the mountains grow.

Lifting the valleys of the sea
my father moved through griefs of joy;
praising a forehead called the moon
singing desire into begin

joy was his song and joy so pure
a heart of star by him could steer
and pure so now and now so yes
the wrists of twilight would rejoice

keen as midsummer's keen beyond
conceiving mind of sun will stand,
so strictly(over utmost him
so hugely)stood my father's dream

his flesh was flesh his blood was blood:
no hungry man but wished him food;
no cripple wouldn't creep one mile
uphill to only see him smile.

Scorning the pomp of must and shall
my father moved through dooms of feel;
his anger was as right as rain
his pity was as green as grain

septembering arms of year extend
less humbly wealth to foe and friend
than he to foolish and to wise
offered immeasurable is

proudly and(by octobering flame
beckoned)as earth will downward climb,
so naked for immortal work
his shoulders marched against the dark

his sorrow was as true as bread:
no liar looked him in the head;
if every friend became his foe
he'd laugh and build a world with snow.

My father moved through theys of we,
singing each new leaf out of each tree
(and every child was sure that spring
danced when she heard my father sing)

then let men kill which cannot share,
let blood and flesh be mud and mire,
scheming imagine,passion willed,
freedom a drug that's bought and sold

giving to steal and cruel kind,
a heart to fear,to doubt a mind,
to differ a disease of same,
conform the pinnacle of am

though dull were all we taste as bright,
bitter all utterly things sweet,
maggoty minus and dumb death
all we inherit,all bequeath

and nothing quite so least as truth
— i say though hate were why men breathe —
because my father lived his soul
love is the whole and more than all

E. E. CUMMINGS
AMERICAN (1894–1962)

The 90th Year

for Lore Segal

High in the jacaranda shines the gilded thread
of a small bird's curlicue of song — too high
for her to see or hear.

                I've learned
not to say, these last years,
'O, look! — O, listen, Mother!'
as I used to.

              (It was she
who taught me to look;
to name the flowers when I was still close to the ground,
my face level with theirs;
or to watch the sublime metamorphoses
unfold and unfold
over the walled back gardens of our street . . .

It had not been given her
to know the flesh as good in itself,
as the flesh of a fruit is good. To her
the human body has been a husk,
a shell in which souls were prisoned.
Yet, from within it, with how much gazing
her life has paid tribute to the world's body!
How tears of pleasure
would choke her, when a perfect voice,
deep or high, clove to its note unfaltering!)

She has swept the crackling seedpods,
the litter of mauve blossoms, off the cement path,
tipped them into the rubbish bucket.
She's made her bed, washed up the breakfast dishes,
wiped the hotplate. I've taken the butter and milkjug
back to the fridge next door — but it's not my place,
visiting here, to usurp the tasks
that weave the day's pattern.

Now she is leaning forward in her chair,
        by the lamp lit in the daylight,
rereading *War and Peace.*
        When I look up
from her wellworn copy of *The Divine Milieu,*
which she wants me to read, I see her hand
loose on the black stem of the magnifying glass,
she is dozing.
'I am so tired,' she has written to me, 'of appreciating
the gift of life.'

DENISE LEVERTOV
AMERICAN (1923–1997)

For My Mother

August 3, 1992

Once more
I summon you
Out of the past
With poignant love,
You who nourished the poet
And the lover.
I see your gray eyes
Looking out to sea
In those Rockport summers,
Keeping a distance
Within the closeness
Which was never intrusive
Opening out
Into the world.
And what I remember
Is how we laughed
Till we cried
Swept into merriment
Especially when times were hard.
And what I remember
Is how you never stopped creating
And how people sent me
Dresses you had designed

With rich embroidery
In brilliant colors
Because they could not bear
To give them away
Or cast them aside.
I summon you now
Not to think of
The ceaseless battle
With pain and ill health,
The frailty and the anguish.
No, today I remember
The creator,
The lion-hearted.

MAY SARTON
AMERICAN (1912–1995)

Portrait

A child draws the outline of a body.
She draws what she can, but it is white all through,
she cannot fill in what she knows is there.
Within the unsupported line, she knows
that life is missing; she has cut
one background from another. Like a child,
she turns to her mother.

And you draw the heart
against the emptiness she has created.

LOUISE GLÜCK
AMERICAN (B. 1943)

Follower

My father worked with a horse-plough,
His shoulders globed like a full sail strung
Between the shafts and the furrow.
The horse strained at his clicking tongue.

An expert. He would set the wing
And fit the bright steel-pointed sock.

The sod rolled over without breaking.
At the headrig, with a single pluck

Of reins, the sweating team turned round
And back into the land. His eye
Narrowed and angled at the ground,
Mapping the furrow exactly.

I stumbled in his hob-nailed wake,
Fell sometimes on the polished sod;
Sometimes he rode me on his back
Dipping and rising to his plod.

I wanted to grow up and plough,
To close one eye, stiffen my arm.
All I ever did was follow
In his broad shadow round the farm.

I was a nuisance, tripping, falling,
Yapping always. But today
It is my father who keeps stumbling
Behind me, and will not go away.

SEAMUS HEANEY
IRISH (B. 1939)

THE FOURTH OF JULY

The New Colossus

Not like the brazen giant of Greek fame,
With conquering limbs astride from land to land;
Here at our sea-washed, sunset gates shall stand
A mighty woman with a torch, whose flame
Is the imprisoned lightning, and her name
Mother of Exiles. From her beacon-hand
Glows world-wide welcome; her mild eyes command
The air-bridged harbor that twin cities frame.

"Keep ancient lands, your storied pomp!" cries she
With silent lips. "Give me your tired, your poor,
Your huddled masses yearning to breathe free,
The wretched refuse of your teeming shore.
Send these, the homeless, tempest-tost to me,
I lift my lamp beside the golden door!"

EMMA LAZARUS
AMERICAN (1849–1887)

America the Beautiful

O beautiful for spacious skies,
 For amber waves of grain,
For purple mountain majesties
 Above the fruited plain!
  America! America!
 God shed His grace on thee
And crown thy good with brotherhood
 From sea to shining sea!

O beautiful for pilgrim feet,
 Whose stern, impassioned stress
A thoroughfare for freedom beat
 Across the wilderness!
  America! America!
 God mend thine every flaw,
Confirm thy soul in self-control,
 Thy liberty in law!

O beautiful for heroes proved
 In liberating strife,
Who more than self their country loved,
 And mercy more than life!
  America! America!
 May God thy gold refine,
Till all success be nobleness,
 And every gain divine!

O beautiful for patriot dream
    That sees beyond the years
Thine alabaster cities gleam
    Undimmed by human tears!
      America! America!
    God shed His grace on thee
And crown thy good with brotherhood
    From sea to shining sea!

KATHARINE LEE BATES
AMERICAN (1859–1929)

I Hear America Singing

I hear America singing, the varied carols I hear,
Those of mechanics, each one singing his as it should be
    blithe and strong,
The carpenter singing his as he measures his plank or
    beam,
The mason singing his as he makes ready for work, or
    leaves off work,
The boatman singing what belongs to him in his boat,
    the deckhand singing on the steamboat deck,
The shoemaker singing as he sits on his bench, the hatter
    singing as he stands,
The wood-cutter's song, the ploughboy's on his way in
    the morning, or at noon intermission or at sundown,
The delicious singing of the mother, or of the young wife
    at work, or of the girl sewing or washing,
Each singing what belongs to him or her and to none else,
The day what belongs to the day — at night the party of
    young fellows, robust, friendly,
Singing with open mouths their strong melodious songs.

WALT WHITMAN
AMERICAN (1819–1892)

I, Too, Sing America

I, too, sing America.

I am the darker brother.
They send me to eat in the kitchen
When company comes,
But I laugh,
And eat well,
And grow strong.

Tomorrow,
I'll be at the table
When company comes.
Nobody'll dare
Say to me,
"Eat in the kitchen,"
Then.

Besides,
They'll see how beautiful I am
And be ashamed —

I, too, am America.

LANGSTON HUGHES
AMERICAN (1902–1967)

Halloween: Phantasms and Hauntings

Witches' Song (I)

From *Macbeth*

Round about the cauldron go:
In the poison'd entrails throw.
Toad, that under cold stone
Days and nights hath thirty one
Swelter'd venom sleeping got,
Boil thou first i' the charmed pot.

Double, double toil and trouble,
Fire burn and cauldron bubble.

Fillet of a fenny snake,
In the cauldron boil and bake;
Eye of newt and toe of frog,
Wool of bat and tongue of dog,
Adder's fork and blind-worm's sting,
Lizard's leg and howlet's wing,
For a charm of powerful trouble,
Like a hell-broth boil and bubble.

Double, double toil and trouble,
Fire burn and cauldron bubble.

WILLIAM SHAKESPEARE
ENGLISH (1564–1616)

Witches' Song (II)

The owl is abroad, the bat, and the toad,
   And so is the cat-a-mountain;
The ant and the mole sit both in a hole,
   And frog peeps out o'the fountain;
The dogs they do bay, and the timbrels play,
   The spindle is now a-turning;
The moon it is red, and the stars are fled,
   But all the sky is a-burning:
The ditch is made, and our nails the spade,
With pictures full, of wax and of wool;
Their livers I stick with needles quick:
There lacks but the blood to make up the flood.

BEN JONSON
ENGLISH (1572–1637)

Dirge

We do lie beneath the grass
    In the moonlight, in the shade
Of the yew-tree. They that pass
    Hear us not. We are afraid
      They would envy our delight,
      In our graves by glow-worm night.
Come follow us, and smile as we;
    We sail to the rock in the ancient waves,
Where the snow falls by thousands into the sea,
    And the drowned and the shipwrecked have
        happy graves.

THOMAS LOVELL BEDDOES
ENGLISH (1803–1849)

The City in the Sea

Lo! Death has reared himself a throne
In a strange city lying alone
Far down within the dim west
Where the good and the bad and the worst and the best
Have gone to their eternal rest.
There shrines and palaces and towers
(Time-eaten towers that tremble not!)
Resemble nothing that is ours.
Around, by lifting winds forgot,
Resignedly beneath the sky
The melancholy waters lie.

No rays from the holy heaven come down
On the long night-time of that town;
But light from out the lurid sea
Streams up the turrets silently,
Gleams up the pinnacles far and free,
Up domes, up spires, up kingly halls,
Up fanes, up Babylon-like walls,
Up shadowy long-forgotten bowers
Of sculptured ivy and stone flowers,

Up many and many a marvellous shrine
Whose wreathèd friezes intertwine
The viol, the violet, and the vine.
Resignedly beneath the sky
The melancholy waters lie.
So blend the turrets and shadows there
That all seem pendulous in air,
While from a proud tower in the town
Death looks gigantically down.

There open fanes and gaping graves
Yawn level with the luminous waves;
But not the riches there that lie
In each idol's diamond eye,
Not the gaily-jewelled dead
Tempt the waters from their bed;
For no ripples curl, alas!
Along that wilderness of glass;
No swellings tell that winds may be
Upon some far-off happier sea;
No heavings hint that winds have been
On seas less hideously serene.

But lo, a stir is in the air!
The wave — there is a movement there!
As if the towers had thrust aside,
In slightly sinking, the dull tide;
As if their tops had feebly given
A void within the filmy heaven.
The waves have now a redder glow;
The hours are breathing faint and low;
And when, amid no earthly moans,
Down, down that town shall settle hence,
Hell, rising from a thousand thrones,
Shall do it reverence.

EDGAR ALLAN POE
AMERICAN (1809–1849)

The Kraken

Below the thunders of the upper deep,
Far, far beneath in the abysmal sea,
His ancient, dreamless, uninvaded sleep
The Kraken sleepeth: faintest sunlights flee
About his shadowy sides; above him swell
Huge sponges of millennial growth and height;
And far away into the sickly light,
From many a wondrous grot and secret cell
Unnumber'd and enormous polypi
Winnow with giant arms the slumbering green.
There hath he lain for ages, and will lie
Battening upon huge sea-worms in his sleep,
Until the latter fire shall heat the deep;
Then once by man and angels to be seen,
In roaring he shall rise and on the surface die.

ALFRED, LORD TENNYSON
ENGLISH (1809–1892)

The Fairies

Up the airy mountain,
    Down the rushy glen,
We daren't go a-hunting
    For fear of little men;
Wee folk, good folk,
    Trooping all together;
Green jacket, red cap,
    And white owl's feather!

Down along the rocky shore
    Some make their home,
They live on crispy pancakes
    Of yellow tide-foam;
Some in the reeds
    Of the black mountain lake,
With frogs for their watch-dogs,
    All night awake.

High on the hill-top
   The old King sits;
He is now so old and gray
   He's nigh lost his wits.
With a bridge of white mist
   Columbkill he crosses,
On his stately journeys
   From Slieveleague to Rosses;
Or going up with music
   On cold starry nights
To sup with the Queen
   Of the gay Northern Lights.

They stole little Bridget
   For seven years long;
When she came down again
   Her friends were all gone.
They took her lightly back,
   Between the night and morrow,
They thought that she was fast asleep,
   But she was dead with sorrow.
They have kept her ever since
   Deep within the lake,
On a bed of flag-leaves,
   Watching till she wake.

By the craggy hill-side,
   Through the mosses bare,
They have planted thorn-trees
   For pleasure here and there.
Is any man so daring
   As dig them up in spite,
He shall find their sharpest thorns
   In his bed at night.

Up the airy mountain,
   Down the rushy glen,

We daren't go a-hunting
  For fear of little men;
Wee folk, good folk,
  Trooping all together;
Green jacket, red cap,
  And white owl's feather!

WILLIAM ALLINGHAM
IRISH (1824—1889)

Little Orphant Annie

Little Orphant Annie's come to our house to stay,
An' wash the cups an' saucers up, an' brush the crumbs away,
An' shoo the chickens off the porch, an' dust the hearth an'
  sweep,
An' make the fire, an' bake the bread, an' earn her board an' keep:
An' all us other children, when the supper things is done,
We set around the kitchen fire an' has the mostest fun
A-list'nin' to the witch tales 'at Annie tells about,
An' the Gobble-uns 'at gits you
                  Ef you
                      Don't
                        Watch
                          Out!

Onc't they was a little boy wouldn't say his pray'rs —
An' when he went to bed 'at night, away up-stairs,
His mammy heerd him holler, an' his daddy heerd him bawl,
An' when they turn't the kivvers down, he wasn't there at all!
An' they seeked him in the rafter-room, an' cubby-hole an' press.
An' seeked him up the chimbly-flue, and every wheres, I guess,
But all they ever found was thist his pants an' roundabout!
An' the Gobble-uns'll git you
                  Ef you
                Don't
                    Watch
                      Out!

An' one time a little girl 'ud allus laugh an' grin,
An' make fun of ever' one an' all her blood an' kin,
An' onc't when they was "company," an' ol' folks was there,
She mocked 'em an' shocked 'em, an' said she didn't care!
An' thist as she kicked her heels, an' turn't to run an' hide,
They was two great big Black Things a-standin' by her side,
An' they snatched her through the ceilin' 'fore she knowed what
   she's about!
An' the Gobble-uns'll git you
                    Ef you
                            Don't
                                    Watch
                                            Out!

An' Little Orphant Annie says, when the blaze is blue,
An' the lampwick splutters, an' the wind goes woo-oo!
An' you hear the crickets quit, an' the moon is gray,
An' the lightnin'-bugs in dew is all squenched away, —
You better mind yer parents, and yer teachers fond and dear,
An' churish them 'at loves you, an' dry the orphant's tear,
An' he'p the pore and needy ones 'at clusters all about,
Er the Gobble-uns'll git you
                    Ef you
                            Don't
                                    Watch
                                            Out!

JAMES WHITCOMB RILEY
AMERICAN (1849–1916)

THANKSGIVING

Grace for a Child

Here a little child I stand,
Heaving up my either hand;
Cold as paddocks though they be,
Here I lift them up to Thee,
For a benison to fall
On our meat, and on us all. *Amen.*

ROBERT HERRICK
ENGLISH (1591–1674)

The Thanksgivings

We who are here present thank the Great Spirit that we are
here to praise Him.

We thank Him that He has created men and women, and
ordered that these beings shall always be living to
multiply the earth.

We thank Him for making the earth and giving these beings
its products to live on.

We thank Him for the water that comes out of the earth and
runs for our lands.

We thank Him for all the animals on the earth.

We thank Him for certain timbers that grow and have fluids
coming from them for us all.

We thank Him for the branches of the trees that grow
shadows for our shelter.

We thank Him for the beings that come from the west, the
thunder and lightning that water the earth.

We thank Him for the light which we call our oldest
brother, the sun that works for our good.

We thank Him for all the fruits that grow on the trees and
vines.

We thank Him for his goodness in making the forests, and
thank all its trees.

We thank Him for the darkness that gives us rest, and for
the kind Being of the darkness that gives us light, the
moon.

We thank Him for the bright spots in the skies that give us
signs, the stars.

We give Him thanks for our supporters, who had charge of
our harvests.

We give thanks that the voice of the Great Spirit can still be
heard through the words of Ga-ne-o-di-o.

We thank the Great Spirit that we have the privilege of this
pleasant occasion.

We give thanks for the persons who can sing the Great
Spirit's music, and hope they will be privileged to
continue in his faith.

We thank the Great Spirit for all the persons who perform
the ceremonies on this occasion.

TRADITIONAL
IROQUOIS
TRANSLATED BY HARRIET MAXWELL CONVERSE

The New-England Boy's Song
about Thanksgiving Day

Over the river, and through the wood,
  To grandfather's house we go;
    The horse knows the way,
    To carry the sleigh,
  Through the white and drifted snow.

Over the river, and through the wood,
  To grandfather's house away!
    We would not stop
    For doll or top,
  For 't is Thanksgiving day.

Over the river, and through the wood,
  Oh, how the wind does blow!
    It stings the toes,
    And bites the nose,
  As over the ground we go.

Over the river, and through the wood,
  With a clear blue winter sky,
    The dogs do bark,
    And children hark,
  As we go jingling by.

Over the river, and through the wood,
  To have a first-rate play —
    Hear the bells ring
    Ting a ling ding,
  Hurra for Thanksgiving day!

Over the river, and through the wood —
  No matter for winds that blow;
    Or if we get
    The sleigh upset,
  Into a bank of snow.

Over the river, and through the wood,
  To see little John and Ann;
    We will kiss them all,
    And play snow-ball,
  And stay as long as we can.

Over the river, and through the wood,
  Trot fast, my dapple grey!
    Spring over the ground
    Like a hunting hound,
  For 't is Thanksgiving day!

Over the river, and through the wood,
  And straight through the barn-yard gate;
    We seem to go
    Extremely slow,
  It is so hard to wait.

Over the river, and through the wood —
  Old Jowler hears our bells;
    He shakes his pow,
    With a loud bow wow,
  And thus the news he tells.

Over the river, and through the wood —
  When grandmother sees us come,
    She will say, Oh dear,
    The children are here,
  Bring a pie for every one.

Over the river, and through the wood —
  Now grandmother's cap I spy!
    Hurra for the fun!
    Is the pudding done?
  Hurra for the pumpkin pie!

LYDIA MARIA CHILD
AMERICAN (1802–1880)

The Pumpkin

O, greenly and fair in the lands of the sun,
The vines of the gourd and the rich melon run,
And the rock and the tree and the cottage enfold,
With broad leaves all greenness and blossoms all gold,
Like that which o'er Nineveh's prophet once grew,
While he waited to know that his warning was true,
And longed for the storm-cloud, and listened in vain
For the rush of the whirlwind and red fire-rain.

On the banks of the Xenil the dark Spanish maiden
Comes up with the fruit of the tangled vine laden;

And the Creole of Cuba laughs out to behold
Through orange-leaves shining the broad spheres of gold;
Yet with dearer delight from his home in the North,
On the fields of his harvest the Yankee looks forth,
Where crook-necks are coiling and yellow fruit shines,
And the sun of September melts down on his vines.

Ah! on Thanksgiving day, when from East and from West,
From North and from South come the pilgrim and guest,
When the gray-haired New-Englander sees round his board
The old broken links of affection restored,
When the care-wearied man seeks his mother once more,
And the worn matron smiles where the girl smiled before,
What moistens the lip and what brightens the eye?
What calls back the past, like the rich Pumpkin pie?

O, — fruit loved of boyhood! — the old days recalling,
When wood-grapes were purpling and brown nuts were falling!
When wild, ugly faces we carved in its skin,
Glaring out through the dark with a candle within!
When we laughed round the corn-heap, with hearts all in tune,
Our chair a broad pumpkin, — our lantern the moon.
Telling tales of the fairy who travelled like steam,
In a pumpkin-shell coach, with two rats for her team!

Then thanks for thy present! — none sweeter or better
E'er smoked from an oven or circled a platter!
Fairer hands never wrought at a pastry more fine,
Brighter eyes never watched o'er its baking, than thine!
And the prayer, which my mouth is too full to express,
Swells my heart that thy shadow may never be less,
That the days of thy lot may be lengthened below,
And the fame of thy worth like a pumpkin-vine grow,
And thy life be as sweet, and its last sunset sky
Golden-tinted and fair as thy own Pumpkin pie!

JOHN GREENLEAF WHITTIER
AMERICAN (1807–1892)

Air a-gittin' cool an' coolah,
   Frost a-comin' in de night,
Hicka' nuts an' wa'nuts fallin',
   Possum keepin' out o' sight.
Tu'key struttin' in de ba'nya'd,
   Nary step so proud ez his;
Keep on struttin', Mistah Tu'key,
   Yo' do' know whut time it is.

Cidah press commence a-squeakin'
   Eatin' apples sto'ed away,
Chillun swa'min' 'roun' lak ho'nets,
   Huntin' aigs ermung de hay,
Mistah Tu'key keep on gobblin'
   At de geese a-flyin' souf,
Oomph! dat bird do' know whut's comin';
   Ef he did he'd shet his mouf.

Pumpkin gittin' good an' yallah
   Mek me open up my eyes;
Seems lak it's a-lookin' at me
   Jes' a-la'in' dah sayin' "Pies."
Tu'key gobbler gwine 'roun' blowin',
   Gwine 'roun' gibbin' sass an' slack;
Keep on talkin', Mistah Tu'key,
   You ain't seed no almanac.

Fa'mer walkin' th'oo de ba'nya'd
   Seein' how things is comin' on,
Sees ef all de fowls is fatt'nin' —
   Good times comin' sho's you bo'n,
Hyeahs dat tu'key gobbler braggin',
   Den his face break in a smile —
Nebbah min', you sassy rascal,
   He's gwine nab you atter while.

Choppin' suet in de kitchen,
   Stonin' raisins in de hall,

Beef a-cookin' fu' de mince meat,
    Spices groun' — I smell 'em all.
Look hyeah, Tu'key, stop dat gobblin',
    You ain' luned de sense ob feah,
You ol' fool, yo' naik's in dangah,
    Do' you know Thanksgibbin's hyeah?

PAUL LAURENCE DUNBAR
AMERICAN (1872–1906)

THE CHRISTMAS SEASON

Make we merry both more and less

Make we merry both more and less,
For now is the time of Christmas.

Let no man come into this hall,
Groom, page, nor yet marshal,
But that some sport he bring withal,
For now is the time of Christmas.

If that he say he cannot sing
Some other sport then let him bring
That it may please at this feasting,
For now is the time of Christmas.

If he say he can nought do,
Then for my love ask him no mo',
But to the stocks then let him go,
For now is the time of Christmas.

ANONYMOUS
ENGLISH (16TH CENTURY)

All you that to feasting and mirth are inclined

All you that to feasting and mirth are inclined,
Come here is good news for to pleasure your mind,
Old Christmas is come for to keep open house,
He scorns to be guilty of starving a mouse:
Then come, boys, and welcome for diet the chief,
Plum-pudding, goose, capon, minced pies, and roast beef.
The holly and ivy about the walls wind
And show that we ought to our neighbors be kind,
Inviting each other for pastime and sport,
And where we best fare, there we most do resort;
We fail not of victuals, and that of the chief,
Plum-pudding, goose, capon, minced pies, and roast beef.
All travellers, as they do pass on their way,
At gentlemen's halls are invited to stay,
Themselves to refresh, and their horses to rest,
Since that he must be Old Christmas's guest;
Nay, the poor shall not want, but have for relief,
Plum-pudding, goose, capon, minced pies, and roast beef.

ANONYMOUS
ENGLISH (MEDIEVAL)

New Prince, New Pomp

Behold a silly tender babe
    In freezing winter night
In homely manger trembling lies:
    Alas! a piteous sight.

The inns are full; no man will yield
    This little pilgrim bed;
But forced he is with silly beasts
    In crib to shroud his head.

Despise not him for lying there;
    First what he is inquire:
An orient pearl is often found
    In depth of dirty mire.

Weigh not his crib, his wooden dish,
    Nor beasts that by him feed;
Weigh not his mother's poor attire,
    Nor Joseph's simple weed.

This stable is a Prince's court,
    This crib his chair of state,
The beasts are parcel of his pomp,
    The wooden dish his plate.

The persons in that poor attire
    His royal liveries wear;
The Prince himself is come from heaven.
    This pomp is prizèd there.

With joy approach, O Christian wight,
    Do homage to thy King;
And highly praise this humble pomp
    Which he from heaven doth bring.

ROBERT SOUTHWELL
ENGLISH (1561–1595)

Come, bring with a noise

Come, bring with a noise,
    My merry, merry boys,
The Christmas log to the firing,
    While my good dame, she
    Bids ye all be free,
And drink to your heart's desiring.

With the last year's brand
    Light the new block, and
For good success in his spending,
    On your psalteries play,
    That sweet luck may
Come while the log is a-tending.

Drink now the strong beer,
Cut the white loaf here,
The while the meat is a-shredding;
For the rare mince-pie,
And the plums stand by,
To fill the paste that's a-kneading.

ROBERT HERRICK
ENGLISH (1591–1674)

A Visit from St. Nicholas

'Twas the night before Christmas, when all through the house
Not a creature was stirring, not even a mouse;
The stockings were hung by the chimney with care,
In hopes that St. Nicholas soon would be there;
The children were nestled all snug in their beds,
While visions of sugar-plums danced in their heads;
And mamma in her kerchief, and I in my cap,
Had just settled our brains for a long winter's nap, —
When out on the lawn there arose such a clatter,
I sprang from my bed to see what was the matter.
Away to the window I flew like a flash,
Tore open the shutters and threw up the sash.
The moon on the breast of the new-fallen snow
Gave a lustre of midday to objects below;
When, what to my wondering eyes should appear,
But a miniature sleigh and eight tiny reindeer,
With a little old driver, so lively and quick
I knew in a moment it must be St. Nick.
More rapid than eagles his coursers they came,
And he whistled and shouted, and called them by name:
"Now, Dasher! now, Dancer! now, Prancer and Vixen!
On, Comet! on, Cupid! on, Donder and Blitzen!
To the top of the porch, to the top of the wall!
Now dash away, dash away, dash away all!"
As dry leaves that before the wild hurricane fly,
When they meet with an obstacle, mount to the sky,
So up to the house-top the coursers they flew,
With the sleigh full of toys, — and St. Nicholas too.

And then in a twinkling I heard on the roof
The prancing and pawing of each little hoof.
As I drew in my head, and was turning around,
Down the chimney St. Nicholas came with a bound.
He was dressed all in fur from his head to his foot,
And his clothes were all tarnished with ashes and soot;
A bundle of toys he had flung on his back,
And he looked like a peddler just opening his pack.
His eyes how they twinkled! his dimples how merry!
His cheeks were like roses, his nose like a cherry;
His droll little mouth was drawn up like a bow,
And the beard on his chin was as white as the snow.
The stump of a pipe he held tight in his teeth,
And the smoke it encircled his head like a wreath.
He had a broad face and a little round belly
That shook, when he laughed, like a bowl full of jelly.
He was chubby and plump, — a right jolly old elf,
And I laughed, when I saw him, in spite of myself.
A wink of his eye and a twist of his head
Soon gave me to know I had nothing to dread.
He spoke not a word, but went straight to his work,
And filled all the stockings; then turned with a jerk,
And laying his finger aside of his nose,
And giving a nod, up the chimney he rose.
He sprang to his sleigh, to his team gave a whistle,
And away they all flew like the down of a thistle;
But I heard him exclaim, ere he drove out of sight,
"Happy Christmas to all, and to all a good-night!"

CLEMENT C. MOORE
AMERICAN (1779–1863)

Christmas Bells

I heard the bells on Christmas Day
Their old, familiar carols play,
   And wild and sweet
   The words repeat
Of peace on earth, good-will to men!

And thought how, as the day had come,
The belfries of all Christendom
   Had rolled along
   The unbroken song
Of peace on earth, good-will to men!

Till, ringing, singing on its way,
The world revolved from night to day,
   A voice, a chime,
   A chant sublime
Of peace on earth, good-will to men!

Then from each black, accursed mouth
The cannon thundered in the South,
   And with the sound
   The carols drowned
Of peace on earth, good-will to men!

It was as if an earthquake rent
The hearth-stones of a continent,
   And made forlorn
   The households born
Of peace on earth, good-will to men!

And in despair I bowed my head;
"There is no peace on earth," I said,
   "For hate is strong,
   And mocks the song
Of peace on earth, good-will to men!"

Then pealed the bells more loud and deep:
"God is not dead, nor doth He sleep!
  The Wrong shall fail,
  The Right prevail,
With peace on earth, good-will to men!"

HENRY WADSWORTH LONGFELLOW
AMERICAN (1807–1882)

The Mahogany Tree

Christmas is here:
Winds whistle shrill,
Icy and chill,
Little care we:
Little we fear
Weather without,
Shelter about
The Mahogany Tree.

Once on the boughs
Birds of rare plume
Sang in its bloom;
Night-birds are we;
Singing like them,
Perched round the stem
Of the jolly old tree.

Here let us sport,
Boys, as we sit;
Laughter and wit
Flashing so free.
Life is but short —
When we are gone,
Let them sing on
Round the old tree.

Evenings we knew,
Happy as this;
Faces we miss,

Pleasant to see.
Kind hearts and true,
Gentle and just,
Peace to your dust!
We sing round the tree.

Care, like a dun,
Lurks at the gate:
Let the dog wait;
Happy we'll be!
Drink, every one;
Pile up the coals,
Fill the red bowls,
Round the old tree!

Drain we the cup, —
Friend, art afraid?
Spirits are laid
In the Red Sea.

Mantle it up;
Empty it yet;
Let us forget,
Round the old tree.

Sorrows, begone!
Life and its ills,
Duns and their bills,
Bid we to flee.
Come with the dawn,
Blue-devil sprite,
Leave us to-night,
Round the old tree.

WILLIAM MAKEPEACE THACKERAY
ENGLISH (1811–1863)

The Oxen

Christmas Eve, and twelve of the clock.
   "Now they are all on their knees,"
An elder said as we sat in a flock
   By the embers in hearthside ease.

We pictured the meek and mild creatures where
   They dwelt in their strawy pen,
Nor did it occur to one of us there
   To doubt they were kneeling then.

So fair a fancy few would weave
   In these years! Yet, I feel,
If someone said on Christmas Eve,
   "Come; see the oxen kneel,

"In the lonely barton by yonder coomb
   Our childhood used to know,"
I should go with him in the gloom,
   Hoping it might be so.

THOMAS HARDY
ENGLISH (1840–1928)

The Cycles of Life

THIS CENTRAL SEGMENT TAKES ITS CATEGORIES FROM THE RHYTHMS OF HUMAN GROWTH AND AGING: ENJOYING OR RECOLLECTING THE IMMEDIACIES OF CHILDHOOD AND youth, looking for the proper mode in which to engage a world of possibilities and challenges, or confronting, in imagination or actuality, one's death. What will be found here is not an endless series of restatements of common themes relating to these milestones — birth, the entry into adulthood, marriage, the plateau of mid-life, aging, grief — but pieces of real and unpredictable experience. Each poem, in a sense, is a life in itself, with its own givens and its own expectations. The dizzying effect of reading them is to live a succession of lives, to be initiated into a multiple awareness of humans caught up in moments of vital change. To register life as a series of transformations — to embody the passage from one age, one state, to another — remains a fundamental task of poetry, rooted in the most ancient ritual forms. But if poetry records the transition, it also makes it possible to return: there is a childhood that lives again in the poems of William Blake, a youth that is pre-served even as its loss is regretted in the poems of Lord Byron and A. E. Housman, an old age that, in William Butler Yeats or William Carlos Williams, is somehow overcome even in the act of acknowledging it.

BIRTH AND INFANCY

Golden slumbers kiss your eyes

Golden slumbers kiss your eyes,
Smiles awake you when you rise.
Sleep, pretty wantons, do not cry,
And I will sing a lullaby:
Rock them, rock them, lullaby.

Care is heavy, therefore sleep you;
You are care, and care must keep you.
Sleep, pretty wantons, do not cry,
And I will sing a lullaby:
Rock them, rock them, lullaby.

THOMAS DEKKER (ATTRIB.)
ENGLISH (1572?–1632?)

The Salutation

1

These little limbs,
These eyes and hands which here I find,
These rosy cheeks wherewith my life begins,
Where have ye been? Behind
What curtain were ye from me hid so long!
Where was, in what abyss, my speaking tongue?

2

When silent I,
So many thousand thousand years,
Beneath the dust did in a chaos lie,
How could I smiles or tears,
Or lips or hands or eyes or ears perceive?
Welcome, ye treasures which I now receive.

3

I that so long
Was nothing from eternity,

Did little think such joys as ear or tongue,
　　To celebrate or see:
Such sounds to hear, such hands to feel, such feet,
Beneath the skies, on such a ground to meet.

4

New burnish'd joys!
　Which yellow gold and pearl excel!
Such sacred treasures are the limbs in boys,
　　In which a soul doth dwell;
Their organized joints, and azure veins
More wealth include, than all the world contains.

5

From dust I rise,
　And out of nothing now awake,
These brighter regions which salute mine eyes,
　　A gift from God I take.
The earth, the seas, the light, the day, the skies,
The sun and stars are mine; if those I prize.

6

Long time before
　I in my mother's womb was born,
A God preparing did this glorious store,
　　The world, for me adorn.
Into this Eden so divine and fair,
So wide and bright, I come His son and heir.

7

A stranger here
　Strange things doth meet, strange glories see;
Strange treasures lodg'd in this fair world appear;
　　Strange all, and new to me.
But that they mine should be, who nothing was,
That strangest is of all, yet brought to pass.

THOMAS TRAHERNE
ENGLISH (1637–1674)

To Miss Charlotte Pulteney
in her Mother's Arms

Timely blossom, infant fair,
Fondling of a happy pair,
Every morn and every night,
Their solicitous delight,
Sleeping, waking, still at ease,
Pleasing, without skill to please,
Little gossip, blithe and hale,
Tattling many a broken tale,
Singing many a tuneless song,
Lavish of a heedless tongue,
Simple maiden, void of art,
Babbling out the very heart,
Yet abandoned to thy will,
Yet imagining no ill,
Yet too innocent to blush,
Like the linlet in the bush,
To the mother-linnet's note
Moduling her slender throat,
Chirping forth thy petty joys,
Wanton in the change of toys,
Like the linnet green in May,
Flitting to each bloomy spray,
Wearied then, and glad of rest,
Like the linlet in the nest.
This thy present happy lot,
This, in time, will be forgot:
Other pleasures, other cares,
Ever-busy time prepares;
And thou shalt in thy daughter see
This picture, once, resembled thee.

AMBROSE PHILIPS
ENGLISH (C. 1675–1749)

The Angel that presided o'er my birth

The Angel that presided o'er my birth
Said, "Little creature, form'd of Joy and Mirth,
"Go love without the help of any Thing on Earth."

WILLIAM BLAKE
ENGLISH (1757–1827)

Infant Joy

"I have no name:
"I am but two days old."
What shall I call thee?
"I happy am,
"Joy is my name."
Sweet joy befall thee!

Pretty joy!
Sweet joy but two days old,
Sweet joy I call thee:
Thou dost smile,
I sing the while,
Sweet joy befall thee!

WILLIAM BLAKE
ENGLISH (1757–1827)

Infant Sorrow

My mother groan'd, my father wept,
Into the dangerous world I leapt;
Helpless, naked, piping loud,
Like a fiend hid in a cloud.

Struggling in my father's hands,
Striving against my swadling bands,
Bound and weary, I thought best
To sulk upon my mother's breast.

WILLIAM BLAKE
ENGLISH (1757–1827)

Nurse's Song

When the voices of children are heard on the green,
And laughing is heard on the hill,
My heart is at rest within my breast,
And everything else is still.

Then come home, my children, the sun is gone down,
And the dews of night arise;
Come, come, leave off play, and let us away,
Till the morning appears in the skies.

No, no, let us play, for it is yet day,
And we cannot go to sleep;
Besides, in the sky the little birds fly,
And the hills are all covered with sheep.

Well, well, go and play till the light fades away,
And then go home to bed.
The little ones leaped and shouted and laughed
And all the hills echoèd.

WILLIAM BLAKE
ENGLISH (1757–1827)

Sweet and low, sweet and low

Sweet and low, sweet and low,
 Wind of the western sea,
Low, low, breathe and blow,
 Wind of the western sea!
Over the rolling waters go,
Come from the dying moon, and blow,
 Blow him again to me;
While my little one, while my pretty one, sleeps.

Sleep and rest, sleep and rest,
    Father will come to thee soon;
Rest, rest, on mother's breast,
    Father will come to thee soon;
Silver sails all out of the west,
    Under the silver moon:
Sleep, my little one, sleep, my pretty one, sleep.

ALFRED, LORD TENNYSON
ENGLISH (1809–1892)

Dutch Lullaby

Wynken, Blynken, and Nod one night
    Sailed off in a wooden shoe, —
Sailed on a river of misty light
    Into a sea of dew.
"Where are you going, and what do you wish?"
    The old moon asked the three.
"We have come to fish for the herring-fish
    That live in this beautiful sea;
    Nets of silver and gold have we,"
        Said Wynken,
        Blynken,
        And Nod.

The old moon laughed and sung a song,
    As they rocked in the wooden shoe;
And the wind that sped them all night long
    Ruffled the waves of dew;
The little stars were the herring-fish
    That lived in the beautiful sea.
"Now cast your nets wherever you wish,
    But never afeard are we!"
    So cried the stars to the fishermen three,
        Wynken,
        Blynken,
        And Nod.

All night long their nets they threw
  For the fish in the twinkling foam,
Then down from the sky came the wooden shoe,
  Bringing the fishermen home;
'T was all so pretty a sail, it seemed
  As if it could not be;
And some folk thought 't was a dream they'd dreamed
  Of sailing that beautiful sea;
  But I shall name you the fishermen three:
    Wynken,
    Blynken,
    And Nod.

Wynken and Blynken are two little eyes,
  And Nod is a little head,
And the wooden shoe that sailed the skies
  Is a wee one's trundle-bed;
So shut your eyes while Mother sings
  Of wonderful sights that be,
And you shall see the beautiful things
  As you rock on the misty sea
  Where the old shoe rocked the fishermen three, —
    Wynken,
    Blynken,
    And Nod.

EUGENE FIELD
AMERICAN (1850–1895)

Seal Lullaby

Oh! hush thee, my baby, the night is behind us,
 And black are the waters that sparkled so green.
The moon, o'er the combers, looks downward to find us
 At rest in the hollows that rustle between.
Where billow meets billow, there soft by the pillow;
 Ah, weary wee flipperling, curl at thy ease!
The storm shall not wake thee, nor shark overtake thee,
 Asleep in the arms of the slow-swinging seas.

RUDYARD KIPLING
ENGLISH (1865–1936)

Labor Pains

I am sick today,
sick in my body,
eyes wide open, silent,
I lie on the bed of childbirth.

Why do I, so used to the nearness of death,
to pain and blood and screaming,
now uncontrollably tremble with dread?

A nice young doctor tried to comfort me,
and talked about the joy of giving birth.
Since I know better than he about this matter,
what good purpose can his prattle serve?

Knowledge is not reality.
Experience belongs to the past.
Let those who lack immediacy be silent.
Let observers be content to observe.

I am all alone,
totally, utterly, entirely on my own,
gnawing my lips, holding my body rigid,
waiting on inexorable fate.

There is only one truth.
I shall give birth to a child,
truth driving outward from my inwardness.
Neither good nor bad; real, no sham about it.

With the first labor pains,
suddenly the sun goes pale.
The indifferent world goes strangely calm.
I am alone.
It is alone I am.

YOSANO AKIKO
JAPANESE (1878–1942)
TRANSLATED BY KENNETH REXROTH

The Birthnight

Dearest, it was a night
That in its darkness rocked Orion's stars;
A sighing wind ran faintly white
Along the willows, and the cedar boughs
Laid their wide hands in stealthy peace across
The starry silence of their antique moss:
No sound save rushing air
Cold, yet all sweet with Spring,
And in thy mother's arms, couched weeping there,
  Thou, lovely thing.

WALTER DE LA MARE
ENGLISH (1873–1956)

By the road to the contagious hospital

By the road to the contagious hospital
under the surge of the blue
mottled clouds driven from the
northeast — a cold wind. Beyond, the
waste of broad, muddy fields
brown with dried weeds, standing and fallen

patches of standing water
the scattering of tall trees

All along the road the reddish
purplish, forked, upstanding, twiggy
stuff of bushes and small trees
with dead, brown leaves under them
leafless vines —

Lifeless in appearance, sluggish
dazed spring approaches —

They enter the new world naked,
cold, uncertain of all
save that they enter. All about them
the cold, familiar wind —

Now the grass, tomorrow
the stiff curl of wildcarrot leaf

One by one objects are defined —
It quickens: clarity, outline of leaf

But now the stark dignity of
entrance — Still, the profound change
has come upon them: rooted, they
grip down and begin to awaken

> WILLIAM CARLOS WILLIAMS
> AMERICAN (1883–1963)

Sara in Her Father's Arms

Cell by cell the baby made herself, the cells
Made cells. That is to say
The baby is made largely of milk. Lying in her father's arms,
    the little seed eyes
Moving, trying to see, smiling for us
To see, she will make a household

To her need of these rooms — Sara, little seed,
Little violent, diligent seed. Come let us look at the world
Glittering: this seed will speak,
Max, words! There will be no other words in the world
But those our children speak. What will she make of a world
Do you suppose, Max, of which she is made.

GEORGE OPPEN
AMERICAN (1908–1984)

Baby Song

From the private ease of Mother's womb
I fall into the lighted room.

Why don't they simply put me back
Where it is warm and wet and black?

But one thing follows on another.
Things were different inside Mother.

Padded and jolly I would ride
The perfect comfort of her inside.

They tuck me in a rustling bed
— I lie there, raging, small, and red.

I may sleep soon, I may forget,
But I won't forget that I regret.

A rain of blood poured round her womb,
But all time roars outside this room.

THOM GUNN
ENGLISH (B. 1929)

CHILDHOOD

Growing an Orchid

I brought a humble orchid into my room
and have since, for years, been intent on nurturing it.
A light shower, and I've taken it outside,
delighting in the sprouting purple buds.
Mornings I watched it, evenings I caressed it,
examining the flower buds a number of times.
I've taken up the brush to paint its piteous figure,
composed poems to praise its lasting grace.
From the care needed to raise an orchid,
I've learned how people bring up children.

EMA SAIKŌ
JAPANESE (1787–1861)
TRANSLATED BY HIROAKI SATO

For sport and play

From the *Ryōjin Hishō*

For sport and play
I think that we are born.
For when I hear
The voices of children at their play,
My limbs, even my
Stiff limbs, are stirred.

ANONYMOUS
JAPANESE (C. 1179)
TRANSLATED BY ARTHUR WALEY

I am called Childhood, in play is all my mind

I am called Childhood, in play is all my mind,
To cast a quoit, a cock-stele, and a ball.
A top can I set, and drive it in his kind.
But would to God these hateful bookès all
Were in a fire burnt to powder small.
Then might I lead my life always in play:
Which life God send me to mine ending day.

SIR THOMAS MORE
ENGLISH (1478–1535)

Methinks 'tis pretty sport to hear a child

Methinks 'tis pretty sport to hear a child
Rocking a word in mouth yet undefiled;
The tender racquet rudely plays the sound
Which, weakly bandied, cannot back rebound;
And the soft air the softer roof doth kiss
With a sweet dying and a pretty miss,
Which hears no answer yet from the white rank
Of teeth not risen from their coral bank.
The alphabet is searched for letters soft
To try a word before it can be wrought;
And when it slideth forth, it goes as nice
As when a man doth walk upon the ice.

THOMAS BASTARD
ENGLISH (1566–1618)

The Retreat

Happy those early days, when I
Shined in my angel-infancy!
Before I understood this place
Appointed for my second race,
Or taught my soul to fancy aught
But a white celestial thought;
When yet I had not walked above
A mile or two from my first love,

And looking back, at that short space,
Could see a glimpse of his bright face;
When on some gilded cloud, or flower,
My gazing soul would dwell an hour,
And in those weaker glories spy
Some shadows of eternity;
Before I taught my tongue to wound
My conscience with a sinful sound,
Or had the black art to dispense
A several sin to every sense,
But felt through all this fleshly dress
Bright shoots of everlastingness.

   O how I long to travel back,
And tread again that ancient track!
That I might once more reach that plain
Where first I left my glorious train;
From whence the enlightened spirit sees
That shady City of Palm-trees.
But ah! my soul with too much stay
Is drunk, and staggers in the way.
Some men a forward motion love,
But I by backward steps would move,
And when this dust falls to the urn
In that state I came, return.

HENRY VAUGHAN
ENGLISH (1622–1695)

Piping down the valleys wild

Piping down the valleys wild,
Piping songs of pleasant glee,
On a cloud I saw a child,
And he laughing said to me:

"Pipe a song about a Lamb!"
So I piped with a merry chear.
"Piper, pipe that song again";
So I piped: he wept to hear.

"Drop thy pipe, thy happy pipe;
Sing thy songs of happy chear":
So I sung the same again,
While he wept with joy to hear.

"Piper, sit thee down and write
In a book, that all may read."
So he vanish'd from my sight,
And I pluck'd a hollow reed,

And I made a rural pen,
And I stain'd the water clear,
And I wrote my happy songs
Every child may joy to hear.

WILLIAM BLAKE
ENGLISH (1757–1827)

Laughing Song

When the green woods laugh, with the voice of joy
And the dimpling stream runs laughing by,
When the air does laugh with our merry wit,
And the green hill laughs with the noise of it.

When the meadows laugh with lively green
And the grasshopper laughs in the merry scene,
When Mary and Susan and Emily,
With their sweet round mouths sing Ha, Ha, He.

When the painted birds laugh in the shade
Where our table with cherries and nuts is spread
Come live & be merry and join with me,
To sing the sweet chorus of Ha, Ha, He.

WILLIAM BLAKE
ENGLISH (1757–1827)

Characteristics of a Child
Three Years Old

Loving she is, and tractable, though wild;
And Innocence hath privilege in her
To dignify arch looks and laughing eyes
And feats of cunning; and the pretty round
Of trespasses, affected to provoke
Mock-chastisement and partnership in play.
And, as a faggot sparkles on the hearth,
Not less if unattended and alone
Than when both young and old sit gathered round
And take delight in its activity;
Even so this happy Creature of herself
Is all-sufficient; solitude to her
Is blithe society, who fills the air
With gladness and involuntary songs.
Light are her sallies as the tripping fawn's
Forth-startled from the fern where she lay couched;
Of the soft breeze ruffling the meadow-flowers,
Unthought-of, unexpected, as the stir
Or from before it chasing wantonly
The many-coloured images imprest
Upon the bosom of a placid lake.

WILLIAM WORDSWORTH
ENGLISH (1770–1850)

I remember, I remember

I remember, I remember,
The house where I was born,
The little window where the sun
Came peeping in at morn;
He never came a wink too soon,
Nor brought too long a day,
But now, I often wish the night
Had borne my breath away!

I remember, I remember,
The roses, red and white,
The vi'lets, and the lily-cups,
Those flowers made of light!
The lilacs where the robin built,
And where my brother set
The laburnum on his birthday, —
The tree is living yet!

I remember, I remember,
Where I was used to swing,
And thought the air must rush as fresh
To swallows on the wing;
My spirit flew in feathers then,
That is so heavy now,
And summer pools could hardly cool
The fever on my brow!

I remember, I remember,
The fir trees dark and high;
I used to think their slender tops
Were close against the sky:
It was a childish ignorance,
But now 'tis little joy
To know I'm farther off from heav'n
Than when I was a boy.

THOMAS HOOD
ENGLISH (1799–1845)

The Children's Hour

Between the dark and the daylight,
    When the night is beginning to lower,
Comes a pause in the day's occupations,
    That is known as the Children's Hour.

I hear in the chamber above me
    The patter of little feet,

The sound of a door that is opened,
  And voices soft and sweet.

From my study I see in the lamplight,
  Descending the broad hall stair,
Grave Alice, and laughing Allegra,
  And Edith with golden hair.

A whisper, and then a silence:
  Yet I know by their merry eyes
They are plotting and planning together
  To take me by surprise.

A sudden rush from the stairway,
  A sudden raid from the hall!
By three doors left unguarded
  They enter my castle wall!

They climb up into my turret
  O'er the arms and back of my chair;
If I try to escape, they surround me;
  They seem to be everywhere.

They almost devour me with kisses,
  Their arms about me entwine,
Till I think of the Bishop of Bingen
  In his Mouse-Tower on the Rhine!

Do you think, O blue-eyed banditti,
  Because you have scaled the wall,
Such an old mustache as I am
  Is not a match for you all!

I have you fast in my fortress,
  And will not let you depart,

But put you down into the dungeon
    In the round-tower of my heart.

And there will I keep you forever,
    Yes, forever and a day,
Till the walls shall crumble to ruin,
    And moulder in dust away!

HENRY WADSWORTH LONGFELLOW
AMERICAN (1807–1882)

The Barefoot Boy

Blessings on thee, little man,
Barefoot boy, with cheek of tan!
With thy turned-up pantaloons,
And thy merry whistled tunes;
With thy red lip, redder still
Kissed by strawberries on the hill;
With the sunshine on thy face,
Through thy torn brim's jaunty grace;
From my heart I give thee joy, —
I was once a barefoot boy!
Prince thou art, — the grown-up man
Only is republican.
Let the million-dollared ride!
Barefoot, trudging at his side,
Thou hast more than he can buy
In the reach of ear and eye, —
Outward sunshine, inward joy:
Blessings on thee, barefoot boy!

Oh for boyhood's painless play,
Sleep that wakes in laughing day,
Health that mocks the doctor's rules,
Knowledge never learned of schools,
Of the wild bee's morning chase,
Of the wild-flower's time and place,
Flight of fowl and habitude
Of the tenants of the wood;

How the tortoise bears his shell,
How the woodchuck digs his cell,
And the ground-mole sinks his well;
How the robin feeds her young,
How the oriole's nest is hung;
Where the whitest lilies blow,
Where the freshest berries grow,
Where the ground-nut trails its vine,
Where the wood-grape's clusters shine;
Of the black wasp's cunning way,
Mason of his walls of clay,
And the architectural plans
Of gray hornet artisans!
For, eschewing books and tasks,
Nature answers all he asks;
Hand in hand with her he walks,
Face to face with her he talks,
Part and parcel of her joy, —
Blessings on the barefoot boy!

Oh for boyhood's time of June,
Crowding years in one brief moon,
When all things I heard or saw,
Me, their master, waited for.
I was rich in flowers and trees,
Humming-birds and honey-bees;
For my sport the squirrel played,
Plied the snouted mole his spade;
For my taste the blackberry cone
Purpled over hedge and stone;
Laughed the brook for my delight
Through the day and through the night,
Whispering at the garden wall,
Talked with me from fall to fall;
Mine the sand-rimmed pickerel pond,
Mine the walnut slopes beyond,
Mine, on bending orchard trees,
Apples of Hesperides!

Still as my horizon grew,
Larger grew my riches too;
All the world I saw or knew
Seemed a complex Chinese toy,
Fashioned for a barefoot boy!

Oh for festal dainties spread,
Like my bowl of milk and bread;
Pewter spoon and bowl of wood,
On the door-stone, gray and rude!
O'er me, like a regal tent,
Cloudy-ribbed, the sunset bent,
Purple-curtained, fringed with gold,
Looped in many a wind-swung fold;
While for music came the play
Of the pied frogs' orchestra;
And, to light the noisy choir,
Lit the fly his lamp of fire.
I was monarch: pomp and joy
Waited on the barefoot boy!

Cheerily, then, my little man,
Live and laugh, as boyhood can!
Though the flinty slopes be hard,
Stubble-speared the new-mown sward,
Every morn shall lead thee through
Fresh baptisms of the dew;
Every evening from thy feet
Shall the cool wind kiss the heat:
All too soon these feet must hide
In the prison cells of pride,
Lose the freedom of the sod,
Like a colt's for work be shod,
Made to tread the mills of toil,
Up and down in ceaseless moil:

Happy if their track be found
Never on forbidden ground;
Happy if they sink not in
Quick and treacherous sands of sin.
Ah! that thou couldst know thy joy,
Ere it passes, barefoot boy!

JOHN GREENLEAF WHITTIER
AMERICAN (1807–1892)

There Was a Child Went Forth

There was a child went forth every day,
And the first object he look'd upon, that object he became,
And that object became part of him for the day or a certain part
of the day,
Or for many years or stretching cycles of years.

The early lilacs became part of this child,
And grass and white and red morning-glories, and white
and red clover, and the song of the phœbe-bird,
And the Third-month lambs and the sow's pink-faint litter,
and the mare's foal and the cow's calf,
And the noisy brood of the barnyard or by the mire of the
pond-side,
And the fish suspending themselves so curiously below
there, and the beautiful curious liquid,
And the water-plants with their graceful flat heads, all
became part of him.

The field-sprouts of Fourth-month and Fifth-month became
part of him,
Winter-grain sprouts and those of the light-yellow corn, and
the esculent roots of the garden,
And the apple-trees cover'd with blossoms and the fruit
afterward, and wood-berries, and the commonest weeds
by the road,
And the old drunkard staggering home from the outhouse
of the tavern whence he had lately risen,
And the schoolmistress that pass'd on her way to the school,

And the friendly boys that pass'd, and the quarrelsome boys,
And the tidy and fresh-cheek'd girls, and the barefoot negro
    boy and girl,
And all the changes of city and country wherever he went.

His own parents, he that had father'd him and she that had
    conceiv'd him in her womb and birth'd him,
They gave this child more of themselves than that,
They gave him afterward every day, they became part of him.

The mother at home quietly placing the dishes on the
    supper-table,
The mother with mild words, clean her cap and gown, a
    wholesome odor falling off her person and clothes as
    she walks by,
The father, strong, self-sufficient, manly, mean, anger'd,
    unjust,
The blow, the quick loud word, the tight bargain, the crafty
    lure,
The family usages, the language, the company, the furniture,
    the yearning and swelling heart,
Affection that will not be gainsay'd, the sense of what is
    real, the thought if after all it should prove unreal,
The doubts of day-time and the doubts of night-time, the
    curious whether and how,
Whether that which appears so is so, or is it all flashes and
    specks?
Men and women crowding fast in the streets, if they are not
    flashes and specks what are they?
The streets themselves and the façades of houses, and goods
    in the windows,
Vehicles, teams, the heavy-plank'd wharves, the huge
    crossing at the ferries,
The village on the highland seen from afar at sunset, the
    river between,
Shadows, aureola and mist, the light falling on roofs and
    gables of white or brown two miles off,
The schooner near by sleepily dropping down the tide, the
    little boat slack-tow'd astern,

The hurrying tumbling waves, quick-broken crests, slapping,
The strata of color'd clouds, the long bar of maroon-tint
  away solitary by itself, the spread of purity it lies
  motionless in,
The horizon's edge, the flying sea-crow, the fragrance of salt
  marsh and shore mud,
These became part of that child who went forth every
  day, and who now goes, and will always go forth
  every day.

WALT WHITMAN
AMERICAN (1819–1892)

The Land of Nod

From breakfast on through all the day
At home among my friends I stay,
But every night I go abroad
Afar into the land of Nod.

All by myself I have to go,
With none to tell me what to do —
All alone beside the streams
And up the mountain-sides of dreams.

The strangest things are there for me,
Both things to eat and things to see,
And many frightening sights abroad
Till morning in the land of Nod.

Try as I like to find the way,
I never can get back by day,
Nor can remember plain and clear
The curious music that I hear.

ROBERT LOUIS STEVENSON
SCOTTISH (1850–1894)

My Bed Is a Boat

My bed is like a little boat;
  Nurse helps me in when I embark;
She girds me in my sailor's coat
  And starts me in the dark.

At night, I go on board and say
  Good-night to all my friends on shore;
I shut my eyes and sail away
  And see and hear no more.

And sometimes things to bed I take,
  As prudent sailors have to do;
Perhaps a slice of wedding-cake,
  Perhaps a toy or two.

All night across the dark we steer:
  But when the day returns at last,
Safe in my room, beside the pier,
  I find my vessel fast.

ROBERT LOUIS STEVENSON
SCOTTISH (1850–1894)

Silly Song

Mama,
I wish I were silver.

Son,
You'd be very cold.

Mama,
I wish I were water.

Son,
You'd be very cold.

Mama,
Embroider me on your pillow.

That, yes!
Right away!

FEDERICO GARCÍA LORCA
SPANISH (1898–1936)
TRANSLATED BY HARRIET DE ONÍS

A Prayer for My Daughter

Once more the storm is howling, and half hid
Under this cradle-hood and coverlid
My child sleeps on. There is no obstacle
But Gregory's wood and one bare hill
Whereby the haystack- and roof-levelling wind,
Bred on the Atlantic, can be stayed;
And for an hour I have walked and prayed
Because of the great gloom that is in my mind.

I have walked and prayed for this young child an hour
And heard the sea-wind scream upon the tower,
And under the arches of the bridge, and scream
In the elms above the flooded stream;
Imagining in excited reverie
That the future years had come,
Dancing to a frenzied drum,
Out of the murderous innocence of the sea.

May she be granted beauty and yet not
Beauty to make a stranger's eye distraught,
Or hers before a looking-glass, for such,
Being made beautiful overmuch,
Consider beauty a sufficient end,
Lose natural kindness and maybe
The heart-revealing intimacy
That chooses right, and never find a friend.

Helen being chosen found life flat and dull
And later had much trouble from a fool,
While that great Queen, that rose out of the spray,
Being fatherless could have her way
Yet chose a bandy-leggèd smith for man.
It's certain that fine women eat
A crazy salad with their meat
Whereby the Horn of Plenty is undone.

In courtesy I'd have her chiefly learned;
Hearts are not had as a gift but hearts are earned
By those that are not entirely beautiful;
Yet many, that have played the fool
For beauty's very self, has charm made wise,
And many a poor man that has roved,
Loved and thought himself beloved,
From a glad kindness cannot take his eyes.

May she become a flourishing hidden tree
That all her thoughts may like the linnet be,
And have no business but dispensing round
Their magnanimities of sound,
Nor but in merriment begin a chase,
Nor but in merriment a quarrel.
O may she live like some green laurel
Rooted in one dear perpetual place.

My mind, because the minds that I have loved,
The sort of beauty that I have approved,
Prosper but little, has dried up of late,
Yet knows that to be choked with hate
May well be of all evil chances chief.
If there's no hatred in a mind
Assault and battery of the wind
Can never tear the linnet from the leaf.

An intellectual hatred is the worst,
So let her think opinions are accursed.
Have I not seen the loveliest woman born

Out of the mouth of Plenty's horn,
Because of her opinionated mind
Barter that horn and every good
By quiet natures understood
For an old bellows full of angry wind?

Considering that, all hatred driven hence,
The soul recovers radical innocence
And learns at last that it is self-delighting,
Self-appeasing, self-affrighting,
And that its own sweet will is Heaven's will;
She can, though every face should scowl
And every windy quarter howl
Or every bellows burst, be happy still.

And may her bridegroom bring her to a house
Where all's accustomed, ceremonious;
For arrogance and hatred are the wares
Peddled in the thoroughfares.
How but in custom and in ceremony
Are innocence and beauty born?
Ceremony's a name for the rich horn,
And custom for the spreading laurel tree.

WILLIAM BUTLER YEATS
IRISH (1865–1939)

in Just-

From *Chansons Innocentes*

    in Just-
    spring   when the world is mud-
    luscious the little
    lame balloonman

    whistles   far   and wee

    and eddieandbill come
    running from marbles and

piracies and it's
spring

when the world is puddle-wonderful

the queer
old balloonman whistles
far   and   wee
and bettyandisbel come dancing

from hop-scotch and jump-rope and

it's
spring
and
      the

            goat-footed

balloonMan   whistles
far
and
wee

E. E. CUMMINGS
AMERICAN (1894–1962)

I am Rose my eyes are blue

I am Rose my eyes are blue
I am Rose and who are you
I am Rose and when I sing
I am Rose like anything.

GERTRUDE STEIN
AMERICAN (1874–1946)

Fern Hill

Now as I was young and easy under the apple boughs
About the lilting house and happy as the grass was green,
  The night above the dingle starry,
   Time let me hail and climb
  Golden in the heydays of his eyes,
And honoured among wagons I was prince of the apple towns
And once below a time I lordly had the trees and leaves
   Trail with daisies and barley
  Down the rivers of the windfall light.

And as I was green and carefree, famous among the barns
About the happy yard and singing as the farm was home,
  In the sun that is young once only,
   Time let me play and be
  Golden in the mercy of his means,
And green and golden I was huntsman and herdsman, the calves
Sang to my horn, the foxes on the hills barked clear and cold,
   And the sabbath rang slowly
  In the pebbles of the holy streams.

All the sun long it was running, it was lovely, the hay
Fields high as the house, the tunes from the chimneys, it was air
  And playing, lovely and watery
   And fire green as grass.
  And nightly under the simple stars
As I rode to sleep the owls were bearing the farm away,
All the moon long I heard, blessed among stables, the nightjars
  Flying with the ricks, and the horses
   Flashing into the dark.

And then to awake, and the farm, like a wanderer white
With the dew, come back, the cock on his shoulder: it was all
  Shining, it was Adam and maiden,
   The sky gathered again
  And the sun grew round that very day.
So it must have been after the birth of the simple light
In the first, spinning place, the spellbound horses walking warm

Out of the whinnying green stable
  On to the fields of praise.

And honoured among foxes and pheasants by the gay house
Under the new made clouds and happy as the heart was long,
  In the sun born over and over,
    I ran my heedless ways,
    My wishes raced through the house high hay
And nothing I cared, at my sky blue trades, that time allows
In all his tuneful turning so few and such morning songs
    Before the children green and golden
      Follow him out of grace,

Nothing I cared, in the lamb white days, that time would take me
Up to the swallow thronged loft by the shadow of my hand,
  In the moon that is always rising,
    Nor that riding to sleep
  I should hear him fly with the high fields
And wake to the farm forever fled from the childless land.
Oh as I was young and easy in the mercy of his means,
    Time held me green and dying
  Though I sang in my chains like the sea.

DYLAN THOMAS
WELSH (1914–1953)

Portrait of Girl with Comic Book

Thirteen's no age at all. Thirteen is nothing.
It is not wit, or powder on the face,
Or Wednesday matinées, or misses' clothing,
Or intellect, or grace.
Twelve has its tribal customs. But thirteen
Is neither boys in battered cars nor dolls,
Not *Sara Crewe*, or movie magazine,
Or pennants on the walls.

Thirteen keeps diaries and tropical fish
(A month, at most); scorns jumpropes in the spring;
Could not, would fortune grant it, name its wish;

Wants nothing, everything;
Has secrets from itself, friends it despises;
Admits none to the terrors that it feels;
Owns half a hundred masks but no disguises;
And walks upon its heels.

Thirteen's anomalous — not that, not this:
Not folded bud, or wave that laps a shore,
Or moth proverbial from the chrysalis.
Is the one age defeats the metaphor.
Is not a town, like childhood, strongly walled
But easily surrounded; is no city.
Nor, quitted once, can it be quite recalled —
Not even with pity.

PHYLLIS McGINLEY
AMERICAN (1905–1978)

In the Waiting Room

In Worcester, Massachusetts,
I went with Aunt Consuelo
to keep her dentist's appointment
and sat and waited for her
in the dentist's waiting room.
It was winter. It got dark
early. The waiting room
was full of grown-up people,
arctics and overcoats,
lamps and magazines.
My aunt was inside
what seemed like a long time
and while I waited I read
the *National Geographic*
(I could read) and carefully
studied the photographs:
the inside of a volcano,
black, and full of ashes;
then it was spilling over
in rivulets of fire.

Osa and Martin Johnson
dressed in riding breeches,
laced boots, and pith helmets.
A dead man slung on a pole
— "Long Pig," the caption said.
Babies with pointed heads
wound round and round with string;
black, naked women with necks
wound round and round with wire
like the necks of light bulbs.
Their breasts were horrifying.
I read it right straight through.
I was too shy to stop.
And then I looked at the cover:
the yellow margins, the date.

Suddenly, from inside,
came an *oh!* of pain
— Aunt Consuelo's voice —
not very loud or long.
I wasn't at all surprised;
even then I knew she was
a foolish, timid woman.
I might have been embarrassed,
but wasn't. What took me
completely by surprise
was that it was *me:*
my voice, in my mouth.
Without thinking at all
I was my foolish aunt,
I — we — were falling, falling,
our eyes glued to the cover
of the *National Geographic,*
February, 1918.

I said to myself: three days
and you'll be seven years old.
I was saying it to stop
the sensation of falling off

the round, turning world
into cold, blue-black space.
But I felt: you are an *I*,
you are an *Elizabeth*,
you are one of *them*.
Why should you be one, too?
I scarcely dared to look
to see what it was I was.
I gave a sidelong glance
— I couldn't look any higher —
at shadowy gray knees,
trousers and skirts and boots
and different pairs of hands
lying under the lamps.
I knew that nothing stranger
had ever happened, that nothing
stranger could ever happen.
Why should I be my aunt,
or me, or anyone?
What similarities —
boots, hands, the family voice
I felt in my throat, or even
the *National Geographic*
and those awful hanging breasts —
held us all together
or made us all just one?
How — I didn't know any
word for it — how "unlikely" . . .
How had I come to be here,
like them, and overhear
a cry of pain that could have
got loud and worse but hadn't?

The waiting room was bright
and too hot. It was sliding
beneath a big black wave,
another, and another.

Then I was back in it.
The War was on. Outside,
in Worcester, Massachusetts,
were night and slush and cold,
and it was still the fifth
of February, 1918.

ELIZABETH BISHOP
AMERICAN (1911–1979)

YOUTH AND ITS PLEASURES

In Youth Is Pleasure

In a herber green, asleep where I lay,
The birds sang sweet in the mids of the day;
I dreamèd fast of mirth and play.
    In youth is pleasure, in youth is pleasure.

Methought I walked still to and fro,
And from her company could not go;
But when I waked it was not so.
    In youth is pleasure, in youth is pleasure.

Therefore my heart is surely pight
Of her alone to have a sight,
Which is my joy and heart's delight.
    In youth is pleasure, in youth is pleasure.

ROBERT WEVER
ENGLISH (C. 1550)

Are they shadows that we see

Are they shadows that we see?
  And can shadows pleasure give?
Pleasures only shadows be,
  Cast by bodies we conceive,
    And are made the things we deem
    In those figures which they seem.

But these pleasures vanish fast,
   Which by shadows are expressed;
Pleasures are not, if they last;
   In their passing is their best.
      Glory is most bright and gay
      In a flash and so away.

Feed apace, then, greedy eyes
   On the wonder you behold;
Take it sudden as it flies,
   Though you take it not to hold.
      When your eyes have done their part,
      Thought must length it in the heart.

SAMUEL DANIEL
ENGLISH (1562?–1619)

Crabbèd Age and Youth

Crabbèd Age and Youth
Cannot live together:
Youth is full of pleasance,
Age is full of care;
Youth like summer morn,
Age like winter weather;
Youth like summer brave,
Age like winter bare.
Youth is full of sport,
Age's breath is short;
Youth is nimble, Age is lame;
Youth is hot and bold,
Age is weak and cold;
Youth is wild, and Age is tame.

Age, I do abhor thee;
Youth, I do adore thee;
O, my Love, my Love is young!
Age, I do defy thee:
O, sweet shepherd, hie thee!
For methinks thou stay'st too long.

WILLIAM SHAKESPEARE (ATTRIB.)
ENGLISH (1564–1616)

To the Virgins, to Make Much of Time

Gather ye rosebuds while ye may,
   Old Time is still a-flying:
And this same flower that smiles to-day
   To-morrow will be dying.

The glorious lamp of heaven, the sun,
   The higher he's a-getting,
The sooner will his race be run,
   And nearer he's to setting.

That age is best which is the first,
   When youth and blood are warmer;
But being spent, the worse, and worst
   Times still succeed the former.

Then be not coy, but use your time,
   And while ye may, go marry:
For having lost but once your prime,
   You may for ever tarry.

ROBERT HERRICK
ENGLISH (1591–1674)

When maidens are young, and in their spring

When maidens are young, and in their spring,
Of pleasure, of pleasure, let 'em take their full swing,
  Full swing, full swing,
And love, and dance, and play, and sing.
For Silvia, believe it, when youth is done,
There's nought but hum-drum, hum-drum, hum-drum,
There's nought but hum-drum, hum-drum, hum-drum.

Then Silvia be wise, be wise, be wise,
The painting and dressing for a while are supplies,
  And may surprise —
But when the fire's going out in your eyes,
It twinkles, it twinkles, it twinkles, and dies,
And then to hear love, to hear love from you,
I'd as live hear an owl cry, *Wit to woo! Wit to woo!*
  Wit to woo!

APHRA BEHN
ENGLISH (1640–1689)

So, we'll go no more a roving

So, we'll go no more a roving
  So late into the night,
Though the heart be still as loving,
  And the moon be still as bright.

For the sword outwears its sheath,
  And the soul wears out the breast,
And the heart must pause to breathe,
  And Love itself have rest.

Though the night was made for loving,
  And the day returns too soon,
Yet we'll go no more a roving
  By the light of the moon.

GEORGE GORDON, LORD BYRON
ENGLISH (1788–1824)

Often I think of the beautiful town
   That is seated by the sea;
Often in thought go up and down
The pleasant streets of that dear old town,
   And my youth comes back to me.
      And a verse of a Lapland song
     Is haunting my memory still:
"A boy's will is the wind's will,
And the thoughts of youth are long, long thoughts."

I can see the shadowy lines of its trees,
   And catch, in sudden gleams,
The sheen of the far-surrounding seas,
And islands that were the Hesperides
   Of all my boyish dreams.
      And the burden of that old song,
     It murmurs and whispers still:
"A boy's will is the wind's will,
And the thoughts of youth are long, long thoughts."

I remember the black wharves and the slips,
   And the sea-tides tossing free
And Spanish sailors with bearded lips,
And the beauty and mystery of the ships,
   And the magic of the sea.
      And the voice of that wayward song
     Is singing and saying still:
"A boy's will is the wind's will,
And the thoughts of youth are long, long thoughts."

I remember the bulwarks by the shore,
   And the fort upon the hill;
The sunrise gun, with its hollow roar,
The drum-beat repeated o'er and o'er,
   And the bugle wild and shrill.
      And the music of that old song
     Throbs in my memory still:

"A boy's will is the wind's will,
And the thoughts of youth are long, long thoughts."

I remember the sea-fight far away,
  How it thundered o'er the tide!
And the dead captains, as they lay
In their graves, o'erlooking the tranquil bay,
  Where they in battle died.
    And the sound of that mournful song
    Goes through me with a thrill:
  "A boy's will is the wind's will,
And the thoughts of youth are long, long thoughts."

I can see the breezy dome of groves,
  The shadows of Deering's Woods;
And the friendships old and the early loves
Come back with a Sabbath sound, as of doves
  In quiet neighborhoods.
    And the verse of that sweet old song,
    It flutters and murmurs still:
  "A boy's will is the wind's will,
And the thoughts of youth are long, long thoughts."

I remember the gleams and glooms that dart
  Across the school-boy's brain;
The song and the silence in the heart,
That in part are prophecies, and in part
  Are longings wild and vain.
    And the voice of that fitful song
    Sings on, and is never still:
  "A boy's will is the wind's will,
And the thoughts of youth are long, long thoughts."

There are things of which I may not speak;
  There are dreams that cannot die;
There are thoughts that make the strong heart weak,
And bring pallor into the cheek,
  And a mist before the eye.
    And the words of that fatal song

Come over me like a chill:
"A boy's will is the wind's will,
And the thoughts of youth are long, long thoughts."

Strange to me now are the forms I meet
  When I visit the dear old town;
But the native air is pure and sweet,
And the trees that o'ershadow each well-known street,
  As they balance up and down,
    Are singing the beautiful song,
    Are sighing and whispering still:
"A boy's will is the wind's will,
And the thoughts of youth are long, long thoughts."

And Deering's Woods are fresh and fair,
  And with joy that is almost pain
My heart goes back to wander there,
And among the dreams of the days that were,
  I find my lost youth again.
    And the strange and beautiful song,
    The groves are repeating it still:
"A boy's will is the wind's will,
And the thoughts of youth are long, long thoughts."

HENRY WADSWORTH LONGFELLOW
AMERICAN (1807–1882)

Awake! for Morning in the Bowl of Night

From *Rubáiyát of Omar Khayyám of Naishápúr*
  Awake! for Morning in the Bowl of Night
  Has flung the Stone that puts the Stars to Flight:
    And Lo! the Hunter of the East has caught
  The Sultán's Turret in a Noose of Light.

  Dreaming when Dawn's Left Hand was in the Sky
  I heard a Voice within the Tavern cry,
    'Awake, my Little ones, and fill the Cup
  Before Life's Liquor in its Cup be dry.'

And, as the Cock crew, those who stood before
The Tavern shouted — 'Open then the Door!
  'You know how little while we have to stay,
And, once departed, may return no more.'

Now the New Year reviving old Desires,
The thoughtful Soul to Solitude retires,
  Where the WHITE HAND OF MOSES on the Bough
Puts out, and Jesus from the Ground suspires.

Irám indeed is gone with all its Rose,
And Jamshýd's Sev'n-ring'd Cup where no one knows;
  But still the Vine her ancient Ruby yields,
And still a Garden by the Water blows.

And David's Lips are lock't; but in divine
High-piping Pehleví, with 'Wine! Wine! Wine!
  Red Wine' — the Nightingale cries to the Rose
That yellow Cheek of hers to incarnadine.

Come, fill the Cup, and in the Fire of Spring
The Winter Garment of Repentance fling:
  The Bird of Time has but a little way
To fly — and Lo! the Bird is on the Wing.

And look — a thousand Blossoms with the Day
Woke — and a thousand scatter'd into Clay:
  And this first Summer Month that brings the Rose
Shall take Jamshýd and Kaikobád away.

But come with old Khayyám, and leave the Lot
Of Kaikobád and Kaikhosrú forgot:
  Let Rustum lay about him as he will,
Or Hátim Tai cry Supper — heed them not.

With me along some Strip of Herbage strown
That just divides the desert from the sown,
  Where name of Slave and Sultán scarce is known,
And pity Sultán Máhmúd on his Throne.

Here with a Loaf of Bread beneath the Bough,
A Flask of Wine, a Book of Verse — and Thou
    Beside me singing in the Wilderness —
And Wilderness is Paradise enow.

'How sweet is mortal Sovranty' — think some:
Others — 'How blest the Paradise to come!'
    Ah, take the Cash in hand and waive the Rest;
Oh, the brave Music of a *distant* Drum!

Look to the Rose that blows about us — 'Lo,
Laughing,' she says, 'into the World I blow:
    At once the silken Tassel of my Purse
Tear, and its Treasure on the Garden throw.'

The Worldly Hope men set their Hearts upon
Turns Ashes — or it prospers; and anon,
    Like Snow upon the Desert's dusty Face
Lighting a little Hour or two — is gone.

And those who husbanded the Golden Grain,
And those who flung it to the Winds like Rain,
    Alike to no such aureate Earth are turn'd
As, buried once, Men want dug up again.

Think, in this batter'd Caravanserai
Whose Doorways are alternate Night and Day,
    How Sultán after Sultán with his Pomp
Abode his Hour or two, and went his way.

They say the Lion and the Lizard keep
The Courts where Jamshýd gloried and drank deep;
    And Bahrám, that great Hunter — the Wild Ass
Stamps o'er his Head, and he lies fast asleep.

I sometimes think that never blows so red
The Rose as where some buried Caesar bled;
    That every Hyacinth the Garden wears
Dropt in its Lap from some once lovely Head.

And this delightful Herb whose tender Green
Fledges the River's Lip on which we lean —
    Ah, lean upon it lightly! for who knows
From what once lovely Lip it springs unseen!

Ah, my Belovèd, fill the Cup that clears
To-DAY of past Regrets and future Fears —
    To-morrow? — Why, To-morrow I may be
Myself with Yesterday's Sev'n Thousand Years.

Lo! some we loved, the loveliest and best
That Time and Fate of all their Vintage prest,
    Have drunk their Cup a Round or two before,
And one by one crept silently to Rest.

And we, that now make merry in the Room
They left, and Summer dresses in new Bloom,
    Ourselves must we beneath the Couch of Earth
Descend, ourselves to make a Couch — for whom?

Ah, make the most of what we yet may spend,
Before we too in the Dust descend;
    Dust into Dust, and under Dust, to lie,
Sans Wine, sans Song, sans Singer, and — sans End!

EDWARD FITZGERALD
ENGLISH (1809–1883)

Live blindly and upon the hour

Live blindly and upon the hour. The Lord,
Who was the Future, died full long ago.
Knowledge which is the Past is folly. Go,
Poor child, and be not to thyself abhorred.
Around thine earth sun-wingèd winds do blow
And planets roll; a meteor draws his sword;
The rainbow breaks his seven-coloured chord
And the long strips of river-silver flow:

Awake! Give thyself to the lovely hours.
Drinking their lips, catch thou the dream in flight
About their fragile hairs' aërial gold.
Thou art divine, thou livest, — as of old
Apollo springing naked to the light,
And all his island shivered into flowers.

TRUMBULL STICKNEY
AMERICAN (1874–1904)

The fairies break their dances

The fairies break their dances
    And leave the printed lawn,
And up from India glances
    The silver sail of dawn.

The candles burn their sockets,
    The blinds let through the day.
The young man feels his pockets
    And wonders what's to pay.

A. E. HOUSMAN
ENGLISH (1859–1936)

Loveliest of trees, the cherry now

Loveliest of trees, the cherry now
Is hung with bloom along the bough,
And stands about the woodland ride
Wearing white for Eastertide.

Now, of my threescore years and ten,
Twenty will not come again,

And take from seventy springs a score,
It only leaves me fifty more.

And since to look at things in bloom
Fifty springs are little room,
About the woodlands I will go
To see the cherry hung with snow.

A. E. HOUSMAN
ENGLISH (1859–1936)

Vitae Summa Brevis Spem Nos Vetat Incohare Longam

They are not long, the weeping and the laughter,
   Love and desire and hate:
I think they have no portion in us after
   We pass the gate.

They are not long, the days of wine and roses:
   Out of a misty dream
Our path emerges for a while, then closes
   Within a dream.

ERNEST DOWSON
ENGLISH (1867–1900)

First Fig

My candle burns at both ends;
   It will not last the night;
But ah, my foes, and oh, my friends —
   It gives a lovely light!

EDNA ST. VINCENT MILLAY
AMERICAN (1892–1950)

Daphnis and Chloe

You found it difficult to woo —
So do we who follow you.

Everyone would like to mate;
Everyone has had to wait.

So much beauty, so much burning!
But ages pass as we are learning.

HANIEL LONG
AMERICAN (1888–1956)

The force that through the green fuse drives the flower

The force that through the green fuse drives the flower
Drives my green age; that blasts the roots of trees
Is my destroyer.
And I am dumb to tell the crooked rose
My youth is bent by the same wintry fever.

The force that drives the water through the rocks
Drives my red blood; that dries the mouthing streams
Turns mine to wax.
And I am dumb to mouth unto my veins
How at the mountain spring the same mouth sucks.

The hand that whirls the water in the pool
Stirs the quicksand; that ropes the blowing wind
Hauls my shroud sail.
And I am dumb to tell the hanging man
How of my clay is made the hangman's lime.

The lips of time leech to the fountain head;
Love drips and gathers, but the fallen blood
Shall calm her sores.
And I am dumb to tell a weather's wind
How time has ticked a heaven round the stars.

And I am dumb to tell the lover's tomb
How at my sheet goes the same crooked worm.

DYLAN THOMAS
WELSH (1914–1953)

INTO ADULTHOOD

All the world's a stage

From *As You Like It*

All the world's a stage,
And all the men and women merely players:
They have their exits and their entrances;
And one man in his time plays many parts,
His acts being seven ages. At first the infant,
Mewling and puking in the nurse's arms,
And then the whining schoolboy, with his satchel,
And shining morning face, creeping like a snail
Unwillingly to school. And then the lover,
Sighing like furnace, with a woful ballad
Made to his mistress' eyebrow. Then a soldier,
Full of strange oaths, and bearded like the pard,
Jealous in honour, sudden and quick in quarrel,
Seeking the bubble reputation
Even in the cannon's mouth. And then the justice,
In fair round belly with good capon lin'd,
With eyes severe, and beard of formal cut,
Full of wise saws and modern instances;
And so he plays his part. The sixth age shifts
Into the lean and slipper'd pantaloon,
With spectacles on nose and pouch on side,
His youthful hose well sav'd, a world too wide

For his shrunk shank; and his big manly voice,
Turning again towards childish treble, pipes
And whistles in his sound. Last scene of all,
That ends this strange eventful history,
Is second childishness, and mere oblivion,
Sans teeth, sans eyes, sans taste, sans everything.

WILLIAM SHAKESPEARE
ENGLISH (1564–1616)

How happy is he born or taught

How happy is he born or taught,
That serveth not another's will;
Whose armour is his honest thought,
And simple truth his highest skill;

Whose passions not his masters are;
Whose soul is still prepared for death,
Untied unto the world with care
Of princes' grace or vulgar breath;

Who envies none whom chance doth raise,
Or vice; who never understood
The deepest wounds are given by praise,
By rule of state, but not of good;

Who hath his life from rumours freed;
Whose conscience is his strong retreat;
Whose state can neither flatterers feed,
Nor ruin make accusers great;

Who God doth late and early pray,
More of his grace than goods to send,

And entertains the harmless day
With a well-chosen book or friend, —

This man is free from servile bands
Of hope to rise or fear to fall;
Lord of himself, though not of lands;
And having nothing, yet hath all.

SIR HENRY WOTTON
ENGLISH (1568–1639)

My heart leaps up when I behold

My heart leaps up when I behold
    A rainbow in the sky;
So was it when my life began;
So is it now I am a man;
So be it when I shall grow old.
    Or let me die!
The Child is father of the Man;
And I could wish my days to be
Bound each to each by natural piety.

WILLIAM WORDSWORTH
ENGLISH (1770–1850)

Abou Ben Adhem

Abou Ben Adhem (may his tribe increase!)
Awoke one night from a deep dream of peace,
And saw, within the moonlight in his room,
Making it rich, and like a lily in bloom,
An angel writing in a book of gold: —
Exceeding peace had made Ben Adhem bold,
And to the presence in the room he said,
    'What writest thou?' — The vision raised its head,
And with a look made of all sweet accord,
Answered, 'The names of those who love the Lord.'
'And is mine one?' said Abou. 'Nay, not so,'
Replied the angel. Abou spoke more low,

But cheerly still; and said, 'I pray thee, then,
Write me as one that loves his fellow men.'
   The angel wrote, and vanished. The next night
It came again with a great wakening light,
And showed the names whom love of God had blest,
And lo! Ben Adhem's name led all the rest.

LEIGH HUNT
ENGLISH (1784–1859)

The Choir Invisible

Oh, may I join the choir invisible
Of those immortal dead who live again
In minds made better by their presence; live
In pulses stirred to generosity,
In deeds of daring rectitude, in scorn
For miserable aims that end with self,
In thoughts sublime that pierce the night like stars,
And with their mild persistence urge men's search
To vaster issues. So to live is heaven:
To make undying music in the world,
Breathing a beauteous order that controls
With growing sway the growing life of man.
So we inherit that sweet purity
For which we struggled, failed, and agonized
With widening retrospect that bred despair.
Rebellious flesh that would not be subdued,
A vicious parent shaming still its child,
Poor anxious penitence, is quick dissolved;
Its discords, quenched by meeting harmonies,
Die in the large and charitable air.
And all our rarer, better, truer self,
That sobbed religiously in yearning song,
That watched to ease the burden of the world,
Laboriously tracing what must be,
And what may yet be better, — saw within
A worthier image for the sanctuary,
And shaped it forth before the multitude,
Divinely human, raising worship so

To higher reverence more mixed with love, —
That better self shall live till human Time
Shall fold its eyelids, and the human sky
Be gathered like a scroll within the tomb
Unread forever. This is life to come, —
Which martyred men have made more glorious
For us who strive to follow. May I reach
That purest heaven, — be to other souls
The cup of strength in some great agony,
Enkindle generous ardor, feed pure love,
Beget the smiles that have no cruelty,
Be the sweet presence of a good diffused,
And in diffusion ever more intense!
So shall I join the choir invisible
Whose music is the gladness of the world.

GEORGE ELIOT
ENGLISH (1819–1880)

Invictus

Out of the night that covers me,
  Black as the Pit from pole to pole,
I thank whatever gods may be
  For my unconquerable soul.

In the fell clutch of circumstance
  I have not winced nor cried aloud.
Under the bludgeonings of chance
  My head is bloody, but unbowed.

Beyond this place of wrath and tears
  Looms but the Horror of the shade,

And yet the menace of the years
    Finds, and shall find, me unafraid.

It matters not how strait the gate,
    How charged with punishments the scroll,
I am the master of my fate:
    I am the captain of my soul.

WILLIAM ERNEST HENLEY
ENGLISH (1849–1903)

If

If you can keep your head when all about you
    Are losing theirs and blaming it on you;
If you can trust yourself when all men doubt you,
    But make allowance for their doubting too:
If you can wait and not be tired by waiting,
    Or, being lied about, don't deal in lies,
Or being hated don't give way to hating,
    And yet don't look too good, nor talk too wise;

If you can dream — and not make dreams your master;
    If you can think — and not make thoughts your aim,
If you can meet with Triumph and Disaster
    And treat those two impostors just the same:
If you can bear to hear the truth you've spoken
    Twisted by knaves to make a trap for fools,
Or watch the things you gave your life to, broken,
    And stoop and build 'em up with worn-out tools;

If you can make one heap of all your winnings
    And risk it on one turn of pitch-and-toss,
And lose, and start again at your beginnings,
    And never breathe a word about your loss:
If you can force your heart and nerve and sinew
    To serve your turn long after they are gone,
And so hold on when there is nothing in you
    Except the Will which says to them: "Hold on!"

If you can talk with crowds and keep your virtue,
   Or walk with Kings — nor lose the common touch,
If neither foes nor loving friends can hurt you,
   If all men count with you, but none too much:
If you can fill the unforgiving minute
   With sixty seconds' worth of distance run,
Yours is the Earth and everything that's in it,
   And — which is more — you'll be a Man, my son!

RUDYARD KIPLING
ENGLISH (1865–1936)

The Road Not Taken

Two roads diverged in a yellow wood,
And sorry I could not travel both
And be one traveler, long I stood
And looked down one as far as I could
To where it bent in the undergrowth;

Then took the other, as just as fair,
And having perhaps the better claim,
Because it was grassy and wanted wear;
Though as for that the passing there
Had worn them really about the same,

And both that morning equally lay
In leaves no step had trodden black.
Oh, I kept the first for another day!
Yet knowing how way leads on to way,
I doubted if I should ever come back.

I shall be telling this with a sigh
Somewhere ages and ages hence:
Two roads diverged in a wood, and I —
I took the one less traveled by,
And that has made all the difference.

ROBERT FROST
AMERICAN (1874–1963)

The City

You said: "I'll go to another country, go to another shore,
find another city better than this one.
Whatever I try to do is fated to turn out wrong
and my heart lies buried as though it were something dead.
How long can I let my mind moulder in this place?
Wherever I turn, wherever I happen to look,
I see the black ruins of my life, here,
where I've spent so many years, wasted them, destroyed
    them totally."

You won't find a new country, won't find another shore.
This city will always pursue you. You will walk
the same streets, grow old in the same neighborhoods,
will turn gray in these same houses.
You will always end up in this city. Don't hope for things
    elsewhere:
there is no ship for you, there is no road.
As you've wasted your life here, in this small corner,
you've destroyed it everywhere else in the world.

C. P. CAVAFY
GREEK (1863–1933)
TRANSLATED BY EDMUND KEELEY
AND PHILIP SHERRARD

Dreams

Hold fast to dreams
For if dreams die
Life is a broken winged bird
That cannot fly.

Hold fast to dreams
For when dreams go
Life is a barren field
Frozen with snow.

LANGSTON HUGHES
AMERICAN (1902–1967)

The Truly Great

I think continually of those who were truly great.
Who, from the womb, remembered the soul's history
Through corridors of light where the hours are suns,
Endless and singing. Whose lovely ambition
Was that their lips, still touched with fire,
Should tell of the Spirit, clothed from head to foot in song.
And who hoarded from the Spring branches
The desires falling across their bodies like blossoms.

What is precious, is never to forget
The essential delight of the blood drawn from ageless springs
Breaking through rocks in worlds before our earth.
Never to deny its pleasure in the morning simple light
Nor its grave evening demand for love.
Never to allow gradually the traffic to smother
With noise and fog, the flowering of the Spirit.

Near the snow, near the sun, in the highest fields,
See how these names are fêted by the waving grass
And by the streamers of white cloud
And whispers of wind in the listening sky.
The names of those who in their lives fought for life,
Who wore at their hearts the fire's centre.
Born of the sun, they travelled a short while toward the sun
And left the vivid air signed with their honour.

STEPHEN SPENDER
ENGLISH (1909–1995)

Catch What You Can

The thing to do is try for that sweet skin
One gets by staying deep inside a thing.
The image that I have is that of fruit —
The stone within the plum or some such pith
As keeps the slender sphere both firm and sound.

Stay with me, mountain flowers I saw
And battering moth against a wind-dark rock,
Stay with me till you build me all around
The honey and the clove I thought to taste
If lingering long enough I lived and got
Your intangible wild essence in my heart.
And whether that's by sight or thought
Or staying deep inside an aerial shed
Till imagination makes the heart-leaf vine
Out of damned bald rock, I cannot guess.
The game is worth the candle if there's flame.

JEAN GARRIGUE
AMERICAN (1912–1972)

Album

This is a hard life you are living
While you are young,
My father said,
As I scratched my casted knees with a paper knife.
By laws of compensation
Your old age should be grand.

Not grand, but of a terrible
Compensation, to perceive
Past the energy of survival
In its sadness
The hard life of the young.

JOSEPHINE MILES
AMERICAN (1911–1985)

MARRIAGE

The maidens came

The maidens came
　　When I was in my mother's bower;
I had all that I would.
　　The bailey beareth the bell away;
　　The lily, the rose, the rose I lay.
The silver is white, red is the gold;
The robes they lay in fold.
　　The bailey beareth the bell away;
　　The lily, the rose, the rose I lay.
And through the glass window shines the sun.
How should I love, and I so young?
　　The bailey beareth the bell away;
　　The lily, the rose, the rose I lay.

ANONYMOUS
ENGLISH (MEDIEVAL)

My true Love hath my heart, and I have his

My true Love hath my heart, and I have his,
By just exchange one for the other given:
I hold his dear, and mine he cannot miss;
There never was a better bargain driven.
His heart in me keeps me and him in one,
My heart in him his thoughts and senses guides:
He loves my heart, for once it was his own;
I cherish his because in me it bides.
His heart his wound receivëd from my sight,
My heart was wounded with his wounded heart;
For as from me, on him his hurt did light,
So still methought in me his hurt did smart.
　　Both, equal hurt, in this change sought our bliss:
　　My true Love hath my heart, and I have his.

SIR PHILIP SIDNEY
ENGLISH (1554–1586)

Ah, what is love? It is a pretty thing,
As sweet unto a shepherd as a king;
    And sweeter too,
For kings have cares that wait upon a crown,
And cares can make the sweetest love to frown;
    Ah then, ah then,
If country loves such sweet desires do gain,
What lady would not love a shepherd swain?

His flocks are folded, he comes home at night,
As merry as a king in his delight;
    And merrier too,
For kings bethink them what the state require,
When shepherds careless carol by the fire:
    Ah then, ah then,
If country loves such sweet desires do gain,
What lady would not love a shepherd swain?

He kisseth first, then sits as blithe to eat
His cream and curds as doth the king his meat;
    And blither too,
For kings have often fears when they do sup,
Where shepherds dread no poison in their cup:
    Ah then, ah then,
If country loves such sweet desires do gain,
What lady would not love a shepherd swain?

To bed he goes, as wanton then, I ween,
As is a king in dalliance with a queen;
    More wanton too,
For kings have many griefs affects to move,
Where shepherds have no greater grief than love:
    Ah then, ah then,
If country loves such sweet desires do gain,
What lady would not love a shepherd swain?

Upon his couch of straw he sleeps as sound,
As doth the king upon his bed of down;
    More sounder too,
For cares cause kings full oft their sleep to spill,
Where weary shepherds lie and snort their fill:
    Ah then, ah then,
If country loves such sweet desires do gain,
What lady would not love a shepherd swain?

Thus with his wife he spends the year, as blithe
As doth the king at every tide or sithe;
    And blither too,
For kings have wars and broils to take in hand,
Where shepherds laugh and love upon the land:
    Ah then, ah then,
If country loves such sweet desires do gain,
What lady would not love a shepherd swain?

ROBERT GREENE
ENGLISH (1560?–1592)

Prothalamion

Calme was the day, and through the trembling ayre
Sweete-breathing Zephyrus did softly play
A gentle spirit, that lightly did delay
Hot Titans beames, which then did glyster fayre;
When I, (whom sullein care,
Through discontent of my long fruitlesse stay
In Princes Court, and expectation vayne
Of idle hopes, which still doe fly away,
Like empty shaddowes, did afflict my brayne,)
Walkt forth to ease my payne
Along the shoare of silver streaming Themmes;
Whose rutty Bancke, the which his River hemmes,
Was paynted all with variable flowers,
And all the meades adorned with daintie gemmes
Fit to decke maydens bowres,
And crowne their Paramours

Against the Brydale day, which is not long:
    Sweete Themmes! runne softly, till I end my Song.

There, in a Meadow, by the Rivers side,
A Flocke of Nymphes I chauncèd to espy,
All lovely Daughters of the Flood thereby,
With goodly greenish locks, all loose untyde,
As each had bene a Bryde;
And each one had a little wicker basket,
Made of the twigs, entraylèd curiously,
In which they gathered flowers to fill their flasket,
And with fine Fingers crept full feateously
The tender stalkes on hye.
Of every sort, which in that Meadow grew,
They gathered some; the Violet, pallid blew,
The little Dazie, that at evening closes,
The virgin Lillie, and the Primrose trew,
With store of vermeil Roses,
To decke their Bridegromes posies
Against the Brydale day, which was not long:
    Sweete Themmes! runne softly, till I end my Song.

With that I saw two Swannes of goodly hewe
Come softly swimming downe along the Lee;
Two fairer Birds I yet did never see;
The snow, which doth the top of Pindus strew,
Did never whiter shew;
Nor Jove himselfe, when he a Swan would be
For love of Leda, whiter did appeare;
Yet Leda was (they say) as white as he,
Yet not so white as these, nor nothing neare;
So purely white they were,
That even the gentle streame, the which them bare,
Seem'd foule to them, and bad his billowes spare
To wet their silken feathers, least they might
Soyle their fayre plumes with water not so fayre,
And marre their beauties bright,
That shone as heavens light,

Against their Brydale day, which was not long:
    Sweete Themmes! runne softly, till I end my Song.

Eftsoones the Nymphes, which now had Flowers their fill
Ran all in haste to see that silver brood,
As they came floating on the Christal Flood;
Whom when they sawe, they stood amazèd still,
Their wondring eyes to fill;
Them seem'd they never saw a sight so fayre,
Of Fowles, so lovely, that they sure did deeme
Them heavenly borne, or to be that same payre
Which through the Skie draw Venus silver Teeme;
For sure they did not seeme
To be begot of any earthly Seede,
But rather Angels, or of Angels breede;
Yet were they bred of Somers-heat, they say,
In sweetest Season, when each Flower and weede
The earth did fresh aray;
So fresh they seem'd as day,
Even as their Brydale day, which was not long:
    Sweete Themmes! runne softly, till I end my Song.

Then forth they all out of their baskets drew
Great store of Flowers, the honour of the field,
That to the sense did fragrant odours yield,
All which upon those goodly Birds they threw
And all the Waves did strew,
That like old Peneus Waters they did seeme,
When downe along by pleasant Tempes shore,
Scattred with Flowres, through Thessaly they streeme.
That they appeare, through Lillies plenteous store,
Like a Brydes Chamber flore.
Two of those Nymphes, meane while, two Garlands bound
Of freshest Flowres which in that Mead they found,
The which presenting all in trim Array,
Their snowie Foreheads therewithall they crownd,
Whil'st one did sing this Lay,
Prepar'd against that Day,

Against their Brydale day, which was not long:
    Sweete Themmes! runne softly, till I end my Song.

'Ye gentle Birdes! the worlds faire ornament,
And heavens glorie, whom this happie hower
Doth leade unto your lovers blisfull bower,
Joy may you have, and gentle hearts content
Of your loves couplement;
And let faire Venus, that is Queene of love,
With her heart-quelling Sonne upon you smile,
Whose smile, they say, hath vertue to remove
All Loves dislike, and friendships faultie guile
For ever to assoile.
Let endlesse Peace your steadfast hearts accord,
And blessèd Plentie wait upon your bord;
And let your bed with pleasures chast abound,
That fruitfull issue may to you afford,
Which may your foes confound,
And make your joyes redound
Upon your Brydale day, which is not long:
    Sweete Themmes! runne softlie, till I end my Song.'

So ended she; and all the rest around
To her redoubled that her undersong,
Which said their brydale daye should not be long:
And gentle Eccho from the neighbour ground
Their accents did resound.
So forth those joyous Birdes did passe along,
Adowne the Lee, that to them murmurde low,
As he would speake, but that he lackt a tong,
Yet did by signes his glad affection show,
Making his streame run slow.
And all the foule which in his flood did dwell
Gan flock about these twaine, that did excell
The rest, so far as Cynthia doth shend
The lesser starres. So they, enrangèd well,
Did on those two attend,
And their best service lend

Against their wedding day, which was not long:
    Sweete Themmes! runne softly, till I end my Song.

At length they all to mery London came,
To mery London, my most kyndly Nurse,
That to me gave this Lifes first native sourse,
Though from another place I take my name,
An house of auncient fame:
There when they came, whereas those bricky towres
The which on Themmes brode agèd backe doe ryde,
Where now the studious Lawyers have their bowers,
There whylome wont the Templer Knights to byde,
Till they decayd through pride:
Next whereunto there standes a stately place,
Where oft I gaynèd giftes and goodly grace
Of that great Lord, which therein wont to dwell,
Whose want too well now feeles my freendles case;
But ah! here fits not well
Olde woes, but joyes, to tell
Against the Brydale daye, which is not long:
    Sweete Themmes! runne softly, till I end my Song.

Yet therein now doth lodge a noble Peer,
Great Englands glory, and the Worlds wide wonder,
Whose dreadfull name late through all Spaine did thunder,
And Hercules two pillars standing neere
Did make to quake and feare:
Faire branch of Honor, flower of Chevalrie!
That fillest England with thy triumphs fame,
Joy have thou of thy noble victorie,
And endlesse happinesse of thine owne name
That promiseth the same;
That through thy prowesse, and victorious armes,
Thy country may be freed from forraine harmes;
And great Elisaes glorious name may ring
Through al the world, fil'd with thy wide Alarmes,
Which some brave muse may sing
To ages following,

Upon the Brydale day, which is not long:
    Sweete Themmes! runne softly, till I end my Song.

From those high Towers this noble Lord issuing,
Like Radiant Hesper, when his golden hayre
In th' Ocean billowes he hath bathèd fayre,
Descended to the Rivers open vewing,
With a great traine ensuing.
Above the rest were goodly to bee seene
Two gentle Knights of lovely face and feature,
Beseeming well the bower of anie Queene,
With gifts of wit, and ornaments of nature,
Fit for so goodly stature,
That like the twins of Jove they seem'd in sight,
Which decke the Bauldricke of the Heavens bright;
They two, forth pacing to the Rivers side,
Received those two faire Brides, their Loves delight;
Which, at th' appointed tyde,
Each one did make his Bryde
Against their Brydale day, which is not long:
    Sweete Themmes! runne softly, till I end my Song.

EDMUND SPENSER
ENGLISH (1552–1599)

Verses Made the Night before He Died

So well I love thee as without thee I
Love nothing; if I might choose, I'd rather die
Than be one day debarred thy company.

Since beasts and plants do grow and live and move,
Beasts are those men that such a life approve:
He only lives that deadly is in love.

The corn, that in the ground is sown, first dies,
And of one seed do many ears arise;
Love, this world's corn, by dying multiplies.

The seeds of love first by thy eyes were thrown
Into a ground untilled, a heart unknown
To bear such fruit, till by thy hands 'twas sown.

Look as your looking-glass by chance may fall,
Divide, and break in many pieces small,
And yet shows forth the selfsame face in all,

Proportions, features, graces, just the same,
And in the smallest piece as well the name
Of fairest one deserves as in the richest frame;

So all my thoughts are pieces but of you,
Which put together makes a glass so true
As I therein no other's face but yours can view.

MICHAEL DRAYTON
ENGLISH (1563–1631)

Let me not to the marriage of true minds

Let me not to the marriage of true minds
Admit impediments. Love is not love
Which alters when it alteration finds,
Or bends with the remover to remove.
O, no! it is an ever-fixèd mark,
That looks on tempests and is never shaken;
It is the star to every wandering bark,
Whose worth's unknown, although his height be taken.
Love's not Time's fool, though rosy lips and cheeks
Within his bending sickle's compass come;
Love alters not with his brief hours and weeks,
But bears it out even to the edge of doom.
If this be error, and upon me proved,
I never writ, nor no man ever loved.

WILLIAM SHAKESPEARE
ENGLISH (1564–1616)

Wedding is great Juno's crown

From *As You Like It*

Wedding is great Juno's crown:
  O blessed bond of board and bed!
'Tis Hymen peoples every town:
  High wedlock then be honouréd:
Honour, high honour and renown,
To Hymen, god of every town!

WILLIAM SHAKESPEARE
ENGLISH (1564–1616)

With thee conversing, I forget all time

From *Paradise Lost*

With thee conversing, I forget all time,
All seasons, and their change, all please alike.
Sweet is the breath of morn, her rising sweet,
With charm of earliest birds; pleasant the sun,
When first on this delightful land he spreads
His orient beams, on herb, tree, fruit, and flower,
Glistering with dew; fragrant the fertile earth
After soft showers; and sweet the coming on
Of grateful evening mild, then silent night
With this her solemn bird, and this fair moon
And these the gems of heaven, her starry train:
But neither breath of morn, when she ascends
With charm of earliest birds, nor rising sun
On this delightful land, nor herb, fruit, flower,
Glistering with dew, nor fragrance after showers,
Nor grateful evening mild, nor silent night
With this her solemn bird, nor walk by moon
Or glittering starlight, without thee is sweet.

JOHN MILTON
ENGLISH (1608–1674)

Even like two little bank-dividing brooks

Even like two little bank-dividing brooks,
 That wash the pebbles with their wanton streams,
And having ranged and searched a thousand nooks,
 Meet both at length in silver-breasted Thames
  Where in a greater current they conjoin:
So I my Best-Beloved's am, so he is mine.

Even so we met; and after long pursuit
 Even so we joined; we both became entire;
No need for either to renew a suit,
 For I was flax and he was flames of fire:
  Our firm united souls did more than twine,
So I my Best-Beloved's am, so he is mine.

If all those glittering monarchs that command
 The servile quarters of this earthly ball
Should tender in exchange their shares of land,
 I would not change my fortunes for them all:
  Their wealth is but a counter to my coin;
The world's but theirs, but my Beloved's mine.

Nay, more: if the fair Thespian ladies all
 Should heap together their diviner treasure,
That treasure should be deemed a price too small
 To buy a minute's lease of half my pleasure.
  'Tis not the sacred wealth of all the Nine
Can buy my heart from him, or his from being mine.

Nor time, nor place, nor chance, nor death can bow
 My least desires unto the least remove;
He's firmly mine by oath, I his by vow;
 He's mine by faith, and I am his by love;
  He's mine by water, I am his by wine;
Thus I my Best-Beloved's am, thus he is mine.

He is my altar, I his holy place;
 I am his guest, and he my living food;

I'm his by penitence, he mine by grace;
    I'm his by purchase, he is mine by blood;
        He's my supporting elm, and I his vine:
Thus I my Best-Beloved's am, thus he is mine.

He gives me wealth, I give him all my vows;
    I give him songs, he gives me length of days;
With wreaths of grace he crowns my conquering brows;
    And I his temples with a crown of praise,
        Which he accepts as an everlasting sign,
That I my Best-Beloved's am; that he is mine.

FRANCIS QUARLES
ENGLISH (1592–1644)

To My Dear and Loving Husband

If ever two were one, then surely we.
If ever man were lov'd by wife, then thee;
If ever wife was happy in a man,
Compare with me ye women if you can.
I prize thy love more than whole mines of gold,
Or all the riches that the East doth hold.
My love is such that rivers cannot quench,
Nor aught but love from thee, give recompense.
Thy love is such I can no way repay,
The heavens reward thee manifold, I pray.
Then while we live, in love lets so persever
That, when we live no more, we may live ever.

ANNE BRADSTREET
AMERICAN (1612–1672)

Oh Wert Thou in the Cauld Blast

Oh, wert thou in the cauld blast,
    On yonder lea, on yonder lea;
My plaidie to the angry airt,
    I'd shelter thee, I'd shelter thee:
Or did misfortune's bitter storms
    Around thee blaw, around thee blaw,

Thy bield should be my bosom,
    To share it a', to share it a'.

Or were I in the wildest waste,
    Sae black and bare, sae black and bare,
The desert were a paradise,
    If thou wert there, if thou wert there.
Or were I monarch o' the globe,
    Wi' thee to reign, wi' thee to reign;
The brightest jewel in my crown,
    Wad be my queen, wad be my queen.

ROBERT BURNS
SCOTTISH (1759–1796)

The River-Merchant's Wife: A Letter

While my hair was still cut straight across my forehead
I played about the front gate, pulling flowers.
You came by on bamboo stilts, playing horse,
You walked about my seat, playing with blue plums.
And we went on living in the village of Chokan:
Two small people, without dislike or suspicion.

At fourteen I married My Lord you.
I never laughed, being bashful.
Lowering my head, I looked at the wall.
Called to, a thousand times, I never looked back.

At fifteen I stopped scowling,
I desired my dust to be mingled with yours
Forever and forever and forever.
Why should I climb the look out?

At sixteen you departed,
You went into far Ku-to-yen, by the river of swirling eddies,

And you have been gone five months.
The monkeys make sorrowful noise overhead.
You dragged your feet when you went out.
By the gate now, the moss is grown, the different mosses,
Too deep to clear them away!
The leaves fall early this autumn, in wind.
The paired butterflies are already yellow with August
Over the grass in the West garden;
They hurt me.   I grow older.
If you are coming down through the narrows of the river Kiang,
Please let me know beforehand,
And I will come out to meet you
          As far as Cho-fu-Sa.

             EZRA POUND (AFTER LI PO)
                AMERICAN (1885–1972)

A Slice of Wedding Cake

Why have such scores of lovely, gifted girls
   Married impossible men?
Simple self-sacrifice may be ruled out,
   And missionary endeavour, nine times out of ten.

Repeat 'impossible men': not merely rustic,
   Foul-tempered or depraved
(Dramatic foils chosen to show the world
   How well women behave, and always have behaved).

Impossible men: idle, illiterate,
   Self-pitying, dirty, sly,
For whose appearance even in City parks
   Excuses must be made to casual passers-by.

Has God's supply of tolerable husbands
    Fallen, in fact, so low?
Or do I always over-value woman
    At the expense of man?
                   Do I?
                      It might be so.

                      ROBERT GRAVES
                  ENGLISH (1895–1985)

The 5:32

She said, If tomorrow my world were torn in two,
Blacked out, dissolved, I think I would remember
(As if transfixed in unsurrendering amber)
This hour best of all the hours I knew:
When cars came backing into the shabby station,
Children scuffing the seats, and the women driving
With ribbons around their hair, and the trains arriving,
And the men getting off with tired but practiced motion.

Yes, I would remember my life like this, she said:
Autumn, the platform red with Virginia creeper,
And a man coming toward me, smiling, the evening paper
Under his arm, and his hat pushed back on his head;
And wood smoke lying like haze on the quiet town,
And dinner waiting, and the sun not yet gone down.

                    PHYLLIS McGINLEY
                 AMERICAN (1905–1978)

The Forms of Love

Parked in the fields
All night
So many years ago,
We saw
A lake beside us
When the moon rose.
I remember

Leaving that ancient car
Together. I remember
Standing in the white grass
Beside it. We groped
Our way together
Downhill in the bright
Incredible light

Beginning to wonder
Whether it could be lake
Or fog
We saw, our heads
Ringing under the stars we walked
To where it would have wet our feet
Had it been water

GEORGE OPPEN
AMERICAN (1908–1984)

The Ache of Marriage

The ache of marriage:

thigh and tongue, beloved,
are heavy with it,
it throbs in the teeth

We look for communion
and are turned away, beloved,
each and each

It is leviathan and we
in its belly
looking for joy, some joy
not to be known outside it

two by two in the ark of
the ache of it.

DENISE LEVERTOV
AMERICAN (1923–1997)

Marriage

Should I get married? Should I be good?
Astound the girl next door with my velvet suit and faustus hood?
Don't take her to movies but to cemeteries
tell all about werewolf bathtubs and forked clarinets
then desire her and kiss her and all the preliminaries
and she going just so far and I understanding why
not getting angry saying You must feel! It's beautiful to feel!
Instead take her in my arms lean against an old crooked
    tombstone
and woo her the entire night the constellations in the sky —

When she introduces me to her parents
back straightened, hair finally combed, strangled by a tie,
should I sit knees together on their 3rd degree sofa
and not ask Where's the bathroom?
How else to feel other than I am,
often thinking Flash Gordon soap —
O how terrible it must be for a young man
seated before a family and the family thinking
We never saw him before! He wants our Mary Lou!
After tea and homemade cookies they ask What do you do for a
    living?

Should I tell them: Would they like me then?
Say All right get married, we're losing a daughter
but we're gaining a son —
And should I then ask Where's the bathroom?

O God, and the wedding! All her family and her friends
and only a handful of mine all scroungy and bearded
just wait to get at the drinks and food —
And the priest! he looking at me as if I masturbated
asking me Do you take this woman for your lawful wedded wife?
And I trembling what to say say Pie Glue!
I kiss the bride all those corny men slapping me on the back
She's all yours, boy! Ha-ha-ha!

And in their eyes you could see some obscene honeymoon going
    on—

Then all that absurd rice and clanky cans and shoes
Niagara Falls! Hordes of us! Husbands! Wives! Flowers!
    Chocolates!

All streaming into cozy hotels
All going to do the same thing tonight
The indifferent clerk he knowing what was going to happen
The lobby zombies they knowing what
The whistling elevator man he knowing
The winking bellboy knowing
Everybody knowing! I'd be almost inclined not to do anything!
Stay up all night! Stare that hotel clerk in the eye!
Screaming: I deny honeymoon! I deny honeymoon!
running rampant into those almost climactic suites
yelling Radio belly! Cat shovel!
O I'd live in Niagara forever! in a dark cave beneath the Falls
I'd sit there the Mad Honeymooner
devising ways to break marriages, a scourge of bigamy
a saint of divorce —

But I should get married I should be good
How nice it'd be to come home to her
and sit by the fireplace and she in the kitchen
aproned young and lovely wanting my baby
and so happy about me she burns the roast beef
and comes crying to me and I get up from my big papa chair
saying Christmas teeth! Radiant brains! Apple deaf!
God what a husband I'd make! Yes, I should get married!
So much to do! like sneaking into Mr Jones' house late at night
and cover his golf clubs with 1920 Norwegian books
Like hanging a picture of Rimbaud on the lawnmower
like pasting Tannu Tuva postage stamps all over the picket fence
like when Mrs Kindhead comes to collect for the Community
    Chest
grab her and tell her There are unfavorable omens in the sky!
And when the mayor comes to get my vote tell him

When are you going to stop people killing whales!
And when the milkman comes leave him a note in the bottle
Penguin dust, bring me penguin dust, I want penguin dust —

Yet if I should get married and it's Connecticut and snow
and she gives birth to a child and I am sleepless, worn,
up for nights, head bowed against a quiet window, the past
    behind me,

finding myself in the most common of situations a trembling
    man
knowledged with responsibility not twig-smear nor Roman coin
    soup —

O what would that be like!
Surely I'd give it for a nipple a rubber Tacitus
For a rattle a bag of broken Bach records
Tack Della Francesca all over its crib
Sew the Greek alphabet on its bib
And build for its playpen a roofless Parthenon

No, I doubt I'd be that kind of father
not rural not snow no quiet window
but hot smelly tight New York City
seven flights up, roaches and rats in the walls
a fat Reichian wife screeching over potatoes Get a job!
And five nose running brats in love with Batman
And the neighbors all toothless and dry haired
like those hag masses of the 18th century
all wanting to come in and watch TV
The landlord wants his rent
Grocery store Blue Cross Gas & Electric Knights of Columbus
Impossible to lie back and dream Telephone snow, ghost
    parking —
No! I should not get married I should never get married!
But — imagine If I were married to a beautiful sophisticated
    woman
tall and pale wearing an elegant black dress and long black gloves

holding a cigarette holder in one hand and a highball in the
    other
and we lived high up in a penthouse with a huge window
from which we could see all of New York and ever farther on
    clearer days
No, can't imagine myself married to that pleasant prison
    dream —

O but what about love? I forget love
not that I am incapable of love
it's just that I see love as odd as wearing shoes —
I never wanted to marry a girl who was like my mother
And Ingrid Bergman was always impossible
And there's maybe a girl now but she's already married
And I don't like men and —
but there's got to be somebody!
Because what if I'm 60 years old and not married,
all alone in a furnished room with pee stains on my underwear
and everybody else is married! All the universe married but me!

Ah, yet well I know that were a woman possible as I am possible
then marriage would be possible —
Like SHE in her lonely alien gaud waiting her Egyptian lover
so I wait — bereft of 2,000 years and the bath of life.

GREGORY CORSO
AMERICAN (1930–2001)

THE PERSPECTIVES OF MIDLIFE

Reading the Book of Hills and Seas

In the month of June the grass grows high
And round my cottage thick-leaved branches sway.
There is not a bird but delights in the place where it rests:
And I too — love my thatched cottage.
I have done my ploughing:
I have sown my seed.
Again I have time to sit and read my books.

In the narrow lane there are no deep ruts:
Often my friends' carriages turn back.
In high spirits I pour out my spring wine
And pluck the lettuce growing in my garden.
A gentle rain comes stealing up from the east
And a sweet wind bears it company.
My thoughts float idly over the story of King Chou
My eyes wander over the pictures of Hills and Seas.
At a single glance I survey the whole Universe.
He will never be happy, whom such pleasures fail to please!

T'AO CH'IEN
CHINESE (372?–427)
TRANSLATED BY ARTHUR WALEY

South of the Yangtze, Thinking of Spring

How many times will I see spring green
again, or yellow birds tireless in song?

The road home ends at the edge of heaven.
Here beyond the river, my old hair white,

my heart flown north to cloudy passes,
I'm shadow in moonlit southern mountains.

My life a blaze of spent abundance, my old
fields and gardens buried in weeds, where

am I going? It's year's-end, and I'm here
chanting long farewells at heaven's gate.

LI PO
CHINESE (701–762)
TRANSLATED BY DAVID HINTON

On Being Sixty

Between thirty and forty, one is distracted by the Five
Lusts;
Between seventy and eighty, one is a prey to a hundred
diseases.
But from fifty to sixty one is free from all ills;
Calm and still — the heart enjoys rest.
I have put behind me Love and Greed; I have done with
Profit and Fame;
I am still short of illness and decay and far from decrepit
age.
Strength of limb I still possess to seek the rivers and hills;
Still my heart has spirit enough to listen to flutes and
strings.
At leisure I open new wine and taste several cups;
Drunken I recall old poems and sing a whole volume.
Meng-te has asked for a poem and herewith I exhort him
Not to complain of three-score, "the time of obedient
ears."

PO CHÜ-I
CHINESE (772–846)
TRANSLATED BY ARTHUR WALEY

Ode I.II

Strive not (Leuconoe) to know what end
The Gods above to thee or me will send:
Nor with Astrologers consult at all,
That thou may'st better know what can befall.
Whether, thou liv'st more winters, or thy last
Be this, which Tyrrhen waves 'gainst rocks do cast;
Be wise, drink free, and in so short a space,
Do not protracted hopes of life embrace.
Whilest we are talking, envious time doth slide:
This day's thine own, the next may be deny'd.

HORACE
LATIN (65–8 B.C.)
TRANSLATED BY SIR THOMAS HAWKINS

When that I was and a little tiny boy

From *Twelfth Night*

When that I was and a little tiny boy,
    With hey, ho, the wind and the rain:
A foolish thing was but a toy,
    For the rain it raineth every day.

But when I came to man's estate,
    With hey, ho, the wind and the rain:
'Gainst knaves and thieves men shut their gate,
    For the rain it raineth every day.

But when I came, alas, to wive,
    With hey, ho, the wind and rain:
By swaggering could I never thrive,
    For the rain it raineth every day.

But when I came unto my beds,
    With hey, ho, the wind and the rain,
With toss-pots still had drunken heads, —
    For the rain it raineth every day.

A great while ago the world begun,
    With hey, ho, the wind and the rain,
But that's all one, our play is done,
    And we'll strive to please you every day.

WILLIAM SHAKESPEARE
ENGLISH (1564–1616)

Half of Life

With its yellow pears
And wild roses everywhere
The shore hangs in the lake,
O gracious swans,
And drunk with kisses
You dip your heads
In the sobering holy water.

Ah, where will I find
Flowers, come winter,
And where the sunshine
And shade of earth?
Walls stand cold
And speechless, in the wind
The weathervanes creak.

FRIEDRICH HÖLDERLIN
GERMAN (1770–1843)
TRANSLATED BY RICHARD SIEBURTH

The Old Familiar Faces

I have had playmates, I have had companions,
In my days of childhood, in my joyful school-days,
All, all are gone, the old familiar faces.

I have been laughing, I have been carousing,
Drinking late, sitting late, with my bosom cronies,
All, all are gone, the old familiar faces.

I loved a love once, fairest among women:
Closed are her doors on me, I must not see her —
All, all are gone, the old familiar faces.

I have a friend, a kinder friend has no man;
Like an ingrate, I left my friend abruptly;
Left him, to muse on the old familiar faces.

Ghost-like I paced round the haunts of my childhood,
Earth seemed a desert I was bound to traverse,
Seeking to find the old familiar faces.

Friend of my bosom, thou more than a brother,
Why wert not thou born in my father's dwelling?
So might we talk of the old familiar faces —

How some they have died, and some they have left me,
And some are taken from me; all are departed;
All, all are gone, the old familiar faces.

CHARLES LAMB
ENGLISH (1775–1834)

Jenny kissed me when we met

Jenny kissed me when we met,
    Jumping from the chair she sat in;
Time, you thief, who love to get
    Sweets into your list, put that in:
Say I'm weary, say I'm sad,
    Say that health and wealth have missed me,
Say I'm growing old, but add
    Jenny kissed me.

LEIGH HUNT
ENGLISH (1784–1859)

Mezzo Cammin

Half of my life is gone, and I have let
    The years slip from me and have not fulfilled
    The aspiration of my youth, to build
    Some tower of song with lofty parapet.
Not indolence, nor pleasure, nor the fret
    Of restless passions that would not be stilled,
    But sorrow, and a care that almost killed,
    Kept me from what I may accomplish yet;

Though, halfway up the hill, I see the Past
 Lying beneath me with its sounds and sights, —
 A city in the twilight dim and vast,
With smoking roofs, soft bells, and gleaming lights, —
 And hear above me on the autumnal blast
 The cataract of Death far thundering from the heights.

HENRY WADSWORTH LONGFELLOW
AMERICAN (1807–1882)

I am a parcel of vain strivings tied

I am a parcel of vain strivings tied
 By a chance bond together,
 Dangling this way and that, their links
  Were made so loose and wide,
   Methinks,
  For milder weather.

A bunch of violets without their roots,
 And sorrel intermixed,
 Encircled by a wisp of straw
  Once coiled about their shoots,
   The law
  By which I'm fixed.

A nosegay which Time clutched from out
 Those fair Elysian fields,
 With weeds and broken stems, in haste,
  Doth make the rabble rout
   That waste
  The day he yields.

And here I bloom for a short hour unseen,
 Drinking my juices up,
 With no root in the land
  To keep my branches green,
   But stand
  In a bare cup.

Some tender buds were left upon my stem
    In mimicry of life,
But ah! the children will not know,
    Till time has withered them,
        The woe
    With which they're rife.

But now I see I was not plucked for naught,
    And after in life's vase
Of glass set while I might survive,
    But by a kind hand brought
        Alive
    To a strange place.

That stock thus thinned will soon redeem its hours,
    And by another year,
Such as God knows, with freer air,
    More fruits and fairer flowers
        Will bear,
    While I droop here.

HENRY DAVID THOREAU
AMERICAN (1817–1862)

As when down some broad river dropping, we

As when down some broad river dropping, we
Day after day behold the assuming shores
Sink and grow dim, as the great watercourse
Pushes his banks apart and seeks the sea:
Benches of pines, high shelf and balcony,
To flats of willow and low sycamores
Subsiding, till where'er the wave we see,
Himself is his horizon utterly.

So fades the portion of our early world,
Still on the ambit hangs the purple air;
Yet while we lean to read the secret there,
The stream that by green shoresides plashed and purled
Expands: the mountains melt to vapors rare,
And life alone circles out flat and bare.

FREDERICK GODDARD TUCKERMAN
AMERICAN (1821–1873)

Dover Beach

The sea is calm to-night.
The tide is full, the moon lies fair
Upon the straits; — on the French coast the light
Gleams and is gone; the cliffs of England stand
Glimmering and vast, out in the tranquil bay.
Come to the window, sweet is the night-air!
Only, from the long line of spray
Where the sea meets the moon-blanch'd land,
Listen! you hear the grating roar
Of pebbles which the waves draw back, and fling,
At their return, up the high strand,
Begin, and cease, and then again begin,
With tremulous cadence slow, and bring
The eternal note of sadness in.

Sophocles long ago
Heard it on the Ægean, and it brought
Into his mind the turbid ebb and flow
Of human misery; we
Find also in the sound a thought,
Hearing it by this distant northern sea.

The Sea of Faith
Was once, too, at the full, and round earth's shore
Lay like the folds of a bright girdle furl'd.
But now I only hear
Its melancholy, long, withdrawing roar,
Retreating, to the breath

Of the night-wind, down the vast edges drear
And naked shingles of the world.

Ah, love, let us be true
To one another! for the world, which seems
To lie before us like a land of dreams,
So various, so beautiful, so new,
Hath really neither joy, nor love, nor light,
Nor certitude, nor peace, nor help for pain;
And we are here as on a darkling plain
Swept with confused alarms of struggle and flight,
Where ignorant armies clash by night.

MATTHEW ARNOLD
ENGLISH (1822–1888)

The passions that we fought with and subdued

The passions that we fought with and subdued
Never quite die. In some maimed serpent's coil
They lurk, ready to spring and vindicate
That power was once our torture and our lord.

TRUMBULL STICKNEY
AMERICAN (1874–1904)

Into my heart an air that kills

Into my heart an air that kills
    From yon far country blows:
What are those blue remembered hills,
    What spires, what farms are those?

That is the land of lost content,
    I see it shining plain,
The happy highways where I went
    And cannot come again.

A. E. HOUSMAN
ENGLISH (1859–1936)

Thursday

I have had my dream — like others —
and it has come to nothing, so that
I remain now carelessly
with feet planted on the ground
and look up at the sky —
feeling my clothes about me,
the weight of my body in my shoes,
the rim of my hat, air passing in and out
at my nose — and decide to dream no more.

WILLIAM CARLOS WILLIAMS
AMERICAN (1883–1963)

What lips my lips have kissed, and where, and why

What lips my lips have kissed, and where, and why,
I have forgotten, and what arms have lain
Under my head till morning; but the rain
Is full of ghosts tonight, that tap and sigh
Upon the glass and listen for reply,
And in my heart there stirs a quiet pain
For unremembered lads that not again
Will turn to me at midnight with a cry.
Thus in the winter stands the lonely tree,
Nor knows what birds have vanished one by one,
Yet knows its boughs more silent than before:
I cannot say what loves have come and gone,
I only know that summer sang in me
A little while, that in me sings no more.

EDNA ST. VINCENT MILLAY
AMERICAN (1892–1950)

A Postcard from the Volcano

Children picking up our bones
Will never know that these were once
As quick as foxes on the hill;

And that in autumn, when the grapes
Made sharp air sharper by their smell
These had a being, breathing frost;

And least will guess that with our bones
We left much more, left what still is
The look of things, left what we felt

At what we saw. The spring clouds blow
Above the shuttered mansion-house,
Beyond our gate and the windy sky

Cries out a literate despair.
We knew for long the mansion's look
And what we said of it became

A part of what it is . . . Children,
Still weaving budded aureoles,
Will speak our speech and never know,

Will say of the mansion that it seems
As if he that lived there left behind
A spirit storming in blank walls,

A dirty house in a gutted world,
A tatter of shadows peaked to white,
Smeared with the gold of the opulent sun.

WALLACE STEVENS
AMERICAN (1879–1955)

Still Here

I've been scared and battered.
My hopes the wind done scattered.
Snow has friz me, sun has baked me.
    Looks like between 'em
    They done tried to make me
Stop laughin', stop lovin', stop livin' —
    But I don't care!
    I'm still here!

LANGSTON HUGHES
AMERICAN (1902–1967)

What I expected was

What I expected was
Thunder, fighting,
Long struggles with men
And climbing.
After continual straining
I should grow strong;
Then the rocks would shake
And I should rest long.

What I had not foreseen
Was the gradual day
Weakening the will
Leaking the brightness away,
The lack of good to touch
The fading of body and soul
Like smoke before wind
Corrupt, unsubstantial.

The wearing of Time,
And the watching of cripples pass
With limbs shaped like questions
In their odd twist,
The pulverous grief
Melting the bones with pity,

The sick falling from earth —
These, I could not foresee.

For I had expected always
Some brightness to hold in trust,
Some final innocence
To save from dust;
That, hanging solid,
Would dangle through all
Like the created poem
Or the dazzling crystal.

STEPHEN SPENDER
ENGLISH (1909–1995)

Not Waving but Drowning

Nobody heard him, the dead man,
But still he lay moaning:
I was much further out than you thought
And not waving but drowning.

Poor chap, he always loved larking
And now he's dead
It must have been too cold for him his heart gave way,
They said.

Oh, no no no, it was too cold always
(Still the dead one lay moaning)
I was much too far out all my life
And not waving but drowning.

STEVIE SMITH
ENGLISH (1902–1971)

One Art

The art of losing isn't hard to master;
so many things seem filled with the intent
to be lost that their loss is no disaster.

Lose something every day. Accept the fluster
of lost door keys, the hour badly spent.
The art of losing isn't hard to master.

Then practice losing farther, losing faster:
places, and names, and where it was you meant
to travel. None of these will bring disaster.

I lost my mother's watch. And look! my last, or
next-to-last, of three loved houses went.
The art of losing isn't hard to master.

I lost two cities, lovely ones. And, vaster,
some realms I owned, two rivers, a continent.
I miss them, but it wasn't a disaster.

— Even losing you (the joking voice, a gesture
I love) I shan't have lied. It's evident
the art of losing's not too hard to master
though it may look like (*Write* it!) like disaster.

ELIZABETH BISHOP
AMERICAN (1911–1979)

To Failure

You do not come dramatically, with dragons
That rear up with my life between their paws
And dash me butchered down beside the wagons,
The horses panicking; nor as a clause
Clearly set out to warn what can be lost,
What out-of-pocket charges must be borne,
Expenses met; nor as a draughty ghost
That's seen, some mornings, running down a lawn.

It is these sunless afternoons, I find,
Instal you at my elbow like a bore.
The chestnut trees are caked with silence. I'm
Aware the days pass quicker than before,
Smell staler too. And once they fall behind
They look like ruin. You have been here some time.

PHILIP LARKIN
ENGLISH (1922–1985)

Life, friends, is boring

Life, friends, is boring. We must not say so.
After all, the sky flashes, the great sea yearns,
we ourselves flash and yearn,
and moreover my mother told me as a boy
(repeatingly) 'Ever to confess you're bored
means you have no

Inner Resources.' I conclude now I have no
inner resources, because I am heavy bored.
Peoples bore me,
literature bores me, especially great literature,
Henry bores me, with his plights & gripes
as bad as achilles,

who loves people and valiant art, which bores me.
And the tranquil hills, & gin, look like a drag
and somehow a dog
has taken itself & its tail considerably away
into mountains or sea or sky, leaving
behind: me, wag.

JOHN BERRYMAN
AMERICAN (1914–1972)

From a Survivor

The pact that we made was the ordinary pact
of men & women in those days

I don't know who we thought we were
that our personalities
could resist the failures of the race

Lucky or unlucky, we didn't know
the race had failures of that order
and that we were going to share them

Like everybody else, we thought of ourselves as special

Your body is as vivid to me
as it ever was: even more

since my feeling for it is clearer:
I know what it could do and could not do

it is no longer
the body of a god
or anything with power over my life

Next year it would have been 20 years
and you are wastefully dead
who might have made the leap
we talked, too late, of making

which I live now
not as a leap
but a succession of brief, amazing movements

each one making possible the next

ADRIENNE RICH
AMERICAN (B. 1929)

I Thought It Was Harry

Excuse me. I thought for a moment you were someone I know.
It happens to me. One time at *The Circle in the Square*
when it *was* still in the Square, I turned my head
when the lights went up and saw me there with a girl
and another couple. Out in the lobby, I looked
right at him and he looked away. I was no one he knew.
Well, it takes two, as they say, and I don't know what
it would prove anyway. Do we know who we are,
do you think? Kids seem to know. One time I asked
a little girl. She said she'd been sick. She said
she'd looked different and felt different. I said,
"Maybe it wasn't you. How do you know?"
"Oh, I was me," she said, "I know I was."

That part doesn't bother me anymore
or not the way it did. I'm nobody else
and nobody anyway. It's all the rest
I don't know. I don't know anything.
It hit me. I thought it was Harry when I saw you
and thought, "I'll ask Harry." I don't suppose
he knows, though. It's not that I get confused.
I don't mean that. If someone appeared and said,
"Ask me questions," I wouldn't know where to start.
I don't have questions even. It's the way I fade
as though I were someone's snapshot left in the light.
And the background fades the way it might if we woke
in the wrong twilight and things got dim and grey
while we waited for them to sharpen. Less and less
is real. No fixed point. Questions fix
a point, as answers do. Things move again
and the only place to move is away. It was wrong:
questions and answers are what to be without
and all we learn is how sound our ignorance is.
That's what I wanted to talk to Harry about.
You looked like him. Thank you anyway.

WILLIAM BRONK
AMERICAN (1918–1999)

RETIREMENT FROM WORK AND FROM THE WORLD

RETIREMENT
FROM WORK
AND FROM THE
WORLD
183

Returning to the Fields

When I was young I was out of tune with the herd:
My only love was for the hills and mountains.
Unwitting I fell into the Web of the World's dust
And was not free until my thirtieth year.
The migrant bird longs for the old wood:
The fish in the tank thinks of its native pool.
I had rescued from wildness a patch of the Southern Moor
And, still rustic, I returned to field and garden.
My ground covers no more than ten acres:
My thatched cottage has eight or nine rooms.
Elms and willows cluster by the eaves:
Peach trees and plum trees grow before the Hall.
Hazy, hazy the distant hamlets of men.
Steady the smoke of the half-deserted village,
A dog barks somewhere in the deep lanes,
A cock crows at the top of the mulberry tree.
At gate and courtyard — no murmur of the World's dust:
In the empty rooms — leisure and deep stillness.
Long I lived checked by the bars of a cage:
Now I have turned again to Nature and Freedom.

T'AO CH'IEN
CHINESE (372?–427)
TRANSLATED BY ARTHUR WALEY

Ease

Lined coat, warm cap and easy felt slippers,
In the little tower, at the low window, sitting over the sunken
    brazier.
Body at rest, heart at peace; no need to rise early.
I wonder if the courtiers at the Western Capital know of these
    things or not?

PO CHÜ-I
CHINESE (772–846)
TRANSLATED BY ARTHUR WALEY

Climb at court for me that will

Climb at court for me that will
Tottering Favor's pinnacle;
All I seek is to lie still.
Settled in some secret nest
In calm leisure let me rest;
And far off the public stage
Pass away my silent age.
Thus when without noise, unknown,
I have lived out all my span,
I shall die, without a groan,
An old honest country man.
Who, exposed to others' eyes,
Into his own heart ne'er pries,
Death to him's a strange surprise.

SENECA
ROMAN (54 B.C.?–39 A.D.)
TRANSLATED BY ANDREW MARVELL

Farewell to the Court

Like truthless dreams, so are my joys expired,
And past return are all my dandled days:
My love misled, and fancy quite retired,
Of all which past the sorrow only stays.

My lost delights now clean from sight of land
Have left me all alone in unknown ways:
My mind to woe, my life in fortune's hand,
Of all which past the sorrow only stays.

As in a country strange without companion
I only wail the wrong of death's delays,
Whose sweet spring spent, whose summer well nigh done,
Of all which past the sorrow only stays:

Whom care forewarns, ere age and winter cold,
To haste me hence to find my fortune's fold.

SIR WALTER RALEGH
ENGLISH (1552?–1618)

The Garden

How vainly men themselves amaze
To win the palm, the oak, or bays,
And their uncessant labours see
Crowned from some single herb or tree,
Whose short and narrow vergèd shade
Does prudently their toils upbraid,
While all flowers and all trees do close
To weave the garlands of repose.

Fair Quiet, have I found thee here,
And Innocence, thy sister dear!
Mistaken long, I sought you then
In busy companies of men.
Your sacred plants, if here below,
Only among the plants will grow.
Society is all but rude,
To this delicious solitude.

No white nor red was ever seen
So am'rous as this lovely green.
Fond lovers, cruel as their flame,
Cut in these trees their mistress' name.
Little, alas, they know, or heed,
How far these beauties hers exceed!
Fair trees! wheres'e'er your barks I wound,
No name shall but your own be found.

When we have run our passion's heat,
Love hither makes his best retreat.
The gods, that mortal beauty chase,
Still in a tree did end their race.
Apollo hunted Daphne so,
Only that she might laurel grow.
And Pan did after Syrinx speed,
Not as a nymph, but for a reed.

What wondrous life is this I lead!
Ripe apples drop about my head;
The luscious clusters of the vine
Upon my mouth do crush their wine;
The nectarene, and curious peach,
Into my hands themselves do reach;
Stumbling on melons, as I pass,
Ensnared with flowers, I fall on grass.

Meanwhile the mind, from pleasures less,
Withdraws into its happiness:
The mind, that ocean where each kind
Does straight its own resemblance find,
Yet it creates, transcending these,
Far other worlds, and other seas,
Annihilating all that's made
To a green thought in a green shade.

Here at the fountain's sliding foot,
Or at some fruit-tree's mossy root,
Casting the body's vest aside,
My soul into the boughs does glide:
There like a bird it sits, and sings,
Then whets, and combs its silver wings;
And, till prepared for longer flight,
Waves in its plumes the various light.

Such was that happy garden-state,
While man there walked without a mate:

After a place so pure, and sweet,
What other help could yet be meet!
But 'twas beyond a mortal's share
To wander solitary there:
Two paradises 'twere in one
To live in paradise alone.

How well the skilful gardener drew
Of flowers and herbs this dial new,
Where from above the milder sun
Does through a fragrant zodiac run;
And, as it works, the industrious bee
Computes its time as well as we.
How could such sweet and wholesome hours
Be reckoned but with herbs and flowers!

ANDREW MARVELL
ENGLISH (1621–1678)

The world is too much with us

The world is too much with us; late and soon,
Getting and spending, we lay waste our powers:
Little we see in Nature that is ours;
We have given our hearts away, a sordid boon!
This Sea that bares her bosom to the moon;
The winds that will be howling at all hours,
And are up-gathered now like sleeping flowers;
For this, for everything, we are out of tune;
It moves us not. — Great God! I'd rather be
A Pagan suckled in a creed outworn;
So might I, standing on this pleasant lea,
Have glimpses that would make me less forlorn;
Have sight of Proteus rising from the sea;
Or hear old Triton blow his wreathèd horn.

WILLIAM WORDSWORTH
ENGLISH (1770–1850)

His heart was in his garden

His heart was in his garden; but his brain
Wandered at will among the fiery stars:
Bards, heroes, prophets, Homers, Hamilcars,
With many angels, stood, his eye to gain;
The devils, too, were his familiars.
And yet the cunning florist held his eyes
Close to the ground, — a tulip-bulb his prize, —
And talked of tan and bone-dust, cutworms, grubs,
As though all Nature held no higher strain;
Or, if he spoke of Art, he made the theme
Flow through box-borders, turf, and flower-tubs;
Or, like a garden-engine's, steered the stream, —
Now spouted rainbows to the silent skies;
Now kept it flat, and raked the walks and shrubs.

FREDERICK GODDARD TUCKERMAN
AMERICAN (1821–1873)

The Last Word

Creep into thy narrow bed,
Creep, and let no more be said!
Vain thy onset! all stands fast.
Thou thyself must break at last.

Let the long contention cease!
Geese are swans, and swans are geese.
Let them have it how they will!
Thou art tired; best be still.

They out-talked thee, hissed thee, tore thee?
Better men fared thus before thee;

Fired their ringing shot and passed,
Hotly charged — and sank at last.

Charge once more, then, and be dumb!
Let the victors, when they come,
When the forts of folly fall,
Find thy body by the wall!

MATTHEW ARNOLD
ENGLISH (1822–1888)

Leisure

What is this life if, full of care,
We have no time to stand and stare.

No time to stand beneath the boughs
And stare as long as sheep or cows.

No time to see, when woods we pass,
Where squirrels hide their nuts in grass.

No time to see, in broad daylight,
Streams full of stars like skies at night.

No time to turn at Beauty's glance,
And watch her feet, how they can dance.

No time to wait till her mouth can
Enrich that smile her eyes began.

A poor life this if, full of care,
We have no time to stand and stare.

W. H. DAVIES
ENGLISH (1871–1940)

Moving In

I moved into my house one day
In a downpour of leaves and rain,
"I took possession," as they say,
With solitude for my domain.

At first it was an empty place
Where every room I came to meet
Watched me in silence like a face:
I heard the whisper of my feet.

So huge the absence walking there
Beside me on the yellow floor,
That one fly buzzing on the air
But made the stillness more and more.

What I possessed was all my own,
Yet not to be possessed at all,
And not a house or even hearthstone,
And never any sheltering wall.

There solitude became my task,
No shelter but a grave demand,
And I must answer, never ask,
Taking this bridegroom by the hand.

I moved into my life one day
In a downpour of leaves in flood,
I took possession as they say,
And knew I was alone for good.

MAY SARTON
AMERICAN (1912–1995)

Written in a Carefree Mood

Old man pushing seventy,
in truth he acts like a little boy,
whooping with delight when he spies some mountain fruits,
laughing with joy, tagging after village mummers;
with the others having fun stacking tiles to make a pagoda,
standing alone staring at his image in a jardiniere pool.
Tucked under his arm, a battered book to read,
just like the time he first set off for school.

LU YU
CHINESE (1125–1210)
TRANSLATED BY BURTON WATSON

That time of year thou may'st in me behold

That time of year thou may'st in me behold
When yellow leaves, or none, or few, do hang
Upon those boughs which shake against the cold,
Bare ruined choirs, where late the sweet birds sang.
In me thou see'st the twilight of such day
As after sunset fadeth in the west;
Which by and by black night doth take away,
Death's second self, that seals up all the rest.
In me thou see'st the glowing of such fire,
That on the ashes of his youth doth lie,
As the death-bed whereon it must expire,
Consumed with that which it was nourished by.
   This thou perceiv'st, which makes thy love more strong,
   To love that well which thou must leave ere long.

WILLIAM SHAKESPEARE
ENGLISH (1564–1616)

Like as the waves make toward the pebbled shore

Like as the waves make toward the pebbled shore,
So do our minutes hasten to their end;
Each changing place with that which goes before,
In sequent toil all forwards do contend.
Nativity, once in the main of light,
Crawls to maturity, wherewith being crowned,
Crooked eclipses 'gainst his glory fight,
And Time that gave doth now his gift confound.
Time doth transfix the flourish set on youth
And delves the parallels in beauty's brow,
Feeds on the rarities of nature's truth,
And nothing stands but for his scythe to mow:
And yet to times in hope my verse shall stand,
Praising thy worth, despite his cruel hand.

WILLIAM SHAKESPEARE
ENGLISH (1564–1616)

Tired with all these, for restful death I cry

Tired with all these, for restful death I cry,
As, to behold desert a beggar born,
And needy nothing trimmed in jollity,
And purest faith unhappily forsworn,
And gilded honour shamefully misplaced,
And maiden virtue rudely strumpeted,
And right perfection wrongfully disgraced,
And strength by limping sway disabled,
And art made tongue-tied by authority,
And folly, doctor-like, controlling skill,
And simple truth miscalled simplicity,
And captive good attending captain ill:
Tired with all these, from these would I be gone,
Save that, to die, I leave my love alone.

WILLIAM SHAKESPEARE
ENGLISH (1564–1616)

The World a-hunting is

The World a-hunting is:
The prey poor Man, the Nimrod fierce is Death;
His speedy greyhounds are
Lust, Sickness, Envy, Care,
Strife that ne'er falls amiss,
With all those ills which haunt us while we breathe.
Now if by chance we fly
Of these the eager chase,
Old Age with stealing pace
Casts up his nets, and there we panting die.

WILLIAM DRUMMOND
SCOTTISH (1585–1649)

Young men dancing, and the old

Young men dancing, and the old
Sporting I with joy behold;
But an old man gay and free
Dancing most I love to see:
Age and youth alike he shares,
For his heart belies his hairs.

THOMAS STANLEY
ENGLISH (1625–1678)

On the Last Verses in the Book

When we for age could neither read nor write,
The subject made us able to indite;
The soul, with nobler resolutions decked,
The body stooping, does herself erect.
No mortal parts are requisite to raise
Her that, unbodied, can her Maker praise.
The seas are quiet when the winds give o'er;
So, calm are we when passions are no more!
For then we know how vain it was to boast
Of fleeting things, so certain to be lost.
Clouds of affection from our younger eyes

Conceal that emptiness which age descries.
The soul's dark cottage, battered and decayed,
Lets in new light through chinks that time has made;
Stronger by weakness, wiser men become,
As they draw near to their eternal home.
Leaving the old, both worlds at once they view,
That stand upon the threshold of the new.

EDMUND WALLER
ENGLISH (1606–1687)

On His Blindness

When I consider how my light is spent,
Ere half my days, in this dark world and wide,
And that one talent which is death to hide,
Lodged with me useless, though my soul more bent
To serve therewith my Maker, and present
My true account, lest He returning chide:
Doth God exact day-labour, light denied,
I fondly ask; but patience to prevent
That murmur, soon replies, God doth not need
Either man's works or His own gifts; who best
Bear His mild yoke, they serve Him best; His state
Is kingly; thousands at His bidding speed
And post o'er land and ocean without rest:
They also serve who only stand and wait.

JOHN MILTON
ENGLISH (1608–1674)

Nature

As a fond mother, when the day is o'er,
   Leads by the hand her little child to bed,
   Half willing, half reluctant to be led,
And leave his broken playthings on the floor,
Still gazing at them through the open door,
   Nor wholly reassured and comforted
   By promises of others in their stead,
Which, though more splendid, may not please him more;

So Nature deals with us, and takes away
    Our playthings one by one, and by the hand
      Leads us to rest so gently, that we go
Scarce knowing if we wish to go or stay,
    Being too full of sleep to understand
      How far the unknown transcends the what we know.

HENRY WADSWORTH LONGFELLOW
AMERICAN (1807–1882)

Terminus

It is time to be old,
To take in sail: —
The god of bounds,
Who sets to seas a shore,
Came to me in his fatal rounds,
And said: 'No more!
No farther spread
Thy broad ambitious branches, and thy root.
Fancy departs: no more invent,
Contract thy firmament
To compass of a tent.
There's not enough for this and that,
Make thy option which of two;
Economize the failing river,
Not the less revere the Giver,
Leave the many and hold the few.
Timely wise accept the terms,
Soften the fall with wary foot;
A little while
Still plan and smile,
And, fault of novel germs,
Mature the unfallen fruit.
Curse, if thou wilt, thy sires,
Bad husbands of their fires,
Who, when they gave thee breath,
Failed to bequeath
The needful sinew stark as once,
The Baresark marrow to thy bones,

But left a legacy of ebbing veins,
Inconstant heat and nerveless reins, —
Amid the Muses, left thee deaf and dumb,
Amid the gladiators, halt and numb.'

As the bird trims her to the gale,
I trim myself to the storm of time,
I man the rudder, reef the sail,
Obey the voice at eve obeyed at prime:
'Lowly faithful, banish fear,
Right onward drive unharmed;
The port, well worth the cruise, is near,
And every wave is charmed.'

RALPH WALDO EMERSON
AMERICAN (1803–1882)

Tithonus

The woods decay, the woods decay and fall,
The vapors weep their burthen to the ground,
Man comes and tills the field and lies beneath,
And after many a summer dies the swan.
Me only cruel immortality
Consumes; I wither slowly in thine arms,
Here at the quiet limit of the world,
A white-hair'd shadow roaming like a dream
The ever-silent spaces of the East,
Far-folded mists, and gleaming halls of morn.
   Alas! for this gray shadow, once a man —
So glorious in his beauty and thy choice,
Who madest him thy chosen, that he seem'd
To his great heart none other than a God!
I ask'd thee, 'Give me immortality.'
Then didst thou grant mine asking with a smile,
Like wealthy men who care not how they give.
But thy strong Hours indignant work'd their wills,
And beat me down and marr'd and wasted me,
And tho' they could not end me, left me maim'd
To dwell in presence of immortal youth,

Immortal age beside immortal youth,
And all I was in ashes. Can thy love,
Thy beauty, make amends, tho' even now,
Close over us, the silver star, thy guide,
Shines in those tremulous eyes that fill with tears
To hear me? Let me go; take back thy gift.
Why should a man desire in any way
To vary from the kindly race of men,
Or pass beyond the goal of ordinance
Where all should pause, as is most meet for all?

   A soft air fans the cloud apart; there comes
A glimpse of that dark world where I was born.
Once more the old mysterious glimmer steals
From thy pure brows, and from thy shoulders pure,
And bosom beating with a heart renew'd.
Thy cheek begins to redden thro' the gloom,
Thy sweet eyes brighten slowly close to mine,
Ere yet they blind the stars, and the wild team
Which love thee, yearning for thy yoke, arise
And shake the darkness from their loosen'd manes,
And beat the twilight into flakes of fire.

   Lo! ever thus thou growest beautiful
In silence, then before thine answer given
Departest, and thy tears are on my cheek.

   Why wilt thou ever scare me with thy tears,
And make me tremble lest a saying learnt,
In days far-off, on that dark earth, be true?
'The Gods themselves cannot recall their gifts.'

   Ay me! ay me! with what another heart
In days far-off, and with what other eyes
I used to watch — if I be he that watch'd —
The lucid outline forming round thee; saw
The dim curls kindle into sunny rings;
Changed with thy mystic change, and felt my blood
Glow with the glow that slowly crimson'd all
Thy presence and thy portals, while I lay,
Mouth, forehead, eyelids, growing dewy-warm
With kisses balmier than half-opening buds
Of April, and could hear the lips that kiss'd

Whispering I knew not what of wild and sweet,
Like that strange song I heard Apollo sing,
While Ilion like a mist rose into towers.

    Yet hold me not for ever in thine East;
How can my nature longer mix with thine?
Coldly thy rosy shadows bathe me, cold
Are all thy lights, and cold my wrinkled feet
Upon thy glimmering thresholds, when the steam
Floats up from those dim fields about the homes
Of happy men that have the power to die,
And grassy barrows of the happier dead.
Release me, and restore me to the ground.
Thou seest all things, thou wilt see my grave;
Thou wilt renew thy beauty morn by morn,
I earth in earth forget these empty courts,
And thee returning on thy silver wheels.

ALFRED, LORD TENNYSON
ENGLISH (1809–1892)

Growing Old

What is it to grow old?
Is it to lose the glory of the form,
The lustre of the eye?
Is it for beauty to forego her wreath?
— Yes, but not this alone.

Is it to feel our strength —
Not our bloom only, but our strength — decay?
Is it to feel each limb
Grow stiffer, every function less exact,
Each nerve more loosely strung?

Yes, this, and more; but not
Ah, 'tis not what in youth we dream'd 'twould be!
'Tis not to have our life
Mellow'd and soften'd as with sunset-glow,
A golden day's decline.

'Tis not to see the world
As from a height, with rapt prophetic eyes,
And heart profoundly stirr'd;
And weep, and feel the fulness of the past,
The years that are no more.

It is to spend long days
And not once feel that we were ever young;
It is to add, immured
In the hot prison of the present, month
To month with weary pain.

It is to suffer this,
And feel but half, and feebly, what we feel.
Deep in our hidden heart
Festers the dull remembrance of a change,
But no emotion — none.

It is — last stage of all —
When we are frozen up within, and quite
The phantom of ourselves,
To hear the world applaud the hollow ghost
Which blamed the living man.

MATTHEW ARNOLD
ENGLISH (1822–1888)

Age

Death, tho I see him not, is near
And grudges me my eightieth year.
Now, I would give him all these last
For one that fifty have run past.
Ah! he strikes all things, all alike,
But bargains: those he will not strike.

WALTER SAVAGE LANDOR
ENGLISH (1775–1864)

I look into my glass

I look into my glass,
And view my wasting skin,
And say, "Would God it came to pass
My heart had shrunk as thin!"

For then, I, undistrest
By hearts grown cold to me,
Could lonely wait my endless rest
With equanimity.

But Time, to make me grieve,
Part steals, lets part abide;
And shakes this fragile frame at eve
With throbbings of noontide.

THOMAS HARDY
ENGLISH (1840–1928)

Mr. Flood's Party

Old Eben Flood, climbing alone one night
Over the hill between the town below
And the forsaken upland hermitage
That held as much as he should ever know
On earth again of home, paused warily.
The road was his with not a native near;
And Eben, having leisure, said aloud,
For no man else in Tilbury Town to hear:

"Well, Mr. Flood, we have the harvest moon
Again, and we may not have many more;
The bird is on the wing, the poet says,
And you and I have said it here before.
Drink to the bird." He raised up to the light
The jug that he had gone so far to fill,
And answered huskily: "Well, Mr. Flood,
Since you propose it, I believe I will."

Alone, as if enduring to the end
A valiant armor of scarred hopes outworn,
He stood there in the middle of the road
Like Roland's ghost winding a silent horn.
Below him, in the town among the trees,
Where friends of other days had honored him,
A phantom salutation of the dead
Rang thinly till old Eben's eyes were dim.

Then, as a mother lays her sleeping child
Down tenderly, fearing it may awake,
He set the jug down slowly at his feet
With trembling care, knowing that most things break;
And only when assured that on firm earth
It stood, as the uncertain lives of men
Assuredly did not, he paced away,
And with his hand extended paused again:

"Well, Mr. Flood, we have not met like this
In a long time; and many a change has come
To both of us, I fear, since last it was
We had a drop together. Welcome home!"
Convivially returning with himself,
Again he raised the jug up to the light;
And with an acquiescent quaver said:
"Well, Mr. Flood, if you insist, I might.

"Only a very little, Mr. Flood —
For auld lang syne. No more, sir; that will do."
So, for the time, apparently it did,
And Eben evidently thought so too;
For soon amid the silver loneliness
Of night he lifted up his voice and sang,
Secure, with only two moons listening,
Until the whole harmonious landscape rang —

"For auld lang syne." The weary throat gave out,
The last word wavered, and the song was done.

He raised again the jug regretfully
And shook his head, and was again alone.
There was not much that was ahead of him,
And there was nothing in the town below —
Where strangers would have shut the many doors
That many friends had opened long ago.

EDWIN ARLINGTON ROBINSON
AMERICAN (1869–1935)

The Lamentation of the Old Pensioner

Although I shelter from the rain
Under a broken tree
My chair was nearest to the fire
In every company
That talked of love or politics,
Ere Time transfigured me.

Though lads are making pikes again
For some conspiracy,
And crazy rascals rage their fill
At human tyranny,
My contemplations are of Time
That has transfigured me.

There's not a woman turns her face
Upon a broken tree,
And yet the beauties that I loved
Are in my memory;
I spit into the face of Time
That has transfigured me.

WILLIAM BUTLER YEATS
IRISH (1865–1939)

When You Are Old

When you are old and grey and full of sleep,
And nodding by the fire, take down this book,
And slowly read, and dream of the soft look
Your eyes had once, and of their shadows deep;

How many loved your moments of glad grace,
And loved your beauty with love false or true,
But one man loved the pilgrim soul in you,
And loved the sorrows of your changing face;

And bending down beside the glowing bars,
Murmur, a little sadly, how Love fled
And paced upon the mountains overhead
And hid his face amid a crowd of stars.

WILLIAM BUTLER YEATS
IRISH (1865–1939)

Sailing to Byzantium

1

That is no country for old men. The young
In one another's arms, birds in the trees
— Those dying generations — at their song,
The salmon-falls, the mackerel-crowded seas,
Fish, flesh, or fowl, commend all summer long
Whatever is begotten, born, and dies.
Caught in that sensual music all neglect
Monuments of unageing intellect.

2

An aged man is but a paltry thing,
A tattered coat upon a stick, unless
Soul clap its hands and sing, and louder sing
For every tatter in its mortal dress,
Nor is there singing school but studying
Monuments of its own magnificence;
And therefore I have sailed the seas and come
To the holy city of Byzantium.

3

O sages standing in God's holy fire
As in the gold mosaic of a wall,
Come from the holy fire, perne in a gyre,
And be the singing-masters of my soul.
Consume my heart away; sick with desire
And fastened to a dying animal
It knows not what it is; and gather me
Into the artifice of eternity.

4

Once out of nature I shall never take
My bodily form from any natural thing,
But such a form as Grecian goldsmiths make
Of hammered gold and gold enamelling
To keep a drowsy Emperor awake;
Or set upon a golden bough to sing
To lords and ladies of Byzantium
Of what is past, or passing, or to come.

WILLIAM BUTLER YEATS
IRISH (1865–1939)

An Old Man's Winter Night

All out of doors looked darkly in at him
Through the thin frost, almost in separate stars,
That gathers on the pane in empty rooms.
What kept his eyes from giving back the gaze
Was the lamp tilted near them in his hand.
What kept him from remembering the need
That brought him to that creaking room was age.
He stood with barrels round him — at a loss.
And having scared the cellar under him
In clomping there, he scared it once again
In clomping off; — and scared the outer night,
Which has its sounds, familiar, like the roar
Of trees and crack of branches, common things,
But nothing so like beating on a box.
A light he was to no one but himself
Where now he sat, concerned with he knew what,

A quiet light, and then not even that.
He consigned to the moon, such as she was,
So late-arising, to the broken moon
As better than the sun in any case
For such a charge, his snow upon the roof,
His icicles along the wall to keep;
And slept. The log that shifted with a jolt
Once in the stove, disturbed him and he shifted,
And eased his heavy breathing, but still slept.
One aged man — one man — can't fill a house,
A farm, a countryside, or if he can,
It's thus he does it of a winter night.

ROBERT FROST
AMERICAN (1874–1963)

The Descent

The descent beckons
　　　　as the ascent beckoned.
　　　　　　　　Memory is a kind
of accomplishment,
　　　　　a sort of renewal
　　　　　　　　　even
an initiation, since the spaces it opens are new places
　　　　inhabited by hordes
　　　　　　　　heretofore unrealized,
of new kinds —
　　　　since their movements
　　　　　　　　are toward new objectives
(even though formerly they were abandoned).

No defeat is made up entirely of defeat — since
the world it opens is always a place

formerly
                    unsuspected. A
world lost,
          a world unsuspected,
                    beckons to new places
and no whiteness (lost) is so white as the memory
of whiteness

With evening, love wakens
          though its shadows
                    which are alive by reason
of the sun shining —
          grow sleepy now and drop away
                    from desire

Love without shadows stirs now
          beginning to awaken
                    as night
advances.

The descent
          made up of despairs
                    and without accomplishment
realizes a new awakening:
                    which is a reversal
of despair.
          For what we cannot accomplish, what
is denied to love,
          what we have lost in the anticipation —
                    a descent follows,
endless and indestructible

WILLIAM CARLOS WILLIAMS
AMERICAN (1883–1963)

The Plain Sense of Things

After the leaves have fallen, we return
To a plain sense of things. It is as if
We had come to an end of the imagination,
Inanimate in an inert savoir.

It is difficult even to choose the adjective
For this blank cold, this sadness without cause.
The great structure has become a minor house.
No turban walks across the lessened floors.

The greenhouse never so badly needed paint.
The chimney is fifty years old and slants to one side.
A fantastic effort has failed, a repetition
In a repetitiousness of men and flies.

Yet the absence of the imagination had
Itself to be imagined. The great pond,
The plain sense of it, without reflections, leaves,
Mud, water like dirty glass, expressing silence

Of a sort, silence of a rat come out to see,
The great pond and its waste of the lilies, all this
Had to be imagined as an inevitable knowledge,
Required, as a necessity requires.

WALLACE STEVENS
AMERICAN (1879–1955)

Hail and Farewell

Waiting to cross the avenue,
I saw a man who had been in school with me:
we had been friendly
and now knew each other at once.
"Hot, isn't it," I said,
as if we had met only yesterday. "It hit ninety-five."
"O no," he answered. "I'm not ninety-five yet!"
Then he smiled a little sadly and said,

"You know I'm so tired
I thought for a moment you were talking about my age."

We walked on together and he asked me what I was doing.
But, of course, he did not care.
Then, politely, I asked him about himself
and he, too, answered briefly.
At the stairs down to the subway station he said,
"I know I ought to be ashamed of myself
but I have forgotten your name."
"Don't be ashamed," I answered,
"I've forgotten yours, too."
With that we both smiled wryly,
gave our names and parted.

CHARLES REZNIKOFF
AMERICAN (1894–1976)

Do not go gentle into that good night

Do not go gentle into that good night,
Old age should burn and rave at close of day;
Rage, rage against the dying of the light.

Though wise men at their end know dark is right,
Because their words had forked no lightning they
Do not go gentle into that good night.

Good men, the last wave by, crying how bright
Their frail deeds might have danced in a green bay,
Rage, rage against the dying of the light.

Wild men who caught and sang the sun in flight,
And learn, too late, they grieved it on its way,
Do not go gentle into that good night.

Grave men, near death, who see with blinding sight
Blind eyes could blaze like meteors and be gay,
Rage, rage against the dying of the light.

And you, my father, there on the sad height,
Curse, bless, me now with your fierce tears, I pray.
Do not go gentle into that good night.
Rage, rage against the dying of the light.

DYLAN THOMAS
WELSH (1914–1953)

The Street

Like slag
              the face,
old,
one who knows he has been banished,
knows his place,
expects no sympathy or interest.

At seeing me
              the face
lit up at once
              and smiled,
expecting a smile:
              You're one of us!

CARL RAKOSI
AMERICAN (B. 1903)

The Language

The fear of dying soon now, the worse fear
of growing old first, yet the need to cling,
though Man seem formed in vain, to the still dear
voices, the hope to see and breathe next Spring —
these crowd in, stifling, clouding, deafening . . .
until fear clears to awe, and one is near
the level sill of silence, listening
tuned by music — by men, divine — to hear

thrilling below thresholds of whispers, low as
a sigh of spider-silk at dawn (new and
still balancing spaced dew between caught flowers),
the language of the intertwining winds
on high among themselves — all vowels —
Holy Holy Holy — the names with no ends —

JONATHAN GRIFFIN
ENGLISH (1906–1990)

Now

I never wanted to kill
myself, never wanted
to die; but now, looking
ahead, thinking of thought
some day going awry
and trickling to a stop,
leaving a smelly shell
high on a dry beach

I think —
            almost
I think —
            but
No. Not yet.

MARY BARNARD
AMERICAN (1909–2000)

Forgetfulness

The name of the author is the first to go
followed obediently by the title, the plot,
the heartbreaking conclusion, the entire novel
which suddenly becomes one you have never read, never
    even heard of,

as if, one by one, the memories you used to harbor
decided to retire to the southern hemisphere of the brain,
to a little fishing village where there are no phones.

Long ago you kissed the names of the nine Muses good-bye
and watched the quadratic equation pack its bag,
and even now as you memorize the order of the planets,

something else is slipping away, a state flower perhaps,
the address of an uncle, the capital of Paraguay.

Whatever it is you are struggling to remember
it is not poised on the tip of your tongue,
not even lurking in some obscure corner of your spleen.

It has floated away down a dark mythological river
whose name begins with an *L* as far as you can recall,
well on your own way to oblivion where you will join those
who have even forgotten how to swim and how to ride a
    bicycle.

No wonder you rise in the middle of the night
to look up the date of a famous battle in a book on war.
No wonder the moon in the window seems to have drifted
out of a love poem that you used to know by heart.

BILLY COLLINS
AMERICAN (B. 1941)

DEATH AND MORTALITY

What has this bugbear death to frighten man

From *On the Nature of Things*

What has this bugbear death to frighten man,
If souls can die, as well as bodies can?
For, as before our birth we felt no pain
When Punic arms infested land and main,
When heav'n and earth were in confusion hurled
For the debated empire of the world,

Which awed with dreadful expectation lay,
Sure to be slaves, uncertain who should sway:
So, when our mortal frame shall be disjoined,
The lifeless lump, uncoupled from the mind,
From sense of grief and pain we shall be free;
We shall not feel, because we shall not be.

LUCRETIUS
LATIN (C. 100 TO 90–C. 55 TO 53 B.C.)
TRANSLATED BY JOHN DRYDEN

Hadrian's Address to His Soul When Dying

Ah! gentle, fleeting, wav'ring sprite,
Friend and associate of this clay!
    To what unknown region borne,
Wilt thou now wing thy distant flight?
No more with wonted humour gay,
    But pallid, cheerless, and forlorn.

THE EMPEROR HADRIAN
LATIN (76–138)
TRANSLATED BY GEORGE GORDON, LORD BYRON

Out of the dark

Out of the dark,
Into a dark path
I now must enter:
Shine on me from afar,
Moon of the mountain fringe!

IZUMI SHIKIBU
JAPANESE (974?–1034?)
TRANSLATED BY ARTHUR WALEY

That it is a road

That it is a road
Which some day we all travel
I had heard before,
Yet I never expected
To take it so soon myself.

ARIWARA NO NARIHARA
JAPANESE (825–880)
TRANSLATED BY RICHARD LANE

Death Song

In the great night my heart will go out.
Toward me the darkness comes rattling,
In the great night my heart will go out.

FRANCES DENSMORE (FROM THE PAPAGO)
AMERICAN (1867–1957)

The silver swan, who living had no note

The silver swan, who living had no note,
When death approached, unlocked her silent throat,
Leaning her breast against the reedy shore,
Thus sung her first and last, and sung no more:
Farewell all joys! O death, come close mine eyes;
More geese than swans now live, more fools than wise.

ANONYMOUS
ENGLISH (16TH CENTURY)

Adieu! Farewell Earth's Bliss!

Adieu! farewell earth's bliss!
This world uncertain is:
Fond are life's lustful joys,
Death proves them all but toys.
None from his darts can fly:
I am sick, I must die.
Lord, have mercy on us!

Rich men, trust not in wealth!
Gold cannot buy you health;
Physic himself must fade;
All things to end are made;
The plague full swift goes by:
I am sick, I must die.
    Lord, have mercy on us!

Beauty is but a flower
Which wrinkles will devour:
Brightness falls from the air;
Queens have died young and fair;
Dust hath closed Helen's eye:
I am sick, I must die.
    Lord, have mercy on us!

Strength stoops unto the grave:
Worms feed on Hector brave;
Swords may not fight with fate;
Earth still holds ope her gate;
Come! come! the bells do cry.
I am sick, I must die.
    Lord, have mercy on us!

Wit with his wantonness
Tasteth death's bitterness:
Hell's executioner
Hath no ears for to hear
What vain art can reply:
I am sick, I must die.
    Lord, have mercy on us!

Haste, therefore, each degree
To welcome destiny:
Heaven is our heritage,
Earth but a player's stage:
Mount we unto the sky.
I am sick, I must die.
> *Lord, have mercy on us!*

THOMAS NASHE
ENGLISH (1567–1601?)

Elegy for Himself, Written in the Tower Before His Execution

My prime of youth is but a frost of cares;
    My feast of joy is but a dish of pain;
My crop of corn is but a field of tares;
    And all my good is but vain hope of gain:
The day is past, and yet I saw no sun;
And now I live, and now my life is done.

My tale was heard, and yet it was not told;
    My fruit is fall'n, and yet my leaves are green;
My youth is spent, and yet I am not old;
    I saw the world, and yet I was not seen:
My thread is cut, and yet it is not spun;
And now I live, and now my life is done.

I sought my death, and found it in my womb;
    I looked for life, and saw it was a shade;
I trod the earth, and knew it was my tomb;
    And now I die, and now I was but made:
My glass is full, and now my glass is run;
And now I live, and now my life is done.

CHIDIOCK TICHBORNE
ENGLISH (C. 1558–1586)

The Passionate Man's Pilgrimage

Give me my scallop-shell of quiet,
My staff of faith to walk upon,
My scrip of joy, immortal diet,
My bottle of salvation,
My gown of glory, hope's true gage,
And thus I'll take my pilgrimage.

Blood must be my body's balmer,
No other balm will there be given,
Whilst my soul like a white palmer
Travels to the land of heaven,
Over the silver mountains,
Where spring the nectar fountains;
And there I'll kiss
The bowl of bliss,
And drink my eternal fill
On every milken hill.
My soul will be a-dry before,
But after it will ne'er thirst more.

And by the happy blissful way
More peaceful pilgrims I shall see,
That have shook off their gowns of clay
And go apparelled fresh like me.
I'll bring them first
To slake their thirst,
And then to taste those nectar suckets,
At the clear wells
Where sweetness dwells,
Drawn up by saints in crystal buckets.

And when our bottles and all we
Are filled with immortality,
Then the holy paths we'll travel,
Strewed with rubies thick as gravel,
Ceilings of diamonds, sapphire floors,
High walls of coral and pearl bowers.

From thence to heaven's bribeless hall
Where no corrupted voices brawl,
No conscience molten into gold,
Nor forged accusers bought and sold,
No cause deferred, nor vain-spent journey,
For there Christ is the King's Attorney,
Who pleads for all without degrees,
And he hath angels, but no fees.

When the grand twelve million jury
Of our sins with sinful fury
'Gainst our souls black verdicts give,
Christ pleads his death, and then we live.
Be thou my speaker, taintless pleader,
Unblotted lawyer, true proceeder;
Thou movest salvation even for alms,
Not with a bribed lawyer's palms.

And this is my eternal plea
To him that made heaven, earth and sea:
Seeing my flesh must die so soon,
And want a head to dine next noon,
Just at the stroke when my veins start and spread,
Set on my soul an everlasting head.
Then am I ready, like a palmer fit,
To tread those blest paths which before I writ.

SIR WALTER RALEGH
ENGLISH (1552?–1618)

What is our life? A play of passion

What is our life? A play of passion,
Our mirth the music of division.
Our mothers' wombs the tiring-houses be,
Where we are dressed for this short comedy.
Heaven the judicious sharp spectator is,
That sits and marks still who doth act amiss.
Our graves that hide us from the searching sun
Are like drawn curtains when the play is done.
Thus march we, playing, to our latest rest.
Only we die in earnest, that's no jest.

SIR WALTER RALEGH
ENGLISH (1552?–1618)

Never weather-beaten sail more willing bent to shore

Never weather-beaten sail more willing bent to shore,
Never tired pilgrim's limbs affected slumber more,
Than my weary sprite now longs to fly out of my troubled
    breast.
Oh, come quickly, sweetest Lord, and take my soul to rest!

Ever blooming are the joys of heaven's high paradise,
Cold age deafs not there our ears nor vapour dims our eyes:
Glory there the sun outshines, whose beams the blessëd only
    see.
Oh, come quickly, glorious Lord, and raise my sprite to thee!

THOMAS CAMPION
ENGLISH (1567–1620)

Thou hast made me, and shall thy work decay

Thou hast made me, and shall thy work decay?
Repair me now, for now mine end doth haste;
I run to death, and death meets me as fast,
And all my pleasures are like yesterday.
I dare not move my dim eyes any way;
Despair behind, and death before doth cast

Such terror, and my feebled flesh doth waste
By sin in it, which it towards hell doth weigh.
Only thou art above, and when towards thee
By thy leave I can look, I rise again;
But our old subtle foe so tempteth me
That not one hour I can myself sustain.
Thy grace may wing me to prevent his art,
And thou like adamant draw mine iron heart.

JOHN DONNE
ENGLISH (1572–1631)

Death, be not proud though some have called thee

Death, be not proud though some have called thee
Mighty and dreadful, for thou art not so,
For those, whom thou think'st thou dost overthrow,
Die not, poor Death, nor yet canst thou kill me.
From rest and sleep, which but thy pictures be,
Much pleasure, then from thee much more must flow,
And soonest our best men with thee do go,
Rest of their bones and soul's delivery.
Thou art slave to Fate, Chance, kings and desperate men,
And dost with poison, war, and sickness dwell,
And poppy or charms can make us sleep as well,
And better than thy stroke; why swell'st thou then?
One short sleep past, we wake eternally,
And death shall be no more; Death, thou shalt die.

JOHN DONNE
ENGLISH (1572–1631)

The Dying Christian to His Soul

Vital spark of heavenly flame!
Quit, oh quit this mortal frame:
Trembling, hoping, lingering, flying,
Oh the pain, the bliss of dying!
Cease, fond Nature, cease thy strife,
And let me languish into life.

Hark! they whisper; Angels say,
Sister Spirit, come away.
    What is this absorbs me quite?
    Steals my senses, shuts my sight,
Drowns my spirits, draws my breath?
Tell me, my Soul, can this be Death?

The world recedes; it disappears!
Heaven opens on my eyes! my ears
    With sounds seraphic ring:
Lend, lend your wings! I mount! I fly!
O Grave! where is thy Victory?
    O Death! where is thy Sting?

ALEXANDER POPE
ENGLISH (1688–1744)

Like to the falling of a star

    Like to the falling of a star,
Or as the flights of eagles are,
Or like the fresh spring's gaudy hue,
Or silver drops of morning dew,
Or like a wind that chafes the flood,
Or bubbles which on water stood:
Even such is man, whose borrowed light
Is straight called in, and paid to night.

    The wind blows out, the bubble dies;
    The spring entombed in autumn lies;
    The dew dries up, the star is shot;
    The flight is past: and man forgot.

HENRY KING
ENGLISH (1592–1669)

The Land o' the Leal

I'm wearin' awa', John
Like snaw-wreaths in thaw, John,
I'm wearin' awa'
To the land o' the leal.
There 's nae sorrow there, John
There 's neither cauld nor care, John,
The day is aye fair
In the land o' the leal.

Our bonnie bairn 's there, John,
She was baith gude and fair, John;
And O! we grudged her sair
To the land o' the leal.
But sorrow's sel' wears past, John,
And joy 's a-coming fast, John,
The joy that 's aye to last
In the land o' the leal.

Sae dear 's the joy was bought, John,
Sae free the battle fought, John,
That sinfu' man e'er brought
To the land o' the leal.
O, dry your glistening e'e, John!
My saul langs to be free, John,
And angels beckon me
To the land o' the leal.

O, haud ye leal and true, John!
Your day it 's wearin' through, John,
And I'll welcome you
To the land o' the leal.
Now fare-ye-weel, my ain John,
This warld's cares are vain, John,
We'll meet, and we'll be fain,
In the land o' the leal.

LADY CAROLINA NAIRNE
SCOTTISH (1766–1845)

I've seen a Dying Eye

I've seen a Dying Eye
Run round and round a Room —
In search of Something — as it seemed —
Then Cloudier become —
And then — obscure with Fog —
And then — be soldered down
Without disclosing what it be
'Twere blessed to have seen —

EMILY DICKINSON
AMERICAN (1830–1886)

Because I could not stop for death

Because I could not stop for Death —
He kindly stopped for me —
The Carriage held but just Ourselves —
And Immortality.

We slowly drove — He knew no haste
And I had put away
My labor and my leisure too,
For His Civility —

We passed the School, where Children strove
At Recess — in the Ring —
We passed the Fields of Gazing Grain —
We passed the Setting Sun —

Or rather — He passed Us —
The Dews drew quivering and chill —
For only Gossamer, my Gown —
My Tippet — only Tulle —

We paused before a House that seemed
A Swelling of the Ground —

The Roof was scarcely visible —
The Cornice — in the Ground —

Since then — 'tis Centuries — and yet
Feels shorter than the Day
I first surmised the Horses' Heads
Were toward Eternity —

EMILY DICKINSON
AMERICAN (1830–1886)

Crossing the Bar

Sunset and evening star,
  And one clear call for me!
And may there be no moaning of the bar,
  When I put out to sea,

But such a tide as moving seems asleep,
  Too full for sound and foam,
When that which drew from out the boundless deep
  Turns again home.

Twilight and evening bell,
  And after that the dark!
And may there be no sadness of farewell,
  When I embark;

For tho' from out our bourne of Time and Place
  The flood may bear me far,
I hope to see my Pilot face to face
  When I have crost the bar.

ALFRED, LORD TENNYSON
ENGLISH (1809–1892)

I strove with none, for none was worth my strife

I strove with none, for none was worth my strife:
    Nature I loved, and next to Nature, Art:
I warmed both hands before the fire of Life;
    It sinks; and I am ready to depart.

WALTER SAVAGE LANDOR
ENGLISH (1775–1864)

Death stands above me

Death stands above me, whispering low
    I know not what into my ear:
Of his strange language all I know
    Is, there is not a word of fear.

WALTER SAVAGE LANDOR
ENGLISH (1775–1864)

Requiem

Under the wide and starry sky,
Dig the grave and let me lie.
Glad did I live and gladly die,
    And I laid me down with a will.

This be the verse you grave for me:
Here he lies where he longed to be;
Home is the sailor, home from sea,
    And the hunter home from the hill.

ROBERT LOUIS STEVENSON
SCOTTISH (1850–1894)

The Lonely Death

In the cold I will rise, I will bathe
In waters of ice; myself
Will shiver, and shrive myself,
Alone in the dawn, and anoint
Forehead and feet and hands;
I will shutter the windows from light,
I will place in their sockets the four
Tall candles and set them a-flame
In the grey of the dawn; and myself
Will lay myself straight in my bed,
And draw the sheet under my chin.

ADELAIDE CRAPSEY
AMERICAN (1878–1914)

Dirge Without Music

I am not resigned to the shutting away of loving hearts in the
    hard ground.
So it is, and so it will be, for so it has been, time out of mind:
Into the darkness they go, the wise and the lovely. Crowned
With lilies and with laurel they go; but I am not resigned.

Lovers and thinkers, into the earth with you.
Be one with the dull, the indiscriminate dust.
A fragment of what you felt, of what you knew,
A formula, a phrase remains, — but the best is lost.

The answers quick and keen, the honest look, the laughter, the
    love, —
They are gone. They are gone to feed the roses. Elegant and
    curled
Is the blossom. Fragrant is the blossom. I know. But I do not
    approve.

More precious was the light in your eyes than all the roses in the
   world.

Down, down, down into the darkness of the grave
Gently they go, the beautiful, the tender, the kind;
Quietly they go, the intelligent, the witty, the brave.
I know. But I do not approve. And I am not resigned.

EDNA ST. VINCENT MILLAY
AMERICAN (1892–1950)

Bavarian Gentians

Not every man has gentians in his house
in soft September, at slow, sad Michaelmas.

Bavarian gentians, big and dark, only dark
darkening of the day-time torch-like with the smoking blueness
   of Pluto's gloom,
ribbed and torch-like, with their blaze of darkness spread blue
down flattening into points, flattened under the sweep of white
   day
torch-flower of the blue-smoking darkness, Pluto's dark-blue
   daze,
black lamps from the halls of Dis, burning dark blue,
giving off darkness, blue darkness, as Demeter's pale lamps give
   off light,
lead me then, lead me the way.

Reach me a gentian, give me a torch
let me guide myself with the blue, forked torch of this flower
down the darker and darker stairs, where blue is darkened on
   blueness,
even where Persephone goes, just now, from the frosted
   September
to the sightless realm where darkness is awake upon the dark

and Persephone herself is but a voice
or a darkness invisible enfolded in the deeper dark
of the arms Plutonic, and pierced with the passion of dense
    gloom,
among the splendour of torches of darkness, shedding darkness
    on the lost bride and her groom.

D. H. LAWRENCE
ENGLISH (1885–1930)

The Bed by the Window

I chose the bed down-stairs by the sea-window for a good
    death-bed
When we built the house; it is ready waiting,
Unused unless by some guest in a twelvemonth, who hardly
    suspects
Its latter purpose. I often regard it,
With neither dislike nor desire: rather with both, so equalled
That they kill each other and a crystalline interest
Remains alone. We are safe to finish what we have to finish;
And then it will sound rather like music
When the patient daemon behind the screen of sea-rock and
    sky
Thumps with his staff, and calls thrice: "Come, Jeffers."

ROBINSON JEFFERS
AMERICAN (1887–1962)

Lemon Elegy

So intensely you had been waiting for lemon.
In the sad, white, light deathbed
you took that one lemon from my hand
and bit it sharply with your bright teeth.
A fragrance rose the color of topaz.
Those heavenly drops of juice
flashed you back to sanity.
Your eyes, blue and transparent, slightly smiled.
You grasped my hand, how vigorous you were.
There was a storm in your throat

but just at the end
Chieko found Chieko again,
all life's love into one moment fallen.
And then once
as once you did on a mountaintop, you let out a great sigh
and with it your engine stopped.
By the cherry blossoms in front of your photograph
today, too, I will put a cool fresh lemon.

TAKAMURA KŌTARŌ
JAPANESE (1883–1956)
TRANSLATED BY HIROAKI SATO

Question

Body my house
my horse my hound
what will I do
when you are fallen

Where will I sleep
How will I ride
What will I hunt

Where can I go
without my mount
all eager and quick
How will I know
in thicket ahead
is danger or treasure
when Body my good
bright dog is dead

How will it be
to lie in the sky
without roof or door
and wind for an eye

With cloud for shift
how will I hide?

MAY SWENSON
AMERICAN (1913–1989)

GRIEF AND MOURNING

To Stella

Thou wert the morning star among the living,
    Ere thy fair light had fled; —
Now, having died, thou art as Hesperus, giving
    New splendor to the dead.

PLATO
GREEK (427?–347 B.C.)
TRANSLATED BY PERCY BYSSHE SHELLEY

In the days when my wife lived

In the days when my wife lived,
We went out to the embankment near by —
We two, hand in hand —
To view the elm trees standing there
With their outspreading branches
Thick with spring leaves. Abundant as their greenery
Was my love. On her leaned my soul.
But who evades mortality?
One morning she was gone, flown like an early bird,
Clad in a heavenly scarf of white,
To the wide fields where the shimmering *kagerō* rises
She went and vanished like the setting sun.

The little babe — the keepsake
My wife has left me —
Cries and clamors.
I have nothing to give; I pick up the child
And clasp it in my arms.

In our chamber, where our two pillows lie,
Where we two used to sleep together,
Days I spend alone, broken-hearted:
Nights I pass, sighing until dawn.

Though I grieve, there is no help;
Vainly I long to see her.
Men tell me that my wife is
In the mountains of Hagai —
Thither I go,
Toiling along the stony path;
But it avails me not,
For of my wife, as she lived in this world,
I find not the faintest shadow.

.   .   .   .

Tonight the autumn moon shines —
The moon that shone a year ago,
But my wife and I who watched it then together
Are divided by ever widening wastes of time.

When leaving my love behind
In the Hikite mountains —
Leaving her there in her grave,
I walk down the mountain path,
I feel like one not living.

KAKINOMOTO NO HITOMARO
JAPANESE (D. C. 708)
TRANSLATED BY RALPH HODGSON AND OTHERS

On the Death of a New Born Child

The flowers in bud on the trees
Are pure like this dead child.
The East wind will not let them last.
It will blow them into blossom,
And at last into the earth.
It is the same with this beautiful life
Which was so dear to me.
While his mother is weeping tears of blood,
Her breasts are still filling with milk.

MEI YAO CH'EN
CHINESE (1002–1060)
TRANSLATED BY KENNETH REXROTH

O grief! even on the bud that fairly flowered

O grief! even on the bud that fairly flowered
    The sun hath lowered;
And at the breast which Love durst never venture
    Bold Death did enter.
Pity, O heavens, that have my Love in keeping,
    My cries and weeping.

ANONYMOUS
ENGLISH (16TH CENTURY)

On My First Son

Farewell, thou child of my right hand, and joy;
My sin was too much hope of thee, loved boy,
Seven years thou wert lent to me, and I thee pay,
Exacted by thy fate, on the just day.
O, could I lose all father, now. For why
Will man lament the state he should envy?

To have so soon 'scaped world's, and flesh's rage,
And, if no other misery, yet age!
Rest in soft peace, and, asked, say here doth lie
Ben Jonson his best piece of poetry.
For whose sake, henceforth, all his vows be such,
As what he loves may never like too much.

BEN JONSON
ENGLISH (1572–1637)

Slow, slow, fresh fount

Slow, slow, fresh fount, keep time with my salt tears;
   Yet, slower, yet; O faintly, gentle springs:
List to the heavy part the music bears,
   Woe weeps out her division, when she sings.
      Droop herbs, and flowers,
      Fall grief in showers,
      Our beauties are not ours:
         O, I could still,
Like melting snow upon some craggy hill,
   Drop, drop, drop, drop,
Since nature's pride is now a withered daffodil.

BEN JONSON
ENGLISH (1572–1637)

They are all gone into the world of light

They are all gone into the world of light!
   And I alone sit ling'ring here;
Their very memory is fair and bright,
   And my sad thoughts doth clear.

It glows and glitters in my cloudy breast
   Like stars upon some gloomy grove,
Or those faint beams in which this hill is dressed,
   After the sun's remove.

I see them walking in an air of glory,
   Whose light doth trample on my days:

My days, which are at best but dull and hoary,
    Mere glimmering and decays.

O holy hope! and high humility,
   High as the Heavens above!
These are your walks, and you have showed them me
    To kindle my cold love.

Dear, beauteous death! the jewel of the just,
   Shining nowhere, but in the dark;
What mysteries do lie beyond thy dust;
    Could man outlook that mark!

He that hath found some fledged bird's nest, may know
   At first sight, if the bird be flown;
But what fair well or grove he sings in now,
    That is to him unknown.

And yet, as Angels in some brighter dreams
   Call to the soul, when man doth sleep:
So some strange thoughts transcend our wonted themes,
    And into glory peep.

If a star were confined into a tomb
   Her captive flames must needs burn there;
But when the hand that locked her up gives room,
    She'll shine through all the sphere.

O Father of eternal life, and all
   Created glories under thee!
Resume thy spirit from this world of thrall
    Into true liberty.

Either disperse these mists, which blot and fill
   My perspective still as they pass,
Or else remove me hence unto that hill,
    Where I shall need no glass.

             HENRY VAUGHAN
        ENGLISH (1622–1695)

What piercing cold I feel

What piercing cold I feel:
    my dead wife's comb, in our bedroom,
      under my heel. . . .

YOSA BUSON
JAPANESE (1716–1783)
TRANSLATED BY HAROLD HENDERSON

On His Deceased Wife

Methought I saw my late espousèd saint
Brought to me like Alcestis from the grave,
Whom Jove's great son to her glad husband gave,
Rescu'd from death by force though pale and faint,
Mine as whom washt from spot of child-bed taint,
Purification in the old Law did save,
And such, as yet once more I trust to have
Full sight of her in Heaven without restraint,
Came vested all in white, pure as her mind:
Her face was vail'd, yet to my fancied sight,
Love, sweetness, goodness, in her person shin'd
So clear, as in no face with more delight.
But O as to embrace me she enclin'd
I wak'd, she fled, and day brought back my night.

JOHN MILTON
ENGLISH (1608–1674)

Coronach

He is gone on the mountain,
    He is lost to the forest,
Like a summer-dried fountain,
    When our need was the sorest.
The font reappearing
    From the raindrops shall borrow;
But to us comes no cheering,
    To Duncan no morrow!

The hand of the reaper
   Takes the ears that are hoary,
But the voice of the weeper
   Wails manhood in glory.
The autumn winds rushing
   Waft the leaves that are serest,
But our flower was in flushing
   When blighting was nearest.

Fleet foot on the correi,
   Sage counsel in cumber,
Red hand in the foray,
   How sound is thy slumber!
Like the dew on the mountain,
   Like the foam on the river,
Like the bubble on the fountain,
   Thou art gone — and for ever!

SIR WALTER SCOTT
SCOTTISH (1771–1832)

Surprised by joy — impatient as the Wind

Surprised by joy — impatient as the Wind
I turned to share the transport — Oh! with whom
But Thee, deep buried in the silent tomb,
That spot which no vicissitude can find?
Love, faithful love, recalled thee to my mind —
But how could I forget thee? Through what power,
Even for the least division of an hour,
Have I been so beguiled as to be blind
To my most grievous loss? — That thought's return
Was the worst pang that sorrow ever bore,
Save one, one only, when I stood forlorn,
Knowing my heart's best treasure was no more;
That neither present time, nor years unborn
Could to my sight that heavenly face restore.

WILLIAM WORDSWORTH
ENGLISH (1770–1850)

Peace, peace! he is not dead, he doth not sleep

From *Adonais*

Peace, peace! he is not dead, he doth not sleep —
He hath awakened from the dream of life —
'Tis we, who lost in stormy visions, keep
With phantoms an unprofitable strife,
And in mad trance, strike with our spirit's knife
Invulnerable nothings. — We decay
Like corpses in a charnel; fear and grief
Convulse us and consume us day by day,
And cold hopes swarm like worms within our living clay.

He has outsoared the shadow of our night;
Envy and calumny and hate and pain,
And that unrest which men miscall delight,
Can touch him not and torture not again;
From the contagion of the world's slow stain
He is secure, and now can never mourn
A heart grown cold, a head grown grey in vain;
Nor, when the spirit's self has ceased to burn,
With sparkless ashes load an unlamented urn.

PERCY BYSSHE SHELLEY
ENGLISH (1792–1822)

The Cross of Snow

In the long, sleepless watches of the night,
    A gentle face — the face of one long dead —
    Looks at me from the wall, where round its head
    The night-lamp casts a halo of pale light.
Here in this room she died; and soul more white
    Never through martyrdom of fire was led
    To its repose; nor can in books be read
    The legend of a life more benedight.

There is a mountain in the distant West
    That, sun-defying, in its deep ravines
    Displays a cross of snow upon its side.
Such is the cross I wear upon my breast
    These eighteen years, through all the changing scenes
    And seasons, changeless since the day she died.

HENRY WADSWORTH LONGFELLOW
AMERICAN (1807–1882)

Sleep brings no joy . . .

    Sleep brings no joy to me,
      Remembrance never dies;
    My soul is given to misery,
      And lives in sighs.

    Sleep brings no rest to me;
      The shadows of the dead,
    My wakening eyes may never see,
      Surround my bed.

    Sleep brings no hope to me,
      In soundest sleep they come,
    And with their doleful imagery
      Deepen the gloom.

    Sleep brings no strength to me,
      No power renewed to brave:
    I only sail a wilder sea,
      A darker wave.

    Sleep brings no friend to me
      To soothe and aid to bear;

They all gaze on — how scornfully!
　And I despair.

Sleep brings no wish to fret
　My harassed heart beneath:
My only wish is to forget
　In endless sleep of death.

EMILY BRONTË
ENGLISH (1818–1848)

Annabel Lee

It was many and many a year ago,
　In a kingdom by the sea,
That a maiden there lived whom you may know
　By the name of ANNABEL LEE;
And this maiden she lived with no other thought
　Than to love and be loved by me.

I was a child and *she* was a child,
　In this kingdom by the sea;
But we loved with a love which was more than love
　I and my Annabel Lee;
With a love that the wingéd seraphs of heaven
　Coveted her and me.

And this was the reason that, long ago,
　In this kingdom by the sea,
A wind blew out of a cloud, chilling
　My beautiful Annabel Lee;
So that her highborn kinsmen came
　And bore her away from me,
To shut her up in a sepulchre
　In this kingdom by the sea.

The angels, not half so happy in heaven,
　Went envying her and me —
Yes! — that was the reason (as all men know,
　In this kingdom by the sea)

That the wind came out of the cloud by night,
    Chilling and killing my Annabel Lee.

But our love it was stronger by far than the love
    Of those who were older than we —
    Of many far wiser than we —
And neither the angels in heaven above,
    Nor the demons down under the sea,
Can ever dissever my soul from the soul
    Of the beautiful Annabel Lee.

For the moon never beams without bringing me dreams
    Of the beautiful Annabel Lee;
And the stars never rise but I feel the bright eyes
    Of the beautiful Annabel Lee;
And so, all the night-tide, I lie down by the side
Of my darling — my darling — my life and my bride,
    In the sepulchre there by the sea,
    In her tomb by the sounding sea.

EDGAR ALLAN POE
AMERICAN (1809–1849)

Break, break, break

Break, break, break,
    On thy cold gray stones, O Sea!
And I would that my tongue could utter
    The thoughts that arise in me.

O well for the fisherman's boy,
    That he shouts with his sister at play!
O well for the sailor lad,
    That he sings in his boat on the bay!

And the stately ships go on
    To their haven under the hill;

But O for the touch of a vanished hand,
  And the sound of a voice that is still!

Break, break, break,
  At the foot of thy crags, O Sea!
But the tender grace of a day that is dead
  Will never come back to me.

ALFRED, LORD TENNYSON
ENGLISH (1809–1892)

Dark house, by which once more I stand

From *In Memoriam*

Dark house, by which once more I stand
  Here in the long unlovely street,
  Doors, where my heart was used to beat
So quickly, waiting for a hand,

A hand that can be clasp'd no more —
  Behold me, for I cannot sleep,
  And like a guilty thing I creep
At earliest morning to the door.

He is not here; but far away
  The noise of life begins again,
  And ghastly thro' the drizzling rain
On the bald street breaks the blank day.

ALFRED, LORD TENNYSON
ENGLISH (1809–1892)

Grief

I tell you, hopeless grief is passionless;
  That only men incredulous of despair,
  Half-taught in anguish, through the midnight air
Beat upward to God's throne in loud access
Of shrieking and reproach. Full desertness
  In souls as countries lieth silent-bare
  Under the blanching, vertical eye-glare

Of the absolute Heavens. Deep-hearted man, express
Grief for thy Dead in silence like to Death —
   Most like a monumental statue set
In everlasting watch and moveless woe
Till itself crumble to the dust beneath.
   Touch it; the marble eyelids are not wet:
If it could weep, it could arise and go.

ELIZABETH BARRETT BROWNING
ENGLISH (1806–1861)

May and Death

I wish that when you died last May,
   Charles, there had died along with you
Three parts of spring's delightful things;
   Ay, and, for me, the fourth part too.

A foolish thought, and worse, perhaps!
   There must be many a pair of friends
Who, arm in arm, deserve the warm
   Moon-births and the long evening-ends.

So, for their sake, be May still May!
   Let their new time, as mine of old,
Do all it did for me: I bid
   Sweet sights and sounds throng manifold.

Only, one little sight, one plant,
   Woods have in May, that starts up green
Save a sole streak which, so to speak,
   Is spring's blood, spilt its leaves between, —

That, they might spare; a certain wood
   Might miss the plant; their loss were small:
But I, — whene'er the leaf grows there,
   Its drop comes from my heart, that's all.

ROBERT BROWNING
ENGLISH (1812–1889)

Requiescat

Strew on her roses, roses,
   And never a spray of yew.
In quiet she reposes:
   Ah! would that I did too.

Her mirth the world required:
   She bathed it in smiles of glee.
But her heart was tired, tired,
   And now they let her be.

Her life was turning, turning,
   In mazes of heat and sound.
But for peace her soul was yearning,
   And now peace laps her round.

Her cabin'd, ample Spirit,
   It flutter'd, and fail'd for breath.
To-night it doth inherit
   The vasty Hall of Death.

MATTHEW ARNOLD
ENGLISH (1822–1888)

Requiescat

Tread lightly, she is near
   Under the snow,
Speak gently, she can hear
   The daisies grow.

All her bright golden hair
   Tarnished with rust,
She that was young and fair
   Fallen to dust.

Lily-like, white as snow,
   She hardly knew
She was a woman, so
   Sweetly she grew.

Coffin board, heavy stone,
    Lie on her breast,
I vex my heart alone,
    She is at rest.

Peace, peace, she cannot hear
    Lyre or sonnet,
All my life's buried here,
    Heap earth upon it.

OSCAR WILDE
IRISH (1854–1900)

The Haunter

He does not think that I haunt here nightly:
    How shall I let him know
That whither his fancy sets him wandering
    I, too, alertly go? —
Hover and hover a few feet from him
    Just as I used to do,
But cannot answer the words he lifts me —
    Only listen thereto!

When I could answer he did not say them:
    When I could let him know
How I would like to join in his journeys
    Seldom he wished to go.
Now that he goes and wants me with him
    More than he used to do,
Never he sees my faithful phantom
    Though he speaks thereto.

Yes, I companion him to places
    Only dreamers know,
Where the shy hares print long paces,
    Where the night rooks go;
Into old aisles where the past is all to him,
    Close as his shade can do,

Always lacking the power to call to him,
 Near as I reach thereto!

What a good haunter I am, O tell him!
 Quickly make him know
If he but sigh since my loss befell him
 Straight to his side I go.
Tell him a faithful one is doing
 All that love can do
Still that his path may be worth pursuing,
 And to bring peace thereto.

THOMAS HARDY
ENGLISH (1840–1928)

The Voice

Woman much missed, how you call to me, call to me,
Saying that now you are not as you were
When you had changed from the one who was all to me,
But as at first, when our day was fair.

Can it be you that I hear? Let me view you, then,
Standing as when I drew near to the town
Where you would wait for me: yes, as I knew you then,
Even to the original air-blue gown!

Or is it only the breeze, in its listlessness
Travelling across the wet mead to me here,
You being ever dissolved to wan wistlessness,
Heard no more again far or near?

 Thus I; faltering forward,
 Leaves around me falling,
Wind oozing thin through the thorn from norward,
 And the woman calling.

THOMAS HARDY
ENGLISH (1840–1928)

His Immortality

I

I saw a dead man's finer part
Shining within each faithful heart
Of those bereft. Then said I: "This must be
His immortality."

II

I looked there as the seasons wore,
And still his soul continuously bore
A life in theirs. But less its shine excelled
Than when I first beheld.

III

His fellow-yearsmen passed, and then
In later hearts I looked for him again;
And found him — shrunk, alas! into a thin
And spectral mannikin.

IV

Lastly I ask — now old and chill —
If aught of him remain unperished still;
And find, in me alone, a feeble spark,
Dying amid the dark.

THOMAS HARDY
ENGLISH (1840–1928)

Little Boy Blue

The little toy dog is covered with dust,
But sturdy and stanch he stands;
And the little toy soldier is red with rust,
And his musket moulds in his hands.
Time was when the little toy dog was new,
And the soldier was passing fair;
And that was the time when our Little Boy Blue
Kissed them and put them there.

"Now, don't you go till I come," he said,
"And don't you make any noise!"
So, toddling off to his trundle-bed,
He dreamt of the pretty toys;

And, as he was dreaming, an angel song
   Awakened our Little Boy Blue —
Oh! the years are many, the years are long,
   But the little toy friends are true!

Ay, faithful to Little Boy Blue they stand,
   Each in the same old place,
Awaiting the touch of a little hand,
   The smile of a little face;
And they wonder, as waiting the long years through
   In the dust of that little chair,
What has become of our Little Boy Blue,
   Since he kissed them and put them there.

EUGENE FIELD
AMERICAN (1850–1895)

To an Athlete Dying Young

The time you won your town the race
We chaired you through the market-place;
Man and boy stood cheering by,
And home we brought you shoulder-high.

To-day, the road all runners come,
Shoulder-high we bring you home,
And set you at your threshold down,
Townsman of a stiller town.

Smart lad, to slip betimes away
From fields where glory does not stay
And early though the laurel grows
It withers quicker than the rose.

Eyes the shady night has shut
Cannot see the record cut,
And silence sounds no worse than cheers
After earth has stopped the ears:

Now you will not swell the rout
Of lads that wore their honours out,
Runners whom renown outran
And the name died before the man.

So set, before its echoes fade,
The fleet foot on the sill of shade,
And hold to the low lintel up
The still-defended challenge-cup.

And round that early-laurelled head
Will flock to gaze the strengthless dead,
And find unwithered on its curls
The garland briefer than a girl's.

A. E. HOUSMAN
ENGLISH (1859–1936)

For a Dead Lady

No more with overflowing light
Shall fill the eyes that now are faded,
Nor shall another's fringe with night
Their woman-hidden world as they did.
No more shall quiver down the days
The flowing wonder of her ways,
Whereof no language may requite
The shifting and the many-shaded.

The grace, divine, definitive,
Clings only as a faint forestalling;
The laugh that love could not forgive
Is hushed, and answers to no calling;
The forehead and the little ears
Have gone where Saturn keeps the years;
The breast where roses could not live
Has done with rising and with falling.

The beauty, shattered by the laws
That have creation in their keeping,

No longer trembles at applause,
Or over children that are sleeping;
And we who delve in beauty's lore
Know all that we have known before
Of what inexorable cause
Makes Time so vicious in his reaping.

EDWIN ARLINGTON ROBINSON
AMERICAN (1869–1935)

The House on the Hill

They are all gone away,
    The House is shut and still,
There is nothing more to say.

Through broken walls and gray
    The winds blow bleak and shrill:
They are all gone away.

Nor is there one to-day
    To speak them good or ill:
There is nothing more to say.

Why is it then we stray
    Around the sunken sill?
They are all gone away,

And our poor fancy-play
    For them is wasted skill:
There is nothing more to say.

There is ruin and decay
    In the House on the Hill:
They are all gone away,
There is nothing more to say.

EDWIN ARLINGTON ROBINSON
AMERICAN (1869–1935)

The Widow's Lament in Springtime

Sorrow is my own yard
where the new grass
flames as it has flamed
often before but not
with the cold fire
that closes round me this year.
Thirtyfive years
I lived with my husband.
The plumtree is white today
with masses of flowers.
Masses of flowers
load the cherry branches
and color some bushes
yellow and some red
but the grief in my heart
is stronger than they
for though they were my joy
formerly, today I notice them
and turn away forgetting.
Today my son told me
that in the meadows,
at the edge of the heavy woods
in the distance, he saw
trees of white flowers.
I feel that I would like
to go there
and fall into those flowers
and sink into the marsh near them.

WILLIAM CARLOS WILLIAMS
AMERICAN (1883–1963)

Shout No More

Stop killing the dead,
Shout no more, don't shout
If you still want to hear them,
If you're hoping not to perish.

Their murmur is imperceptible,
The sound they make no louder
Than growing grass,
Happy where men don't pass.

GIUSEPPE UNGARETTI
ITALIAN (1888–1970)
TRANSLATED BY ANDREW FRISARDI

While I Slept

While I slept, while I slept and the night grew colder
She would come to my room, stepping softly
And draw a blanket about my shoulder
While I slept.

While I slept, while I slept in the dark, still heat
She would come to my bedside, stepping coolly
And smooth the twisted, troubled sheet
While I slept.

Now she sleeps, sleeps under quiet rain
While nights grow warm or nights grow colder.
And I wake, and sleep, and wake again
While she sleeps.

ROBERT FRANCIS
AMERICAN (1901–1987)

The Human Condition

―――――――

*I*F POETRY IS (AMONG OTHER THINGS, BUT PERHAPS PRIMARILY) AN EXERCISE IN THE CLEAR DEFINITION OF FEELING, THEN THIS PART OF THE BOOK CAN BE TAKEN AS A partial lexicon of such definitions. Approaching analogous situations at different times and from different angles, individual poets open up altogether distinct perspectives. Immense nouns — *passion, love, separation, solitude, sorrow, survival* — stand like symbolic arches as emblems for our lives. By long overexposure — precisely like monuments that one passes every day on the street — the words that ought to carry the weightiest import come to be drained of any effect at all. The work of poets is to demonstrate that those nouns can, after all, possess specific and unavoidable meaning. That meaning is not to be confused with some kind of didactic message: what the poem nails, often by the simplest of means, is not essentially paraphrasable. It's in the sounds and textures, in the proportions and the shape of the poem that meaning is embedded, and it's by totally grasping what is going on at all the poet's levels that the reader may discover an experience of unexampled richness in what might otherwise seem a bald statement. Indeed, the extravagant intimacy of poetry is perhaps best measured by those occasions when the poem seems to engage merely the most ordinary recurrences of existence. Indeed, it is precisely at those moments when the poet appears to be fine-tuning a perception of sheer humdrum blankness — like the speaker in Robert Frost's "The Most of It," who "thought he kept the universe alone" — that the inexplicable comes crashing through like the great buck in that poem who "stumbled through the rocks with horny tread, / And forced the underbrush — and that was all." The poems of spiritual awakening with which this section concludes address the infinitely large through the immediate and transient, as when George Herbert, in his great poem "The Flower," describes an inner restoration in the simplest terms: "I once more smell the dew and rain"; or when Walt Whitman finds the deepest possible image of his own soul's quest in a spider spinning its web: "It launched forth filament, filament, filament, out of itself / Ever unreeling them, ever tirelessly speeding them."

To an Old Comrade in the Army of Brutus

Dear friend who fought so often, together with me,
In the ranks of Brutus in hardship and in danger,
Under whose sponsorship have you come back,
A citizen again, beneath our sky?

Pompey, we drank together so many times,
And we were together in the Philippi fight,
The day I ran away, leaving my shield,
And Mercury got me out of it, carrying me

In a cloud, in a panic, right through the enemy rage;
But the undertow of a wave carried you back
Into the boiling waters of the war.
Come, stretch your weary legs out under this tree;

Let's dedicate a feast to Jupiter
Just as we told each other we'd do someday.
I've got good food to eat, good wine to drink;
Come celebrate old friendship under the laurel.

HORACE
LATIN (65–8 B.C.)
TRANSLATED BY DAVID FERRY

Inviting a Friend to Supper

Tonight, grave sir, both my poor house and I
Do equally desire your company:
Not that we think us worthy such a guest,
But that your worth will dignify our feast
With those that come; whose grace may make that seem
Something, which else could hope for no esteem.
It is the fair acceptance, sir, creates
The entertainment perfect: not the cates.
Yet shall you have, to rectify your palate,

An olive, capers, or some better salad
Ushering the mutton; with a short-legged hen,
If we can get her, full of eggs, and then
Lemons, and wine for sauce; to these, a cony
Is not to be despaired of for our money;
And though fowl now be scarce, yet there are clerks,
The sky not falling, think we may have larks.
I'll tell you of more, and lie, so you will come:
Of partridge, pheasant, woodcock, of which some
May yet be there; and godwit, if we can;
Knat, rail and ruff too. Howsoe'er, my man
Shall read a piece of Virgil, Tacitus,
Livy, or of some better book to us,
Of which we'll speak our minds, amidst our meat;
And I'll profess no verses to repeat:
To this, if aught appear which I not know of,
That will the pastry, not my paper show of.
Digestive cheese and fruit there sure will be;
But that which most doth take my Muse and me
Is a pure cup of rich canary wine,
Which is the Mermaid's now, but shall be mine;
Of which had Horace or Anacreon tasted,
Their lives, as do their lines, till now had lasted.
Tobacco, nectar, or the Thespian spring
Are all but Luther's beer, to this I sing.
Of this we will sup free, but moderately,
And we will have no Pooly or Parrot by;
Nor shall our cups make any guilty men,
But at our parting we will be as when
We innocently met. No simple word
That shall be uttered at our mirthful board
Shall make us sad next morning, or affright
The liberty that we'll enjoy tonight.

BEN JONSON
ENGLISH (1572–1637)

This is the spot: — how mildly does the sun
Shine in between the fading leaves! the air
In the habitual silence of this wood
Is more than silent; and this bed of heath —
Where shall we find so sweet a resting-place?
Come, let me see thee sink into a dream
Of quiet thoughts, protracted till thine eye
Be calm as water when the winds are gone
And no one can tell whither. My sweet Friend,
We two have had such happy hours together
That my heart melts in me to think of it.

WILLIAM WORDSWORTH
ENGLISH (1770–1850)

This Lime-Tree Bower My Prison

ADDRESSED TO CHARLES LAMB, OF THE INDIA HOUSE, LONDON

*In the June of 1797 some long-expected friends paid a visit to the author's
cottage; and on the morning of their arrival, he met with an accident,
which disabled him from walking during the whole time of their stay.
One evening, when they had left him for a few hours, he composed the
following lines in the garden-bower.*

Well, they are gone, and here must I remain,
This lime-tree bower my prison! I have lost
Beauties and feelings, such as would have been
Most sweet to my remembrance even when age
Had dimmed mine eyes to blindness! They, meanwhile,
Friends, whom I never more may meet again,
On springy heath, along the hill-top edge,
Wander in gladness, and wind down, perchance,
To that still roaring dell, of which I told;
The roaring dell, o'erwooded, narrow, deep,
And only speckled by the mid-day sun;
Where its slim trunk the ash from rock to rock
Flings arching like a bridge; — that branchless ash,
Unsunned and damp, whose few poor yellow leaves
Ne'er tremble in the gale, yet tremble still,

Fanned by the water-fall! and there my friends
Behind the dark green file of long lank weeds,
That all at once (a most fantastic sight!)
Still nod and drip beneath the dripping edge
Of the blue clay-stone.

           Now, my friends emerge
Beneath the wide wide Heaven — and view again
The many-steepled tract magnificent
Of hilly fields and meadows, and the sea,
With some fair bark, perhaps, whose sails light up
The slip of smooth clear blue betwixt two Isles
Of purple shadow! Yes! they wander on
In gladness all; but thou, methinks, most glad,
My gentle-hearted Charles! for thou hast pined
And hungered after Nature, many a year,
In the great City pent, winning thy way
With sad yet patient soul, through evil and pain
And strange calamity! Ah! slowly sink
Behind the western ridge, thou glorious Sun!
Shine in the slant beams of the sinking orb,
Ye purple heath-flowers! richlier burn, ye clouds!
Live in the yellow light, ye distant groves!
And kindle, thou blue Ocean! So my friend
Struck with deep joy, may stand, as I have stood,
Silent with swimming sense; yea, gazing round
On the wide landscape, gaze till all doth seem
Less gross than bodily, and of such hues
As veil the Almighty Spirit, when yet he makes
Spirits perceive his presence.

           A delight
Comes sudden on my heart, and I am glad
As I myself were there! Nor in this bower,
This little lime-tree bower, have I not marked
Much that has soothed me. Pale beneath the blaze
Hung the transparent foliage; and I watched
Some broad and sunny leaf, and loved to see
The shadow of the leaf and stem above

Dappling its sunshine! And that walnut-tree
Was richly tinged, and a deep radiance lay
Full on the ancient ivy, which usurps
Those fronting elms, and now, with blackest mass
Makes their dark branches gleam a lighter hue
Through the late twilight: and though now the bat
Wheels silent by, and not a swallow twitters,
Yet still the solitary humble-bee
Sings in the bean-flower! Henceforth I shall know
That Nature ne'er deserts the wise and pure;
No plot so narrow, be but Nature there,
No waste so vacant, but may well employ
Each faculty of sense, and keep the heart
Awake to Love and Beauty! and sometimes
'Tis well to be bereft of promised good,
That we may lift the soul, and contemplate
With lively joy the joys we cannot share.
My gentle-hearted Charles! when the last rook
Beat its straight path along the dusky air
Homewards, I blest it! deeming its black wing
(Now a dim speck, now vanishing in light)
Had crossed the mighty Orb's dilated glory,
While thou stood'st gazing; or, when all was still,
Flew creeking o'er thy head, and had a charm
For thee, my gentle-hearted Charles, to whom
No sound is dissonant which tells of Life.

SAMUEL TAYLOR COLERIDGE
ENGLISH (1772–1834)

The Fire of Drift-Wood

Devereux Farm, Near Marblehead

We sat within the farm-house old,
  Whose windows, looking o'er the bay,
Gave to the sea-breeze damp and cold,
  An easy entrance, night and day.

Not far away we saw the port,
  The strange, old-fashioned, silent town,

The lighthouse, the dismantled fort,
   The wooden houses, quaint and brown.

We sat and talked until the night,
   Descending, filled the little room;
Our faces faded from the sight,
   Our voices only broke the gloom.

We spake of many a vanished scene,
   Of what we once had thought and said,
Of what had been, and might have been,
   And who was changed, and who was dead;

And all that fills the hearts of friends,
   When first they feel, with secret pain,
Their lives thenceforth have separate ends,
   And never can be one again;

The first slight swerving of the heart,
   That words are powerless to express,
And leave it still unsaid in part,
   Or say it in too great excess.

The very tones in which we spake
   Had something strange, I could but mark;
The leaves of memory seemed to make
   A mournful rustling in the dark.

Oft died the words upon our lips,
   As suddenly, from out the fire
Built of the wreck of stranded ships,
   The flames would leap and then expire.

And, as their splendor flashed and failed,
   We thought of wrecks upon the main,
Of ships dismasted, that were hailed
   And sent no answer back again.

The windows, rattling in their frames,
   The ocean, roaring up the beach,
The gusty blast, the bickering flames,
   All mingled vaguely in our speech;

Until they made themselves a part
   Of fancies floating through the brain,
The long-lost ventures of the heart,
   That send no answers back again.

O flames that glowed! O hearts that yearned!
   They were indeed too much akin,
The drift-wood fire without that burned,
   The thoughts that burned and glowed within.

HENRY WADSWORTH LONGFELLOW
AMERICAN (1807–1882)

Sonnet — To a Friend

When we were idlers with the loitering rills,
   The need of human love we little noted:
   Our love was nature; and the peace that floated
On the white mist, and dwelt upon the hills,
To sweet accord subdued our wayward wills:
   One soul was ours, one mind, one heart devoted,
   That, wisely doting, ask'd not why it doted,
And ours the unknown joy, which knowing kills.
But now I find how dear thou wert to me;
   That man is more than half of nature's treasure,
Of that fair beauty which no eye can see,
   Of that sweet music which no ear can measure;
   And now the streams may sing for others' pleasure,
The hills sleep on in their eternity.

HARTLEY COLERIDGE
ENGLISH (1796–1849)

They told me, Heraclitus, they told me you were dead

They told me, Heraclitus, they told me you were dead,
They brought me bitter news to hear and bitter tears to shed.
I wept as I remembered how often you and I
Had tired the sun with talking and sent him down the sky.

And now that thou art lying, my dear old Carian guest,
A handful of grey ashes, long, long ago at rest,
Still are thy pleasant voices, thy nightingales, awake;
For Death, he taketh all away, but them he cannot take.

WILLIAM CORY
ENGLISH (1823–1892)

Monody

To have known him, to have loved him
    After loneness long;
And then to be estranged in life,
    And neither in the wrong;
And now for death to set his seal —
    Ease me, a little ease, my song!

By wintry hills his hermit-mound
    The sheeted snow-drifts drape,
And houseless there the snow-bird flits
    Beneath the fir-trees' crape:
Glazed now with ice the cloistral vine
    That hid the shyest grape.

HERMAN MELVILLE
AMERICAN (1819–1891)

They say that in the unchanging place,
    Where all we loved is always dear,
We meet our morning face to face
    And find at last our twentieth year . . .

They say (and I am glad they say)
    It is so; and it may be so:
It may be just the other way,
    I cannot tell. But this I know:

From quiet homes and first beginning,
    Out to the undiscovered ends,
There's nothing worth the wear of winning,
    But laughter and the love of friends.

                        HILAIRE BELLOC
                    ENGLISH (1870–1953)

Exile's Letter

To So-Kin of Rakuyo, ancient friend, Chancellor of Gen.
Now I remember that you built me a special tavern
By the south side of the bridge at Ten-Shin.
With yellow gold and white jewels, we paid for songs and
    laughter
And we were drunk for month on month, forgetting the kings
    and princes.
Intelligent men came drifting in from the sea and from the west
    border,
And with them, and with you especially
There was nothing at cross purpose,
And they made nothing of sea-crossing or of mountain-crossing,
If only they could be of that fellowship,
And we all spoke out our hearts and minds, and without regret.

And then I was sent off to South Wei, smothered in laurel
    groves,
And you to the north of Raku-hoku,
Till we had nothing but thoughts and memories in common.
And then, when separation had come to its worst,
We met, and travelled into Sen-Go,
Through all the thirty-six folds of the turning and twisting
    waters,
Into a valley of the thousand bright flowers,
That was the first valley;
And into ten thousand valleys full of voices and pine-winds.
And with silver harness and reins of gold,
Out came the East of Kan foreman and his company.
And there came also the "True man" of Shi-yo to meet me,
Playing on a jewelled mouth-organ.
In the storied houses of San-Ko they gave us more Sennin music,
Many instruments, like the sound of young phœnix broods.
The foreman of Kan Chu, drunk, danced because his long sleeves
    wouldn't keep still
With that music playing,
And I, wrapped in brocade, went to sleep with my head on his
    lap,
And my spirit so high it was all over the heavens,
And before the end of the day we were scattered like stars, or
    rain.
I had to be off to So, far away over the waters,
You back to your river-bridge.

And your father, who was brave as a leopard,
Was governor in Hei Shu, and put down the barbarian rabble.
And one May he had you send for me,
    despite the long distance.

And what with broken wheels and so on, I won't say it wasn't
   hard going,
Over roads twisted like sheep's guts.
And I was still going, late in the year,
     in the cutting wind from the North,
And thinking how little you cared for the cost,
     and you caring enough to pay it.
And what a reception:
Red jade cups, food well set on a blue jewelled table,
And I was drunk, and had no thought of returning.
And you would walk out with me to the western corner of the
   castle,
To the dynastic temple, with water about it clear as blue jade,
With boats floating, and the sound of mouth-organs and drums,
With ripples like dragon-scales, going grass green on the water,
Pleasure lasting, with courtezans, going and coming without
   hindrance,
With the willow flakes falling like snow,
And the vermilioned girls getting drunk about sunset,
And the water, a hundred feet deep, reflecting green eyebrows
— Eyebrows painted green are a fine sight in young moonlight,
Gracefully painted —
And the girls singing back at each other,
Dancing in transparent brocade,
And the wind lifting the song, and interrupting it,
Tossing it up under the clouds.
     And all this comes to an end.
     And is not again to be met with.
I went up to the court for examination,
Tried Layu's luck, offered the Choyo song,
And got no promotion,
     and went back to the East Mountains
     White-headed.

And once again, later, we met at the South bridge-head.
And then the crowd broke up, you went north to San palace,
And if you ask how I regret that parting:
It is like the flowers falling at Spring's end
    Confused, whirled in a tangle.
What is the use of talking, and there is no end of
    talking,
There is no end of things in the heart.
I call in the boy,
Have him sit on his knees here
    To seal this,
And send it a thousand miles, thinking.

EZRA POUND (AFTER LI PO)
AMERICAN (1885–1972)

Friendship and Illness

Through the silences,
The long empty days
You have sat beside me
Watching the finches feed,
The tremor in the leaves.
You have not left my mind.

Friendship supplied the root —
It was planted years ago —
To bring me flowers and seed
Through the long drought.

Far-flung as you are
You have seemed to sit beside me.
You have not left my mind.

Will you come in the new year?
To share the wind in the leaves
And the finches lacing the air
To savor the silence with me?
It's been a long time.

MAY SARTON
AMERICAN (1912–1995)

CONTENTMENT

Idle Thoughts

Thatch gate works all right but I never open it,
afraid people walking might scuff the green moss.
Fine days bit by bit convince me spring's on the way;
fair winds come now and then, wrapped up with market sounds.
Studying the Classics, my wife asks about words she doesn't know;
tasting the wine, my son pours till the cup overflows.
If only I could get a little garden, half an acre wide —
I'd have yellow plums and green damsons growing all at once!

LU YU
CHINESE (1125–1210)
TRANSLATED BY BURTON WATSON

The things that make a life to please

The things that make a life to please
(Sweetest Martial), they are these:
Estate inherited, not got:
A thankful field, hearth always hot:
City seldom, law-suits never:
Equal friends agreeing ever:
Health of body, peace of mind:

Sleeps that till the morning bind:
Wise simplicity, plain fare:
Not drunken nights, yet loos'd from care:
A sober, not a sullen spouse:
Clean strength, not such as his that ploughs;
Wish only what thou art, to be;
Death neither wish, nor fear to see.

MARTIAL
LATIN (C. 40–C. 103)
TRANSLATED BY SIR RICHARD FANSHAWE

'Tis mirth that fills the veins with blood

'Tis mirth that fills the veins with blood,
More than wine, or sleep, or food;
Let each man keep his heart at ease;
No man dies of that disease.
He that would his body keep
From diseases, must not weep;
But whoever laughs and sings,
Never he his body brings
Into fevers, gouts, or rheums,
Or lingeringly his lungs consumes;
Or meets with achës in the bone,
Or catarrhs, or griping stone:
But contented lives for aye;
The more he laughs, the more he may.

FRANCIS BEAUMONT (ATTRIB.)
ENGLISH (1584?–1616)

Art thou poor, yet hast thou golden slumbers

Art thou poor, yet hast thou golden slumbers?
    O sweet content!
Art thou rich, yet is thy mind perplexed?
    O punishment!
Dost thou laugh to see how fools are vexed
To add to golden numbers, golden numbers?

O sweet content! O sweet, O sweet content!
   Work apace, apace, apace, apace;
    Honest labour bears a lovely face;
  Then hey nonny nonny, hey nonny nonny!

Canst drink the waters of the crispëd spring?
    O sweet content!
Swimm'st thou in wealth, yet sink'st in thine own tears?
    O punishment!
Then he that patiently want's burden bears
No burden bears, but is a king, a king!
O sweet content! O sweet, O sweet content!
   Work apace, apace, apace, apace;
    Honest labour bears a lovely face;
  Then hey nonny nonny, hey nonny nonny!

              THOMAS DEKKER (ATTRIB.)
              ENGLISH (1572?–1632?)

The Man of Life Upright

The man of life upright,
  Whose guiltless heart is free
From all dishonest deeds
  And thought of vanity:

The man whose silent days
  In harmless joys are spent,
Whom hopes cannot delude
  Nor sorrow discontent:

That man needs neither towers
  Nor armour for defence,
Nor secret vaults to fly
  From thunder's violence.

He only can behold
  With unaffrighted eyes
The horrors of the deep
  And terrors of the skies.

Thus scorning all the cares
  That fate or fortune brings,
He makes the heaven his book,
  His wisdom heavenly things,

Good thoughts his only friends,
  His wealth a well-spent age,
The earth his sober inn
  And quiet pilgrimage.

THOMAS CAMPION
ENGLISH (1567–1620)

The Wish

Well then! I now do plainly see
This busy world and I shall ne'er agree.
The very honey of all earthly joy
Does of all meats the soonest cloy;
  And they, methinks, deserve my pity
Who for it can endure the stings,
The crowd, and buzz, and murmurings,
  Of this great hive, the city.

Ah, yet, ere I descend to the grave,
May I a small house and large garden have;
And a few friends, and many books, both true,
Both wise, and both delightful too!
  And since love ne'er will from me flee,
A Mistress moderately fair,
And good as guardian angels are,
  Only beloved and loving me.

O fountains! when in you shall I
Myself eased of unpeaceful thoughts espy?
O fields! O woods! when, when shall I be made
The happy tenant of your shade?
  Here's the spring-head of Pleasure's flood:
Here's wealthy Nature's treasury,

Where all the riches lie that she
   Has coin'd and stamp'd for good.

Pride and ambition here
Only in far-fetch'd metaphors appear;
Here nought but winds can hurtful murmurs scatter,
And nought but Echo flatter.
   The gods, when they descended, hither
From heaven did always choose their way:
And therefore we may boldly say
   That 'tis the way too thither.

How happy here should I
And one dear She live, and embracing die!
She who is all the world, and can exclude
In deserts solitude.
   I should have then this only fear:
Lest men, when they my pleasures see,
Should hither throng to live like me,
   And so make a city here.

ABRAHAM COWLEY
ENGLISH (1618–1667)

I Murder Hate by Field or Flood

1

I murder hate by field or flood,
   Tho' Glory's name may screen us,
In wars at hame I'll spend my blood —
   Life-giving wars of Venus.
The deities that I adore
   Are Social Peace and Plenty:
I'm better pleas'd to make one more
   Than be the death of twenty.

2

I would not die like Socrates,
   For all the fuss of Plato;

Nor would I with Leonidas,
   Nor yet would I with Cato;
The zealots of the Church and State
   Shall ne'er my mortal foes be;
But let me have bold Zimri's fate
   Within the arms of Cozbi.

ROBERT BURNS
SCOTTISH (1759–1796)

He who binds to himself a joy

He who binds to himself a joy
Does the winged life destroy;
But he who kisses the joy as it flies
Lives in Eternity's sun rise.

WILLIAM BLAKE
ENGLISH (1757–1827)

Inscription for the Entrance to a Wood

Stranger, if thou hast learned a truth which needs
No school of long experience, that the world
Is full of guilt and misery, and hast seen
Enough of all its sorrows, crimes, and cares,
To tire thee of it, enter this wild wood
And view the haunts of Nature. The calm shade
Shall bring a kindred calm, and the sweet breeze
That makes the green leaves dance, shall waft a balm
To thy sick heart. Thou wilt find nothing here
Of all that pained thee in the haunts of men,
And made thee loathe thy life. The primal curse
Fell, it is true, upon the unsinning earth,
But not in vengeance. God hath yoked to Guilt
Her pale tormentor, Misery. Hence these shades
Are still the abodes of gladness; the thick roof
Of green and stirring branches is alive
And musical with birds, that sing and sport
In wantonness of spirit; while below
The squirrel, with raised paws and form erect,

Chirps merrily. Throngs of insects in the shade
Try their thin wings and dance in the warm beam
That waked them into life. Even the green trees
Partake the deep contentment; as they bend
To the soft winds, the sun from the blue sky
Looks in and sheds a blessing on the scene.
Scarce less the cleft-born wild-flower seems to enjoy
Existence, than the winged plunderer
That sucks its sweets. The mossy rocks themselves,
And the old and ponderous trunks of prostrate trees
That lead from knoll to knoll a causey rude,
Or bridge the sunken brook, and their dark roots,
With all their earth upon them, twisting high,
Breathe fixed tranquillity. The rivulet
Sends forth glad sounds, and tripping o'er its bed
Of pebbly sands, or leaping down the rocks,
Seems, with continuous laughter, to rejoice
In its own being. Softly tread the marge,
Lest from her midway perch thou scare the wren
That dips her bill in water. The cool wind,
That stirs the stream in play, shall come to thee,
Like one that loves thee nor will let thee pass
Ungreeted, and shall give its light embrace.

WILLIAM CULLEN BRYANT
AMERICAN (1794–1878)

To a Friend Whose Work Has Come to Nothing

Now all the truth is out,
Be secret and take defeat
From any brazen throat,
For how can you compete,
Being honour bred, with one
Who, were it proved he lies,
Were neither shamed in his own
Nor in his neighbors' eyes?
Bred to harder thing
Than Triumph, turn away

And like a laughing string
Whereon mad fingers play
Amid a place of stone,
Be secret and exult,
Because of all things known
That is most difficult.

WILLIAM BUTLER YEATS
IRISH (1865–1939)

THE WORKING LIFE

On Money

Give money me, take friendship whoso list,
For friends are gone come once adversity,
When money yet remaineth safe in chest,
That quickly can thee bring from misery.
Fair face show friends when riches do abound;
Come time of proof, farewell, they must away;
Believe me well, they are not to be found
If God but send thee once a lowering day.
Gold never starts aside, but in distress,
Finds ways enough to ease thine heaviness.

BARNABE GOOGE
ENGLISH (1540–1594)

He that is down needs fear no fall

He that is down needs fear no fall,
He that is low, no pride;
He that is humble ever shall
Have God to be his guide.

I am content with what I have,
Little be it or much:

And, Lord, contentment still I crave,
Because Thou savest such.

Fullness to such a burden is
That go on pilgrimage:
Here little, and hereafter bliss,
Is best from age to age.

                    JOHN BUNYAN
                ENGLISH (1628–1688)

On the Death of Mr Robert Levet

A Practiser in Physic

Condemned to Hope's delusive mine,
As on we toil from day to day,
By sudden blasts, or slow decline,
Our social comforts drop away.

Well tried through many a varying year,
See Levet to the ground descend;
Officious, innocent, sincere,
Of every friendless name the friend.

Yet still he fills affection's eye,
Obscurely wise, and coarsely kind;
Nor, lettered arrogance, deny
Thy praise to merit unrefined.

When fainting nature called for aid,
And hovering death prepared the blow,
His vigorous remedy displayed
The power of art without the show.

In misery's darkest caverns known,
His useful care was ever nigh,
Where hopeless anguish poured his groan,
And lonely want retired to die.

No summons mocked by chill delay,
No petty gain disdained by pride,
The modest wants of every day
The toil of every day supplied.

His virtues walked their narrow round,
Nor made a house, nor left a void;
And sure the Eternal Master found
The single talent well employed.

The busy day, the peaceful night,
Unfelt, uncounted, glided by;
His frame was firm, his powers were bright,
Though now his eightieth year was nigh,

Then with no fiery throbbing pain,
No cold gradations of decay,
Death broke at once the vital chain,
And freed his soul the nearest way.

SAMUEL JOHNSON
ENGLISH (1709–1784)

Work without Hope

All Nature seems at work. Slugs leave their lair —
The bees are stirring — birds are on the wing —
And Winter, slumbering in the open air,
Wears on his smiling face a dream of Spring!
And I, the while, the sole unbusy thing,
Nor honey make, nor pair, nor build, nor sing.

Yet well I ken the banks where amaranths blow,
Have traced the fount whence streams of nectar flow.

Bloom, O ye amaranths! bloom for whom ye may,
For me ye bloom not! Glide, rich streams, away!
With lips unbrightened, wreathless brow, I stroll:
And would you learn the spells that drowse my soul?
Work without Hope draws nectar in a sieve,
And Hope without an object cannot live.

SAMUEL TAYLOR COLERIDGE
ENGLISH (1772–1834)

When I have fears that I may cease to be

When I have fears that I may cease to be
  Before my pen has gleaned my teeming brain,
Before high-piled books, in charactery,
  Hold like rich garners the full ripened grain;
When I behold, upon the night's starred face,
  Huge cloudy symbols of a high romance,
And think that I may never live to trace
  Their shadows, with the magic hand of chance;
And when I feel, fair creature of an hour,
  That I shall never look upon thee more,
Never have relish in the faery power
  Of unreflecting love; — then on the shore
Of the wide world I stand alone, and think
Till love and fame to nothingness do sink.

JOHN KEATS
ENGLISH (1795–1821)

My life has been the poem I would have writ

My life has been the poem I would have writ,
But I could not both live and utter it.

HENRY DAVID THOREAU
AMERICAN (1817–1862)

The Village Blacksmith

Under a spreading chestnut-tree
　　The village smithy stands;
The smith, a mighty man is he,
　　With large and sinewy hands;
And the muscles of his brawny arms
　　Are strong as iron bands.

His hair is crisp, and black, and long,
　　His face is like the tan;
His brow is wet with honest sweat,
　　He earns whate'er he can,
And looks the whole world in the face,
　　For he owes not any man.

Week in, week out, from morn till night,
　　You can hear his bellows blow;
You can hear him swing his heavy sledge
　　With measured beat and slow,
Like a sexton ringing the village bell,
　　When the evening sun is low.

And children coming home from school
　　Look in at the open door;
They love to see the flaming forge,
　　And hear the bellows roar,
And catch the burning sparks that fly
　　Like chaff from a threshing-floor.

He goes on Sunday to the church,
　　And sits among his boys;
He hears the parson pray and preach,
　　He hears his daughter's voice,
Singing in the village choir,
　　And it makes his heart rejoice.

It sounds to him like her mother's voice,
　　Singing in Paradise!

He needs must think of her once more,
How in the grave she lies;
And with his hard, rough hand he wipes
A tear out of his eyes.

Toiling, — rejoicing, — sorrowing,
Onward through life he goes;
Each morning sees some task begin,
Each evening sees its close;
Something attempted, something done,
Has earned a night's repose.

Thanks, thanks to thee, my worthy friend,
For the lesson thou hast taught!
Thus at the flaming forge of life
Our fortunes must be wrought;
Thus on its sounding anvil shaped
Each burning deed and thought.

HENRY WADSWORTH LONGFELLOW
AMERICAN (1807–1882)

The Wasted Day

Another day let slip! Its hours have run,
Its golden hours, with prodigal excess,
All run to waste. A day of life the less;
Of many wasted days, alas, but one!

Through my west window streams the setting sun.
I kneel within my chamber, and confess
My sin and sorrow, filled with vain distress,
In place of honest joy for work well done.

At noon I passed some labourers in a field.
The sweat ran down upon each sunburnt face,
Which shone like copper in the ardent glow.
And one looked up, with envy unconcealed,
Beholding my cool cheeks and listless pace,
Yet he was happier, though he did not know.

ROBERT F. MURRAY
ENGLISH (1863–1893)

Seams

I was sewing a seam one day —
Just this way —
Flashing four silver stitches there
With thread, like this, fine as a hair,
And then four here, and there again,
When
The seam I sewed dropped out of sight . . .
I saw the sea come rustling in,
Big and grey, windy and bright . . .
Then my thread that was as thin
As hair, tangled up like smoke
And broke.
I threaded up my needle, then —
Four here, four there, and here again.

HAZEL HALL
AMERICAN (1886–1924)

Sea-Fever

I must down to the seas again, to the lonely sea and the sky,
And all I ask is a tall ship and a star to steer her by,
And the wheel's kick and the wind's song and the white sail's
    shaking,
And a grey mist on the sea's face and a grey dawn breaking.

I must down to the seas again, for the call of the running tide
Is a wild call and a clear call that may not be denied;
And all I ask is a windy day with the white clouds flying,

And the flung spray and the blown spume, and the sea-gulls
   crying.

I must down to the seas again to the vagrant gypsy life.
To the gull's way and the whale's way where the wind's like a
   whetted knife;
And all I ask is a merry yarn from a laughing fellow-rover,
And quiet sleep and a sweet dream when the long trick's over.

JOHN MASEFIELD
ENGLISH (1878–1967)

Mesh cast for mackerel

Mesh cast for mackerel,
by guess and the sheen's tremor,
imperceptible if you havent the knack —
a difficult job,

hazardous and seasonal:
many shoals all of a sudden,
it would tax the Apostles to take the lot;
then drowse for months,

nets on the shingle,
a pint in the tap.
Likewise the pilchards come unexpectedly,
startle the man on the cliff.

Remember us to the teashop girls.
Say we have seen no legs better than theirs,
we have the sea to stare at,
its treason, copiousness, tedium.

BASIL BUNTING
ENGLISH (1900–1985)

Blue Monday

No use in my going
Downtown to work today,
  It's eight,
  I'm late —
And it's marked down that-a-way.

Saturday and Sunday's
Fun to sport around.
But no use denying —
Monday'll get you down.

That old blue Monday
Will surely get you down.

LANGSTON HUGHES
AMERICAN (1902–1967)

Pitcher

His art is eccentricity, his aim
How not to hit the mark he seems to aim at,

His passion how to avoid the obvious,
His technique how to vary the avoidance.

The others throw to be comprehended. He
Throws to be a moment misunderstood.

Yet not too much. Not errant, arrant, wild,
But every seeming aberration willed.

Not to, yet still, still to communicate
Making the batter understand too late.

ROBERT FRANCIS
AMERICAN (1901–1987)

Hay for the Horses

He had driven half the night
From far down San Joaquin
Through Mariposa, up the
Dangerous mountain roads,
And pulled in at eight a.m.
With his big truckload of hay
    behind the barn.
With winch and ropes and hooks
We stacked the bales up clean
To splintery redwood rafters
High in the dark, flecks of alfalfa
Whirling through shingle-cracks of light,
Itch of haydust in the
    sweaty shirt and shoes.
At lunchtime under Black oak
Out in the hot corral,
— The old mare nosing lunchpails,
Grasshoppers crackling in the weeds —
"I'm sixty-eight" he said,
"I first bucked hay when I was seventeen.
I thought, that day I started,
I sure would hate to do this all my life.
And dammit, that's just what
I've gone and done."

GARY SNYDER
AMERICAN (B. 1930)

Where I Am Now

Every morning I look
Into the world
And there is no renewal.
Every night, my lids clamped,
I concentrate
On the renewal to come.

I am on the lookout for
A great illumining,
Prepared to recognize it
Instantly and put it to use
Even among the desks
And chairs of the office, should
It come between nine and five.

HARVEY SHAPIRO
AMERICAN (B. 1925)

LOVE AND PASSION

Love of you is mixed deep in my vitals

Love of you is mixed deep in my vitals,
    like water stirred into flour for bread,
Like simples compound in a sweet-tasting drug,
    like pastry and honey mixed to perfection.

Oh, hurry to look at your love!
    Be like horses charging in battle,
Like a gardener up with the sun
    burning to watch his prize bud open.

High heaven causes a girl's lovelonging.
    It is like being too far from the light,
Far from the hearth of familiar arms.
    It is this being so tangled in you.

ANONYMOUS
EGYPTIAN (ANCIENT)
TRANSLATED BY JOHN L. FOSTER

He is more than a hero

He is more than a hero

He is a god in my eyes —
the man who is allowed
to sit beside you — he

who listens intimately
to the sweet murmur of
your voice, the enticing

laughter that makes my own
heart beat fast. If I meet
you suddenly, I can't

speak — my tongue is broken;
a thin flame runs under
my skin; seeing nothing,

hearing only my own ears
drumming, I drip with sweat;
trembling shakes my body

and I turn paler than
dry grass. At such times
death isn't far from me

SAPPHO
GREEK (C. 612 B.C.)
TRANSLATED BY MARY BARNARD

Flowers for Heliodora

White violets I will weave
with myrtle and tender narcissus;
I will weave laughing lilies too,
and soft crocus and purple hyacinths
with roses, flower of lovers,

that I may come to decorate her brow
and brighten her perfumed hair
in a rain of flowers.

MELEAGROS
GREEK (C. 140–70 B.C.)
TRANSLATED BY WILLIS BARNSTONE

Lesbia for ever on me rails

Lesbia for ever on me rails,
To talk of me, she never fails,
Now, hang me, but for all her art
I find that I have gained her heart.
My proof is this: I plainly see
The case is just the same with me;
I curse her every hour sincerely,
Yet, hang me, but I love her dearly.

CATULLUS
LATIN (84?–54? B.C.)
TRANSLATED BY JONATHAN SWIFT

Carmina 85

I hate and love, wouldst thou the reason know?
I know not, but I burn and feel it so.

CATULLUS
LATIN (84?–54? B.C.)
TRANSLATED BY RICHARD LOVELACE

Her quick eyes

Her quick eyes
and animated mouth
unsettle me.
So, of course,
her lifted breasts,
full lips —
soft fruits of desire.
But why should a
single wisp of hair,
stroked beneath her
navel like
some unforgettable
line of poetry,
reduce me to such
anguish?

BHARTRIHARI
INDIAN (570?–651?)
TRANSLATED BY ANDREW SCHELLING

Through the whole night we slowly

Through the whole night we slowly
made love,
body pressed against body,
cheek against cheek.
We spoke every thought that came into mind.
Lost in each other's arms
lost in words, we never noticed
dawn had come
      the night flown.

BHAVABHUTI
INDIAN (FL. 700)
TRANSLATED BY ANDREW SCHELLING

This night of no moon

This night of no moon
There is no way to meet him.
I rise in longing —
My breast pounds, a leaping flame,
My heart is consumed in fire.

ONO NO KOMACHI
JAPANESE (C. 833–857)
TRANSLATED BY DONALD KEENE

My ghostly father, I me confess

My ghostly father, I me confess,
First to God and then to you,
That at a window — wot ye how?
I stole a kiss of great sweetness,
Which done was without avisedness;
But it is done, not undone, now.
My ghostly father, I me confess,
First to God and then to you.
But I restore it shall doubtless
Again, if so be that I mow;
And that to God I make a vow,
And else I ask forgiveness.
My ghostly father, I me confess,
First to God and then to you,
That at a window — wot ye how?
I stole a kiss of great sweetness.

CHARLES OF ORLEANS
FRENCH (1394?–1465)

I must go walk the wood so wild

I must go walk the wood so wild,
    And wander here and there
    In dread and deadly fear;
For where I trusted I am beguiled,
    And all for one.

Thus am I banished from my bliss
    By craft and false pretense,
    Faultless without offense;
As of return no certain is,
    And all for fear of one.

My bed shall be under the greenwood tree,
    A tuft of brakes under my head,
    As one from joy were fled;
Thus from my life day by day I flee,
    And all for one.

The running streams shall be my drink,
    Acorns shall be my food;
    Nothing may do me good
But when of thy beauty I do think —
    And all for love of one.

ANONYMOUS
ENGLISH (15TH CENTURY)

When to my lone soft bed at eve returning

When to my lone soft bed at eve returning
Sweet desir'd sleep already stealeth o'er me,
My spirit flieth to the fairy-land of her tyrannous love.

Him then I think fondly to kiss, to hold him
Frankly then to my bosom; I that all day
Have looked for him suffering, repining, yea many long days.

O bless'd sleep, with flatteries beguile me;
So, if I ne'er may of a surety have him,
Grant to my poor soul amorous the dark gift of this illusion.

LOUISE LABÉ
FRENCH (1526–1566)
TRANSLATED BY ROBERT BRIDGES

Love Will Find Out the Way

Over the mountains
  And under the waves,
Under the fountains
  And under the graves;
Under floods that are deepest,
  Which Neptune obey,
Over rocks that are steepest,
  Love will find out the way.

When there is no place
  For the glow-worm to lie,
Where there is no space
  For receipt of a fly;
Where the midge dares not venture
  Lest herself fast she lay,
If Love come, he will enter
  And will find out the way.

You may esteem him
  A child for his might;

Or you may deem him
  A coward from his flight:
But if she whom Love doth honour
  Be conceal'd from the day —
Set a thousand guards upon her,
  Love will find out the way.

Some think to lose him
  By having him confined;
And some do suppose him,
  Poor heart! To be blind;
But if ne'er so close ye wall him,
  Do the best that you may,
Blind Love, if so you call him,
  Will find out his way.

You may train the eagle
  To stoop to your fist;
Or you may inveigle
  The Phoenix of the east;
The lioness, ye may move her
  To give over her prey;
But you'll ne'er stop a lover —
  He will find out his way.

If the earth it should part him,
  He would gallop it o'er;
If the seas should o'erthwart him,
  He would swim to the shore;
Should his Love become a swallow,
  Through the air to stray,
Love will lend wings to follow,
  And will find out the way.

There is no striving
  To cross his intent;

There is no contriving
  His plots to prevent;
But if once the message greet him
  That his True Love doth stay,
If Death should come and meet him,
  Love will find out the way!

ANONYMOUS
ENGLISH (17TH CENTURY)

Ovid's Fifth Elegy

In summer's heat and mid-time of the day
To rest my limbs upon a bed I lay,
One window shut, the other open stood,
Which gave such light as twinkles in a wood,
Like twilight glimpse at setting of the sun,
Or night being past and yet not day begun.
Such light to shame-faced maidens must be shown,
Where they may sport, and seem to be unknown.
Then came Corinna in a long loose gown,
Her white neck hid with tresses hanging down:
Resembling fair Semiramis going to bed
Or Laïs of a thousand wooers sped.
I snatched her gown; being thin, the harm was small,
Yet striv'd she to be covered there withal;
And striving thus, as one that would be cast,
Betray'd herself and yielded at the last.
Stark naked as she stood before mine eye,
Not one wen in her body could I spy.
What arms and shoulders did I touch and see,
How apt her breasts were to be pressed by me?
How smooth a belly under her waist saw I?
How large a leg, and what a lusty thigh?
To leave the rest, all liked me passing well:
I cling'd her naked body, down she fell.
Judge you the rest: being tired she bade me kiss,
Jove send me more such afternoons as this.

CHRISTOPHER MARLOWE
ENGLISH (1564–1593)

It lies not in our power to love or hate

From *Hero and Leander*

It lies not in our power to love or hate,
For will in us is over-ruled by fate.
When two are stripped, long ere the course begin,
We wish that one should lose, the other win;
And one especially do we affect
Of two gold ingots, like in each respect.
The reason no man knows; let it suffice,
What we behold is censured by our eyes.
Where both deliberate, the love is slight;
Who ever loved, that loved not at first sight?

CHRISTOPHER MARLOWE
ENGLISH (1564–1593)

The Passionate Shepherd to His Love

Come live with me and be my Love,
And we will all the pleasures prove
That hills and valleys, dales and fields,
Or woods or steepy mountain yields.

And we will sit upon the rocks,
And see the shepherds feed their flocks
By shallow rivers, to whose falls
Melodious birds sing madrigals.

And I will make thee beds of roses
And a thousand fragrant posies;
A cap of flowers, and a kirtle
Embroider'd all with leaves of myrtle.

A gown made of the finest wool
Which from our pretty lambs we pull;
Fair-linèd slippers for the cold,
With buckles of the purest gold.

A belt of straw and ivy-buds
With coral clasps and amber studs:
And if these pleasures may thee move,
Come live with me and be my Love.

The shepherd swains shall dance and sing
For thy delight each May morning:
If these delights thy mind may move,
Then live with me and be my Love.

CHRISTOPHER MARLOWE
ENGLISH (1564–1593)

The Nymph's Reply to the Shepherd

If all the world and love were young,
And truth in every shepherd's tongue,
These pretty pleasures might me move
To live with thee and be thy Love.

But Time drives flocks from field to fold;
When rivers rage and rocks grow cold;
And Philomel becometh dumb;
The rest complains of cares to come.

The flowers do fade, and wanton fields
To wayward Winter reckoning yields:
A honey tongue, a heart of gall,
Is fancy's spring, but sorrow's fall.

Thy gowns, thy shoes, thy beds of roses,
Thy cap, thy kirtle, and thy posies,
Soon break, soon wither — soon forgotten,
In folly ripe, in reason rotten.

Thy belt of straw and ivy-buds,
Thy coral clasps and amber studs, —
All these in me no means can move
To come to thee and be thy Love.

But could youth last, and love still breed,
Had joys no date, nor age no need,
Then these delights my mind might move
To live with thee and be thy Love.

SIR WALTER RALEGH
ENGLISH (1552?–1618)

Shall I compare thee to a summer's day

Shall I compare thee to a summer's day?
Thou art more lovely and more temperate:
Rough winds do shake the darling buds of May,
And summer's lease hath all too short a date:
Sometime too hot the eye of heaven shines,
And often is his gold complexion dimmed;
And every fair from fair sometime declines,
By chance, or nature's changing course untrimmed;
But thy eternal summer shall not fade,
Nor lose possession of that fair thou owest,
Nor shall Death brag thou wanderest in his shade,
When in eternal lines to time thou growest;
So long as men can breathe, or eyes can see,
So long lives this, and this gives life to thee.

WILLIAM SHAKESPEARE
ENGLISH (1564–1616)

When in disgrace with fortune and men's eyes

When in disgrace with fortune and men's eyes
I all alone beweep my outcast state,
And trouble deaf heaven with my bootless cries,
And look upon myself, and curse my fate,
Wishing me like to one more rich in hope,
Featured like him, like him with friends possessed,
Desiring this man's art, and that man's scope,
With what I most enjoy contented least;
Yet in these thoughts myself almost despising,
Haply I think on thee, and then my state,
Like to the lark at break of day arising
From sullen earth, sing hymns at heaven's gate;
For thy sweet love remembered such wealth brings
That then I scorn to change my state with kings.

WILLIAM SHAKESPEARE
ENGLISH (1564–1616)

There is a garden in her face

There is a garden in her face
   Where roses and white lilies grow;
A heavenly paradise is that place
   Wherein all pleasant fruits do flow.
There cherries grow which none may buy,
Till 'cherry-ripe' themselves do cry.

Those cherries fairly do enclose
   Of orient pearl a double row,
Which when her lovely laughter shows,
   They look like rosebuds filled with snow.
Yet them nor peer nor prince can buy,
Till 'cherry-ripe' themselves do cry.

Her eyes like angels watch them still,
   Her brows like bended bows do stand,
Threatening with piercing frowns to kill
   All that attempt, with eye or hand,
Those sacred cherries to come nigh,
Till 'cherry-ripe' themselves do cry.

THOMAS CAMPION
ENGLISH (1567–1620)

Thrice Toss These Oaken Ashes

Thrice toss these oaken ashes in the air,
Thrice sit thou mute in this enchanted chair;
Then thrice-three times tie up this true love's knot,
And murmur soft 'She will or she will not.'

Go burn these poisonous weeds in yon blue fire,
These screech-owl's feathers and this prickling brier,

This cypress gathered at a dead man's grave,
That all thy fears and cares an end may have.

Then come, you Fairies! dance with me a round!
Melt her hard heart with your melodious sound! —
In vain are all the charms I can devise:
She hath an art to break them with her eyes.

THOMAS CAMPION
ENGLISH (1567–1620)

My sweetest Lesbia, let us live and love

My sweetest Lesbia, let us live and love,
And though the sager sort our deeds reprove,
Let us not weigh them. Heaven's great lamps do dive
Into their west, and straight again revive;
But, soon as once set is our little light,
Then must we sleep one ever-during night.

If all would lead their lives in love like me,
Then bloody swords and armour should not be;
No drum nor trumpet peaceful sleeps should move,
Unless alarm came from the camp of love.
But fools do live and waste their little light,
And seek with pain their ever-during night.

When timely death my life and fortune ends,
Let not my hearse be vexed with mourning friends;
But let all lovers, rich in triumph, come
And with sweet pastimes grace my happy tomb:
And, Lesbia, close up thou my little light,
And crown with love my ever-during night.

THOMAS CAMPION
ENGLISH (1567–1620)

To Celia

Drink to me only with thine eyes,
　And I will pledge with mine;
Or leave a kiss but in the cup
　And I'll not look for wine.
The thirst that from the soul doth rise
　Doth ask a drink divine;
But might I of Jove's nectar sup,
　I would not change for thine.

I sent thee late a rosy wreath,
　Not so much honoring thee
As giving it a hope that there
　It could not withered be;
But thou thereon didst only breathe,
　And sent'st it back to me;
Since when it grows, and smells, I swear,
　Not of itself but thee!

BEN JONSON
ENGLISH (1572–1637)

The Good-Morrow

I wonder, by my troth, what thou and I
Did, till we loved: were we not weaned till then?
But sucked on country pleasures, childishly?
Or snorted we in the Seven Sleepers' den?
'Twas so; but this, all pleasures fancies be;
If ever any beauty I did see,
Which I desired, and got, 'twas but a dream of thee.

And now good-morrow to our waking souls,
Which watch not one another out of fear;
For love all love of other sights controls,
And makes one little room an everywhere.
Let sea-discoverers to new worlds have gone;
Let maps to other, worlds on worlds have shown,
Let us possess one world; each hath one, and is one.

My face in thine eye, thine in mine appears,
And true plain hearts do in the faces rest;
Where can we find two better hemispheres
Without sharp north, without declining west?
What ever dies, was not mixed equally;
If our two loves be one, or thou and I
Love so alike that none do slacken, none can die.

JOHN DONNE
ENGLISH (1572–1631)

The Sun Rising

      Busy old fool, unruly sun,
      Why dost thou thus
Through windows and through curtains call on us?
Must to thy motions lovers' seasons run?
      Saucy pedantic wretch, go chide
      Late schoolboys and sour prentices,
   Go tell court huntsmen that the king will ride,
   Call country ants to harvest offices;
Love, all alike, no season knows, nor clime,
Nor hours, days, months, which are the rags of time.

      Thy beams so reverend and strong
      Why shouldst thou think?
I could eclipse and cloud them with a wink,
But that I would not lose her sight so long:
      If her eyes have not blinded thine,
      Look, and tomorrow late, tell me
   Whether both th' Indias of spice and mine
   Be where thou left'st them, or lie here with me.
Ask for those kings whom thou saw'st yesterday
And thou shalt hear: All here in one bed lay.

      She is all states, and all princes I:
      Nothing else is.
Princes do but play us; compar'd to this,
All honor's mimic; all wealth alchemy.

Thou, sun, art half as happy as we,
In that the world's contracted thus;
Thine age asks ease, and since thy duties be
To warm the world, that's done in warming us.
Shine here to us, and thou art everywhere:
This bed thy center is, these walls thy sphere.

JOHN DONNE
ENGLISH (1572–1631)

To His Mistress Going to Bed

Come, Madam, come, all rest my powers defy,
Until I labour, I in labour lie.
The foe oft-times having the foe in sight,
Is tir'd with standing though he never fight.
Off with that girdle, like heaven's zone glistering,
But a far fairer world incompassing.
Unpin that spangled breastplate which you wear,
That th'eyes of busy fools may be stopped there.
Unlace your self, for that harmonious chime,
Tells me from you, that now it is bed time.
Off with that happy busk, which I envy,
That still can be, and still can stand so nigh.
Your gown going off, such beauteous state reveals,
As when from flowry meads th'hill's shadow steals.
Off with that wiry Coronet and show
The hairy diadem which on you doth grow:
Now off with those shoes, and then safely tread
In this love's hallow'd temple, this soft bed.
In such white robes, heaven's angels us'd to be
Receiv'd by men; thou angel bringst with thee
A heaven like Mahomet's paradise; and though
Ill spirits walk in white, we eas'ly know,
By this these angels from an evil sprite,
Those set our hairs, but these our flesh upright.
    Licence my roving hands, and let them go,
Before, behind, between, above, below.
O my America! my new-found-land,
My kingdom, safeliest when with one man mann'd,

My mine of precious stones, my empery,
How blest am I in this discovering thee!
To enter in these bonds, is to be free;
Then where my hand is set, my seal shall be.
    Full nakedness! All joys are due to thee,
As souls unbodied, bodies uncloth'd must be,
To taste whole joys. Gems which you women use
Are like Atlanta's balls, cast in men's views,
That when a fool's eye lighteth on a gem,
His earthly soul may covet theirs, not them.
Like pictures, or like books' gay coverings made
For lay-men, are all women thus array'd;
Themselves are mystic books, which only we
(Whom their imputed grace will dignify)
Must see reveal'd. Then since that I may know;
As liberally, as to a midwife, show
Thyself: cast all, yea, this white linen hence,
Here is no penance, much less innocence.
    To teach thee, I am naked first; why then
What needst thou have more covering than a man?

JOHN DONNE
ENGLISH (1572–1631)

The Ecstasy

Where, like a pillow on a bed,
    A pregnant bank swelled up, to rest
The violet's reclining head,
    Sat we two, one another's best.

Our hands were firmly cemented
    With a fast balm, which thence did spring
Our eye-beams twisted, and did thread
    Our eyes upon one double string;

So to entergraft our hands, as yet
    Was all our means to make us one,
And pictures on our eyes to get
    Was all our propagation.

As 'twixt two equal armies Fate
  Suspends uncertain victory,
Our souls (which to advance their state
  Were gone out) hung 'twixt her and me.

And whilst our souls negotiate there,
  We like sepulchral statues lay;
All day the same our postures were,
  And we said nothing all the day.

If any, so by love refined
  That he soul's language understood,
And by good love were grown all mind,
  Within convenient distance stood,

He (though he knew not which soul spake,
  Because both meant, both spake the same)
Might thence a new concoction take,
  And part far purer than he came.

This ecstasy doth unperplex
  (We said) and tell us what we love,
We see by this, it was not sex,
  We see, we saw not what did move:

But as all several souls contain
  Mixture of things, they know not what,
Love these mixed souls doth mix again,
  And makes both one, each this and that.

A single violet transplant,
  The strength, the colour, and the size,
(All which before was poor and scant)
  Redoubles still, and multiplies.

When love with one another so
  Interinanimates two souls,
That abler soul, which thence doth flow,
  Defects of loneliness controls.

We then, who are this new soul, know
 Of what we are composed, and made,
For the atomies of which we grow
 Are souls, whom no change can invade.

But, O alas! so long, so far
 Our bodies why do we forbear?
They are ours, though they are not we; we are
 The intelligences, they the sphere.

We owe them thanks, because they thus
 Did us, to us, at first convey,
Yielded their forces, sense, to us,
 Nor are dross to us, but allay.

On man heaven's influence works not so,
 But that it first imprints the air;
So soul into the soul may flow,
 Though it to body first repair.

As our blood labours to beget
 Spirits, as like souls as it can;
Because such fingers need to knit
 That subtle knot, which makes us man;

So must pure lovers' souls descend
 To affections, and to faculties,
Which sense may reach and apprehend,
 Else a great Prince in prison lies.

To our bodies turn we then, that so
 Weak men on love revealed may look;

Love's mysteries in souls do grow,
But yet the body is his book.

And if some lover, such as we,
Have heard this dialogue of one,
Let him still mark us, he shall see
Small change, when we're to bodies gone.

JOHN DONNE
ENGLISH (1572–1631)

Song

Ask me no more where Jove bestows
When June is past, the fading rose;
For in your beauties' orient deep
These flowers as in their causes sleep.

Ask me no more whither do stray
The golden atoms of the day;
For in pure love Heaven did prepare
These powders to enrich your hair.

Ask me no more whither doth haste
The nightingale when May is past;
For in your sweet dividing throat
She winters and keeps warm her note.

Ask me no more where those stars light
That downwards fall in dead of night;
For in your eyes they sit and there
Fixéd become, as in their sphere.

Ask me no more if east or west
The phoenix builds her spicy nest;
For unto you at last she flies
And in your fragrant bosom dies.

THOMAS CAREW
ENGLISH (1595?–1645?)

Clothes Do but Cheat and Cozen Us

Away with silks, away with lawn,
I'll have no scenes or curtains drawn:
Give me my mistress as she is,
Dress'd in her nak't simplicities:
For as my heart, e'en so my eye
Is won with flesh, not drapery.

ROBERT HERRICK
ENGLISH (1591–1674)

To Anthea, Who May Command Him Any Thing

Bid me to live, and I will live
  Thy Protestant to be:
Or bid me love, and I will give
  A loving heart to thee.

A heart as soft, a heart as kind,
  A heart as sound and free,
As in the whole world thou canst find,
  That heart I'll give to thee.

Bid that heart stay, and it will stay,
  To honor thy decree:
Or bid it languish quite away,
  And't shall do so for thee.

Bid me to weep, and I will weep,
  While I have eyes to see:
And having none, yet I will keep
  A heart to weep for thee.

Bid me despair, and I'll despair,
  Under that cypress tree:

Or bid me die, and I will dare
　E'en Death, to die for thee.

Thou art my life, my love, my heart,
　The very eyes of me:
And hast command of every part,
　To live and die for thee.

ROBERT HERRICK
ENGLISH (1591–1674)

The Fifth Ode of Horace, Book I

What slender youth bedew'd with liquid odours
Courts thee on roses in some pleasant cave,
　Pyrrha? for whom bindst thou
　In wreaths thy golden hair,
Plain in thy neatness? O how oft shall he
On faith and changed gods complain: and seas
　Rough with black winds and storms
　Unwonted shall admire:
Who now enjoys thee credulous, all gold,
Who always vacant, always amiable
　Hopes thee; of flattering gales
　Unmindful. Hapless they
To whom thou untried seem'st fair. Me in my vow'd
Picture the sacred wall declares t' have hung
　My dank and dropping weeds
　To the stern God of Sea.

JOHN MILTON
ENGLISH (1608–1674)

All my past Life is mine no more

All my past life is mine no more,
　The flying hours are gone:
Like transitory dreams giv'n o're,
Whose images are kept in store,
　By memory alone.

The time that is to come is not,
   How can it then be mine?
The present moment's all my lot,
And that, as fast as it is got,
   Phillis, is only thine.

Then talk not of inconstancy,
   False hearts, and broken vows:
If I, by miracle, can be
This live-long minute true to thee,
   'Tis all that Heav'n allows.

JOHN WILMOT, EARL OF ROCHESTER
ENGLISH (1647–1680)

Why so pale and wan, fond lover

Why so pale and wan, fond lover?
   Prithee, why so pale?
Will, when looking well can't win her,
   Looking ill prevail?
   Prithee, why so pale?

Why so dull and mute, young sinner?
   Prithee, why so mute?
Will, when speaking well can't win her,
   Saying nothing do't?
   Prithee, why so mute?

Quit, quit for shame, this will not move;
   This cannot take her.
If of herself she will not love,
   Nothing can make her;
   The devil take her!

JOHN SUCKLING
ENGLISH (1609–1642)

To His Coy Mistress

Had we but world enough and time,
This coyness, lady, were no crime.
We would sit down, and think which way
To walk, and pass our long love's day.
Thou by the Indian Ganges' side
Should'st rubies find: I by the tide
Of Humber would complain. I would
Love you ten years before the flood;
And you should if you please refuse
Till the conversion of the Jews.
My vegetable love should grow
Vaster than empires and more slow.
A hundred years should go to praise
Thine eyes, and on thy forehead gaze.
Two hundred to adore each breast;
But thirty thousand to the rest.
An age at least to every part,
And the last age should show your heart.
For, lady, you deserve this state,
Nor would I love at lower rate.
   But at my back I always hear
Time's wingéd chariot hurrying near;
And yonder all before us lie
Deserts of vast eternity.
Thy beauty shall no more be found,
Nor in thy marble vault shall sound
My echoing song; then worms shall try
That long preserved virginity,
And your quaint honour turn to dust,
And into ashes all my lust.
The grave's a fine and private place,
But none I think do there embrace.
   Now therefore while the youthful hue
Sits on thy skin like morning dew,
And while thy willing soul transpires
At every pore with instant fires,
Now let us sport us while we may;

And now like amorous birds of prey
Rather at once our time devour
Than languish in his slow-chapped power.
Let us roll all our strength and all
Our sweetness up into one ball,
And tear our pleasures with rough strife
Thorough the iron gates of life.
Thus, though we cannot make our sun
Stand still, yet we will make him run.

ANDREW MARVELL
ENGLISH (1621–1678)

The Prince of Love

How sweet I roamed from field to field,
   And tasted all the summer's pride,
'Till I the prince of love beheld,
   Who in the sunny beams did glide!

He showed me lilies for my hair,
   And blushing roses for my brow;
He led me through his gardens fair,
   Where all his golden pleasures grow.

With sweet May dews my wings were wet,
   And Phoebus fired my vocal rage;
He caught me in his silken net,
   And shut me in his golden cage.

He loves to sit and hear me sing,
   Then, laughing, sports and plays with me;
Then stretches out my golden wing,
   And mocks my loss of liberty.

WILLIAM BLAKE
ENGLISH (1757–1827)

A Red, Red Rose

My luve is like a red, red rose,
    That's newly sprung in June:
My luve is like the melodie,
    That's sweetly play'd in tune.
As fair art thou, my bonnie lass,
    So deep in luve am I,
And I will luve thee still, my dear,
    Till a' the seas gang dry.

Till a' the seas gang dry, my dear,
    And the rocks melt wi' the sun!
And I will luve thee still, my dear,
    While the sands o' life shall run.
And fare-thee-weel, my only luve,
    And fare-thee-weel a while!
And I will come again, my luve,
    Tho' it were ten-thousand mile.

ROBERT BURNS
SCOTTISH (1759–1796)

Lang Hae We Parted Been

Chorus:
Near me, near me,
    Lassie, lie near me!
Lang hast thou lien thy lane,
    Lassie, lie near me.

Lang hae we parted been,
    Lassie, my dearie;
Now we are met again,

Lassie, lie near me!
(*Chorus*)

A' that I hae endured,
    Lassie, my dearie,
Here in thy arms is cured —
    Lassie, lie near me!
    (*Chorus*)

ROBERT BURNS
SCOTTISH (1759–1796)

She was a Phantom of delight

She was a Phantom of delight
When first she gleamed upon my sight;
A lovely Apparition, sent
To be a moment's ornament;
Her eyes as stars of Twilight fair;
Like Twilight's, too, her dusky hair;
But all things else about her drawn
From May-time and the cheerful Dawn;
A dancing Shape, an Image gay,
To haunt, to startle, and way-lay.

I saw her upon nearer view,
A Spirit, yet a Woman too!
Her household motions light and free,
And steps of virgin-liberty;
A countenance in which did meet
Sweet records, promises as sweet;
A Creature not too bright or good
For human nature's daily food;
For transient sorrows, simple wiles,
Praise, blame, love, kisses, tears, and smiles.

And now I see with eye serene
The very pulse of the machine;
A Being breathing thoughtful breath,
A Traveller between life and death;

The reason firm, the temperate will,
Endurance, foresight, strength, and skill;
A perfect Woman, nobly planned,
To warn, to comfort, and command;
And yet a Spirit still, and bright
With something of angelic light.

WILLIAM WORDSWORTH
ENGLISH (1770–1850)

She Walks in Beauty

She walks in beauty, like the night
  Of cloudless climes and starry skies;
And all that's best of dark and bright
  Meet in her aspect and her eyes:
Thus mellow'd to that tender light
  Which heaven to gaudy day denies.

One shade the more, one ray the less,
  Had half impair'd the nameless grace
Which waves in every raven tress,
  Or softly lightens o'er her face;
Where thoughts serenely sweet express
  How pure, how dear their dwelling-place.

And on that cheek, and o'er that brow,
  So soft, so calm, yet eloquent,
The smiles that win, the tints that glow,
  But tell of days in goodness spent,
A mind at peace with all below,
  A heart whose love is innocent!

GEORGE GORDON, LORD BYRON
ENGLISH (1788–1824)

To ———

Music, when soft voices die,
Vibrates in the memory;
Odors, when sweet violets sicken,
Live within the sense they quicken.

Rose leaves, when the rose is dead,
Are heaped for the belovèd's bed;
And so thy thoughts, when thou art gone,
Love itself shall slumber on.

PERCY BYSSHE SHELLEY
ENGLISH (1792–1822)

Bright star! would I were steadfast as thou art

Bright star! would I were steadfast as thou art —
   Not in lone splendour hung aloft the night,
And watching, with eternal lids apart,
   Like Nature's patient, sleepless Eremite,
The moving waters at their priestlike task
   Of pure ablution round earth's human shores,
Or gazing on the new soft fallen mask
   Of snow upon the mountains and the moors —
No — yet still steadfast, still unchangeable,
   Pillowed upon my fair love's ripening breast,
To feel for ever its soft fall and swell,
   Awake for ever in a sweet unrest,
Still, still to hear her tender-taken breath,
And so live ever — or else swoon to death.

JOHN KEATS
ENGLISH (1795–1821)

Lines Supposed to Have Been Addressed To Fanny Brawne

This living hand, now warm and capable
Of earnest grasping, would, if it were cold
And in the icy silence of the tomb,
So haunt thy days and chill thy dreaming nights
That thou wouldst wish thine own heart dry of blood
So in my veins red life might stream again,
And thou be conscience-calm'd — see here it is —
I hold it towards you.

JOHN KEATS
ENGLISH (1795–1821)

Give all to love

Give all to love;
Obey thy heart;
Friends, kindred, days,
Estate, good-fame,
Plans, credit and the Muse, —
Nothing refuse.

'Tis a brave master;
Let it have scope:
Follow it utterly,
Hope beyond hope:
High and more high
It dives into noon,
With wing unspent,
Untold intent;
But it is a god,
Knows its own path
And the outlets of the sky.

It was never for the mean;
It requireth courage stout.
Souls above doubt,
Valor unbending,
It will reward, —

They shall return
More than they were,
And ever ascending.

Leave all for love;
Yet, hear me, yet,
One word more thy heart behoved,
One pulse more of firm endeavor, —
Keep thee to-day,
To-morrow, forever,
Free as an Arab
Of thy beloved.

Cling with life to the maid;
But when the surprise,
First vague shadow of surmise
Flits across her bosom young,
Of a joy apart from thee,
Free be she, fancy-free;
Nor thou detain her vesture's hem,
Nor the palest rose she flung
From her summer diadem.

Though thou loved her as thyself,
As a self of purer clay,
Though her parting dims the day,
Stealing grace from all alive;
Heartily know,
When half-gods go,
The gods arrive.

RALPH WALDO EMERSON
AMERICAN (1803–1882)

Say over again, and yet once over again

Say over again, and yet once over again,
That thou dost love me. Though the word repeated
Should seem 'a cuckoo song,' as thou dost treat it,
Remember, never to the hill or plain,
Valley and wood, without her cuckoo-strain
Comes the fresh Spring in all her green completed.
Belovèd, I, amid the darkness greeted
By a doubtful spirit-voice, in that doubt's pain,
Cry 'Speak once more — thou lovest!' Who can fear
Too many stars, though each in heaven shall roll,
Too many flowers, though each shall crown the year?
Say thou dost love me, love me, love me — toll
The silver iterance! — only minding, Dear,
To love me also in silence with thy soul.

ELIZABETH BARRETT BROWNING
ENGLISH (1806–1861)

If thou must love me, let it be for nought

If thou must love me, let it be for nought
Except for love's sake only. Do not say
"I love her for her smile — her look — her way
Of speaking gently, — for a trick of thought
That falls in well with mine, and certes brought
A sense of pleasant ease on such a day" —
For these things in themselves, Belovéd, may
Be changed, or change for thee, — and love, so wrought
May be unwrought so. Neither love me for
Thine own dear pity's wiping my cheeks dry, —
A creature might forget to weep, who bore
Thy comfort long, and lose thy love thereby!
But love me for love's sake, that evermore
Thou mayst love on, through love's eternity.

ELIZABETH BARRETT BROWNING
ENGLISH (1806–1861)

How do I love thee? Let me count the ways

How do I love thee? Let me count the ways.
I love thee to the depth and breadth and height
My soul can reach, when feeling out of sight
For the ends of Being and ideal Grace.
I love thee to the level of everyday's
Most quiet need, by sun and candle-light.
I love thee freely, as men strive for Right;
I love thee purely, as they turn from Praise.
I love thee with the passion put to use
In my old griefs, and with my childhood's faith.
I love thee with a love I seemed to lose
With my lost saints, — I love thee with the breath,
Smiles, tears, of all my life! — and, if God choose,
I shall but love thee better after death.

ELIZABETH BARRETT BROWNING
ENGLISH (1806–1861)

Now sleeps the crimson petal, now the white

Now sleeps the crimson petal, now the white;
Nor waves the cypress in the palace walk;
Nor winks the gold fin in the porphyry font:
The firefly wakens: waken thou with me.

Now droops the milk-white peacock like a ghost,
And like a ghost she glimmers on to me.

Now lies the Earth all Danaë to the stars,
And all thy heart lies open unto me.

Now slides the silent meteor on, and leaves
A shining furrow, as thy thoughts in me.

Now folds the lily all her sweetness up,
And slips into the bosom of the lake:
So fold thyself, my dearest, thou, and slip
Into my bosom and be lost in me.

ALFRED, LORD TENNYSON
ENGLISH (1809–1892)

Sudden Light

I have been here before,
    But when or how I cannot tell:
I know the grass beyond the door,
    The sweet keen smell,
The sighing sound, the lights around the shore.

You have been mine before, —
    How long ago I may not know:
But just when at that swallow's soar
    Your neck turned so,
Some veil did fall, — I knew it all of yore.

Has this been thus before?
    And shall not thus time's eddying flight
Still with our lives our love restore
    In death's despite,
And day and night yield one delight once more?

DANTE GABRIEL ROSSETTI
ENGLISH (1828–1882)

Wild Nights!

Wild nights! Wild nights!
Were I with thee,
Wild nights should be
Our luxury!

Futile the winds
To a heart in port, —
Done with the compass,
Done with the chart.

Rowing in Eden.
Ah! the sea!
Might I but moor
Tonight in thee!

EMILY DICKINSON
AMERICAN (1830–1886)

My delight and thy delight

My delight and thy delight
Walking, like two angels white,
In the gardens of the night:

My desire and thy desire
Twining to a tongue of fire,
Leaping live, and laughing higher;
Thro' the everlasting strife
In the mystery of life.

Love, from whom the world begun,
Hath the secret of the sun.

Love can tell, and love alone,
Whence the million stars were strewn,
Why each atom knows its own,
How, in spite of woe and death,
Gay is life, and sweet is breath:

This he taught us, this we know,
Happy in his science true,
Hand in hand as we stood
Neath the shadows of the wood,
Heart to heart as we lay
In the dawning of the day.

ROBERT BRIDGES
ENGLISH (1844–1930)

White Heliotrope

The feverish room and that white bed,
The tumbled skirts upon a chair,
The novel flung half-open, where
Hat, hair-pins, puffs, and paints, are spread;

The mirror that has sucked your face
Into its secret deep of deeps,
And there mysteriously keeps
Forgotten memories of grace;

And you, half dressed and half awake,
Your slant eyes strangely watching me,
And I, who watch you drowsily,
With eyes that, having slept not, ache;

This (need one dread? nay, dare one hope?)
Will rise, a ghost of memory, if
Ever again my handkerchief
Is scented with White Heliotrope.

ARTHUR SYMONS
ENGLISH (1865–1945)

Non Sum Qualis Eram Bonae sub Regno Cynarae

Last night, ah, yesternight, betwixt her lips and mine
There fell thy shadow, Cynara! thy breath was shed
Upon my soul between the kisses and the wine;
And I was desolate and sick of an old passion,
   Yea, I was desolate and bow'd my head:
I have been faithful to thee, Cynara! in my fashion.

All night upon mine heart I felt her warm heart beat,
Night-long within mine arms in love and sleep she lay;
Surely the kisses of her bought red mouth were sweet;
But I was desolate and sick of an old passion,
   When I awoke and found the dawn was gray:
I have been faithful to thee, Cynara! in my fashion.

I have forgot much, Cynara! gone with the wind,
Flung roses, roses, riotously with the throng,
Dancing, to put thy pale lost lilies out of mind;
But I was desolate and sick of an old passion,
   Yea, all the time, because the dance was long:
I have been faithful to thee, Cynara! in my fashion.

I cried for madder music and for stronger wine,
But when the feast is finish'd and the lamps expire,
Then falls thy shadow, Cynara! the night is thine;
And I am desolate and sick of an old passion,
   Yea, hungry for the lips of my desire:
I have been faithful to thee, Cynara! in my fashion.

ERNEST DOWSON
ENGLISH (1867–1900)

Love Song

How should I hold my spirit back, how weight
it lest it graze your own? How should I raise
it high above your head to other things?
Oh gladly I would simply relegate
my soul to something lost that darkly clings
to a strange silent place, a place that stays

quite still when your own inmost depths vibrate.
But all that grazes us, yourself and me,
is like a bow to us and joins two strings
together, so that one voice only sings.
To what stringed instrument have we been bound?
And in what player's hands do we resound?
Sweet melody.

RAINER MARIA RILKE
GERMAN (1875–1926)
TRANSLATED BY MICHAEL HAMBURGER

The Look

Strephon kissed me in the spring,
   Robin in the fall,
But Colin only looked at me
   And never kissed at all.

Strephon's kiss was lost in jest,
   Robin's lost in play,
But the kiss in Colin's eyes
   Haunts me night and day.

SARA TEASDALE
AMERICAN (1884–1933)

Summer Night, Riverside

In the wild soft summer darkness
How many and many a night we two together
Sat in the park and watched the Hudson
Wearing her lights like golden spangles
Glinting on black satin.
The rail along the curving pathway
Was low in a happy place to let us cross,
And down the hill a tree that dripped with bloom
Sheltered us
While your kisses and the flowers,
Falling, falling,
Tangled my hair. . . .

The frail white stars moved slowly over the sky.

And now, far off
In the fragrant darkness
The tree is tremulous again with bloom
For June comes back.

To-night what girl
When she goes home,
Dreamily before her mirror shakes from her hair
This year's blossoms, clinging in its coils?

SARA TEASDALE
AMERICAN (1884–1933)

Black hair

Black hair
Tangled in a thousand strands.
Tangled my hair and
Tangled my tangled memories
Of our long nights of love making.

YOSANO AKIKO
JAPANESE (1878–1942)
TRANSLATED BY KENNETH REXROTH

Terminus

Wonderful was the long secret night you gave me, my Lover,
Palm to palm, breast to breast in the gloom. The faint red
lamp
Flushing with magical shadows the common-place room of
the inn,
With its dull impersonal furniture, kindled a mystic flame
In the heart of the swinging mirror, the glass that has seen
Faces innumerous and vague of the endless travelling
automata
Whirled down the ways of the world like dust-eddies swept
through a street,
Faces indifferent or weary, frowns of impatience or pain,

Smiles (if such there were ever) like your smile and mine
    when they met
Here, in this self-same glass, while you helped me to loosen
    my dress,
And the shadow-mouths melted to one, like sea-birds that
    meet in a wave —
Such smiles, yes, such smiles the mirror perhaps has reflected;
And the low wide bed, as rutted and worn as a high-road,
The bed with its soot-sodden chintz, the grime of its brasses,
That has born the weight of fagged bodies, dust-stained,
    averted in sleep,
The hurried, the restless, the aimless — perchance it has also
    thrilled
With the pressure of bodies ecstatic, bodies like ours,
Seeking each other's souls in the depths of unfathomed
    caresses,
And through the long windings of passion emerging again to
    the stars . . .
Yes, all this through the room, the passive and featureless
    room,
Must have flowed with the rise and fall of the human
    unceasing current,
And lying there hushed in your arms, as the waves of rapture
    receded,
And far down the margin of being we heard the low beat of
    the soul,
I was glad as I thought of those others, the nameless, the
    many,
Who perhaps thus had lain and loved for an hour on the
    brink of the world,
Secret and fast in the heart of the whirlwind of travel,
The shaking and shrieking of trains, the night-long shudder
    of traffic;
Thus, like us they have lain and felt, breast to breast in the
    dark,
The fiery rain of possession descend on their limbs while
    outside
The black rain of midnight pelted the roof of the station;

And thus some woman like me waking alone before dawn,

While her lover slept, as I woke and heard the calm stir of
your breathing,

Some woman has heard as I heard the farewell shriek of the
trains

Crying good-bye to the city and staggering out into darkness,

And shaken at heart has thought: "So must we forth in the
darkness,

Sped down the fixed rail of habit by the hand of implacable
fate —"

So shall we issue to life, and the rain, and the dull dark
dawning;

You to the wide flair of cities, with windy garlands and
shouting,

Carrying to populous places the freight of holiday throngs;

I, by waste land and stretches of low-skied marsh,

To a harbourless wind-bitten shore, where a dull town
moulders and shrinks,

And its roofs fall in, and the sluggish feet of the hours

Are printed in grass in its streets; and between the featureless
houses

Languid the town-folk glide to stare at the entering train,

The train from which no one descends; till one pale evening
of winter,

When it halts on the edge of the town, see, the houses have
turned into grave-stones,

The streets are the grassy paths between the low roofs of the
dead;

And as the train glides in ghosts stand by the doors of the
carriages;

And scarcely the difference is felt — yes, such is the life I
return to . . . !

Thus may another have thought; thus, as I turned, may have
turned

To the sleeping lips at her side, to drink, as I drank there,
oblivion.

EDITH WHARTON
AMERICAN (1862–1937)

Alba

When the nightingale to his mate
Sings day-long and night late
My love and I keep state
In bower,
In flower,
'Till the watchman on the tower
Cry:
    "Up! Thou rascal, Rise,
    I see the white
        Light
        And the night
            Flies."

EZRA POUND
AMERICAN (1885–1972)

Vernal Equinox

The scent of hyacinths, like a pale mist, lies between me and
    my book;
And the South Wind, washing through the room,
Makes the candles quiver.
My nerves sting at a spatter of rain on the shutter,
And I am uneasy with the thrusting of green shoots
Outside, in the night.

Why are you not here to overpower me with your tense and
    urgent love?

AMY LOWELL
AMERICAN (1874–1925)

Fragment 113

"Neither honey nor bee for me." — *Sappho*

Not honey,
not the plunder of the bee
from meadow or sand-flower
or mountain bush;
from winter-flower or shoot
born of the later heat:
not honey, not the sweet
stain on the lips and teeth:
not honey, not the deep
plunge of soft belly
and the clinging of the gold-edged
pollen-dusted feet;

not so —
though rapture blind my eyes,
and hunger crisp
dark and inert my mouth,
not honey, not the south,
not the tall stalk
of red twin-lilies,
nor light branch of fruit tree
caught in flexible light branch;

not honey, not the south;
ah flower of purple iris,
flower of white,
or of the iris, withering the grass —
for fleck of the sun's fire,
gathers such heat and power,
that shadow-print is light,
cast through the petals
of the yellow iris flower;

not iris — old desire — old passion —
old forgetfulness — old pain —
not this, nor any flower,

but if you turn again,

seek strength of arm and throat,

touch as the god;

neglect the lyre-note;

knowing that you shall feel,

about the frame,

no trembling of the string

but heat, more passionate

of bone and the white shell

and fiery tempered steel.

H.D.
AMERICAN (1886–1961)

Recuerdo

We were very tired, we were very merry —
We had gone back and forth all night on the ferry.
It was bare and bright, and smelled like a stable —
But we looked into a fire, we leaned across a table,
We lay on the hill-top underneath the moon;
And the whistles kept blowing, and the dawn came soon.

We were very tired, we were very merry —
We had gone back and forth all night on the ferry;
And you ate an apple, and I ate a pear,
From a dozen of each we had bought somewhere;
And the sky went wan, and the wind came cold,
And the sun rose dripping, a bucketful of gold.

We were very tired, we were very merry,
We had gone back and forth all night on the ferry.
We hailed, "Good morrow, mother!" to a shawl-covered head,
And bought a morning paper, which neither of us read;
And she wept, "God bless you!" for the apples and the pears,
And we gave her all our money but our subway fares.

EDNA ST. VINCENT MILLAY
AMERICAN (1892–1950)

I Want to Die While You Love Me

I want to die while you love me,
  While yet you hold me fair,
While laughter lies upon my lips
  And lights are in my hair.

I want to die while you love me,
  And bear to that still bed
Your kisses turbulent, unspent,
  To warm me when I'm dead.

I want to die while you love me,
  Oh, who would care to live
Till love has nothing more to ask
  And nothing more to give?

I want to die while you love me,
  And never, never see
The glory of this perfect day
  Grow dim or cease to be!

GEORGIA DOUGLAS JOHNSON
AMERICAN (1886–1966)

in spite of everything

in spite of everything
which breathes and moves,since Doom
(with white longest hands
neatening each crease)
will smooth entirely our minds

— before leaving my room
i turn,and(stooping
through the morning)kiss
this pillow,dear
where our heads lived and were.

E. E. CUMMINGS
AMERICAN (1894–1962)

somewhere i have never travelled . . .

somewhere i have never travelled,gladly beyond
any experience,your eyes have their silence:
in your most frail gesture are things which enclose me,
or which i cannot touch because they are too near

your slightest look easily will unclose me
though i have closed myself as fingers,
you open always petal by petal myself as Spring opens
(touching skilfully,mysteriously)her first rose

or if your wish be to close me,i and
my life will shut very beautifully,suddenly,
as when the heart of this flower imagines
the snow carefully everywhere descending;

nothing which we are to perceive in this world equals
the power of your intense fragility:whose texture
compels me with the colour of its countries,
rendering death and forever with each breathing

(i do not know what it is about you that closes
and opens;only something in me understands
the voice of your eyes is deeper than all roses)
nobody,not even the rain,has such small hands

E. E. CUMMINGS
AMERICAN (1894–1962)

Lay your sleeping head, my love

Lay your sleeping head, my love,
Human on my faithless arm;
Time and fevers burn away
Individual beauty from
Thoughtful children, and the grave
Proves the child ephemeral:
But in my arms till break of day
Let the living creature lie,

Mortal, guilty, but to me
The entirely beautiful.

Soul and body have no bounds:
To lovers as they lie upon
Her tolerant enchanted slope
In their ordinary swoon,
Grave the vision Venus sends
Of supernatural sympathy,
Universal love and hope;
While an abstract insight wakes
Among the glaciers and the rocks
The hermit's sensual ecstasy.

Certainty, fidelity
On the stroke of midnight pass
Like vibrations of a bell,
And fashionable madmen raise
Their pedantic boring cry:
Every farthing of the cost,
All the dreaded cards foretell,
Shall be paid, but from this night
Not a whisper, not a thought,
Not a kiss nor look be lost.

Beauty, midnight, vision dies:
Let the winds of dawn that blow
Softly round your dreaming head
Such a day of sweetness show
Eye and knocking heart may bless,
Find the mortal world enough;
Noons of dryness see you fed
By the involuntary powers,
Nights of insult let you pass
Watched by every human love.

W. H. AUDEN
ENGLISH (1907–1973)

The Kimono

When I returned from lovers' lane
My hair was white as snow.
Joy, incomprehension, pain
I'd seen like seasons come and go.
How I got home again
Frozen half dead, perhaps you know.

You hide a smile and quote a text:
Desires ungratified
Persist from one life to the next.
Hearths we strip ourselves beside
Long, long ago were x'd
On blueprints of "consuming pride."

Times out of mind, the bubble-gleam
To our charred level drew
April back. A sudden beam . . .
— Keep talking while I change into
The pattern of a stream
Bordered with rushes white on blue.

JAMES MERRILL
AMERICAN (1926–1995)

Having a Coke with You

is even more fun than going to San Sebastian, Irún, Hendaye,
  Biarritz, Bayonne
or being sick to my stomach on the Travesera de Gracia in
  Barcelona
partly because in your orange shirt you look like a better happier
  St. Sebastian
partly because of my love for you, partly because of your love for
  yoghurt
partly because of the fluorescent orange tulips around the birches
partly because of the secrecy our smiles take on before people
  and statuary
it is hard to believe when I'm with you that there can be
  anything as still

as solemn as unpleasantly definitive as statuary when right in
    front of it
in the warm New York 4 o'clock light we are drifting back and
    forth
between each other like a tree breathing through its spectacles

and the portrait show seems to have no faces in it at all, just
    paint
you suddenly wonder why in the world anyone ever did them
                                       I look
at you and I would rather look at you than all the portraits in
    the world
except possibly for the *Polish Rider* occasionally and anyway it's in
    the Frick
which thank heavens you haven't gone to yet so we can go
    together the first time
and the fact that you move so beautifully more or less takes care
    of Futurism
just as at home I never think of the *Nude Descending a Staircase*
    or
at a rehearsal a single drawing of Leonardo or Michelangelo that
    used to wow me
and what good does all the research of the Impressionists do
    them
when they never got the right person to stand near the tree when
    the sun sank
or for that matter Marino Marini when he didn't pick the rider
    as carefully
as the horse
                it seems they were all cheated of some marvellous
    experience
which is not going to go wasted on me which is why I'm telling
    you about it

FRANK O'HARA
AMERICAN (1926–1966)

23rd Street Runs into Heaven

You stand near the window as lights wink
On along the street. Somewhere a trolley, taking
Shop-girls and clerks home, clatters through
This before-supper Sabbath. An alley cat cries
To find the garbage cans sealed; newsboys
Begin their murder-into-pennies round.

We are shut in, secure for a little, safe until
Tomorrow. You slip your dress off, roll down
Your stockings, careful against runs. Naked now,
With soft light on soft flesh, you pause
For a moment; turn and face me —
Smile in a way that only women know
Who have lain long with their lover
And are made more virginal.

Our supper is plain but we are very wonderful.

KENNETH PATCHEN
AMERICAN (1911–1972)

Elegy

Body, beloved, yes; we know each other you and I.

Perhaps I ran to meet you
like a cloud heavy with lightning.

Ah, that fleeting light, that fulmination,
that vast silence that succeeds catastrophe.

Whoever looks at us now (dark stones, bits
and pieces of used matter)
won't know that for an instant our name was love
and that in eternity they call us destiny.

ROSARIO CASTELLANOS
MEXICAN (1925–1974)
TRANSLATED BY MAGDA BOGIN

I crave your mouth, your voice, your hair.
Silent and starving, I prowl through the streets.
Bread does not nourish me, dawn disrupts me, all day
I hunt for the liquid measure of your steps.

I hunger for your sleek laugh,
your hands the color of a savage harvest,
hunger for the pale stones of your fingernails,
I want to eat your skin like a whole almond.

I want to eat the sunbeam flaring in your lovely body,
the sovereign nose of your arrogant face,
I want to eat the fleeting shade of your lashes,

and I pace around hungry, sniffing the twilight,
hunting for you, for your hot heart,
like a puma in the barrens of Quitratue.

PABLO NERUDA
CHILEAN (1904–1973)
TRANSLATED BY STEPHEN TAPSCOTT

DISAPPOINTMENT

Hate whom ye list, for I care not

Hate whom ye list, for I care not:
Love whom ye list and spare not:
Do what ye list and dread not:
Think what ye list, I fear not:
For as of me, I am not,
But even as one that recks not
Whether ye hate or hate not:
For in your love I dote not:
Wherefore I pray you forget not,
But love whom ye list, for I care not.

SIR THOMAS WYATT
ENGLISH (C. 1503–1542)

What meaneth this? When I lie alone

What meaneth this? When I lie alone,
I toss, I turn, I sigh, I groan;
My bed me seems as hard as stone:
    What meaneth this?

I sigh, I plain continually;
The clothes that on my bed do lie
Always methinks they lie awry:
    What meaneth this?

In slumbers oft for fear I quake;
For heat and cold I burn and shake;
For lack of sleep my head doth ache:
    What meaneth this?

At mornings then when I do rise
I turn unto my wonted guise;
All day after muse and devise:
    What meaneth this?

And if perchance by me there pass
She unto whom I sue for grace,
The cold blood forsaketh my face:
    What meaneth this?

But if I sit near her by,
With loud voice my heart doth cry,
And yet my mouth is dumb and dry:
    What meaneth this?

To ask for help no heart I have,
My tongue doth fail what I should crave,

Yet inwardly I rage and rave:
    What meaneth this?

Thus have I passèd many a year
And many a day, though nought appear
But most of that that most I fear:
    What meaneth this?

SIR THOMAS WYATT
ENGLISH (C. 1503–1542)

The Lover Showeth How He Is Forsaken of Such as He Sometime Enjoyed

They flee from me that sometime did me seek
    With naked foot stalking in my chamber:
I have seen them gentle, tame, and meek
    That now are wild and do not remember
    That sometime they put themself in danger
To take bread at my hand; and now they range
Busily seeking with a continual change.

Thanked be fortune, it hath been otherwise
    Twenty times better; but once in special,
In thin array after a pleasant guise,
    When her loose gown from her shoulders did fall,
    And she me caught in her arms long and small:
Therewithal sweetly did me kiss,
And softly said, "Dear heart, how like you this?"

It was no dream: I lay broad waking.
    But all is turned thorough my gentleness
Into a strange fashion of forsaking;
    And I have leave to go of her goodness,
    And she also to use new fangleness.
But since that I so kindely am served,
I would fain know what she hath deserved.

SIR THOMAS WYATT
ENGLISH (C. 1503–1542)

To My Lord Biron's Tune of "Adieu Phillis"

'Tis true, our life is but a long disease,
Made up of real pain and seeming ease;
You stars, who these entangled fortunes give,
   O tell me why
   It is so hard to die,
      Yet such a task to live?
If with some pleasure we our griefs betray,
It costs us dearer than it can repay:
For time or fortune all things so devours;
   Our hopes are crossed,
   Or else the object lost,
      Ere we can call it ours.

KATHERINE PHILIPS
ENGLISH (1631–1664)

And if I did what then

And if I did what then?
Are you aggrieved therefore?
The sea hath fish for every man,
And what would you have more?

Thus did my mistress once
Amaze my mind with doubt:
And popped a question for the nonce
To beat my brains about.

Whereto I thus replied:
Each fisherman can wish
That all the sea at every tide
Were his alone to fish.

And so did I (in vain),
But since it may not be,
Let such fish there as find the gain,
And leave the loss for me.

And with such luck and loss
I will content myself:
Till tides of turning time may toss
Such fishers on the shelf.

And when they stick on sands,
That every man may see,
Then will I laugh and clap my hands
As they do now at me.

GEORGE GASCOIGNE
ENGLISH (C. 1539–1577)

An evil spirit, your beauty haunts me still

An evil spirit, your beauty haunts me still,
Wherewith, alas, I have been long possessed,
Which ceaseth not to tempt me to each ill,
Nor gives me once but one poor minute's rest;
In me it speaks, whether I sleep or wake,
And when by means to drive it out I try,
With greater torments then it me doth take,
And tortures me in most extremity;
Before my face it lays down my despairs,
And hastes me on unto a sudden death,
Now tempting me to drown myself in tears,
And then in sighing to give up my breath.
   Thus am I still provoked to every evil
   By this good wicked spirit, sweet angel-devil.

MICHAEL DRAYTON
ENGLISH (1563–1631)

I saw my lady weep

   I saw my lady weep,
And Sorrow proud to be advancéd so
In those fair eyes where all perfections keep.
   Her face was full of woe,
But such a woe (believe me) as wins more hearts
Than Mirth can do with her enticing parts.

Sorrow was there made fair,
And Passion wise; Tears a delightful thing;
Silence beyond all speech, a wisdom rare;
   She made her sighs to sing,
And all things with so sweet a sadness move
As made my heart at once both grieve and love.

   O fairer than aught else
The world can show, leave off in time to grieve.
Enough, enough; your joyful look excels:
   Tears kill the heart, believe.
O strive not to be excellent in woe,
Which only breeds your beauty's overthrow.

ANONYMOUS
ENGLISH (C. 1600)

The expense of spirit in a waste of shame

The expense of spirit in a waste of shame
Is lust in action; and till action, lust
Is perjured, murderous, bloody, full of blame,
Savage, extreme, rude, cruel, not to trust;
Enjoyed no sooner but despisèd straight;
Past reason hunted; and no sooner had,
Past reason hated, as a swallowed bait,
On purpose laid to make the taker mad:
Mad in pursuit, and in possession so;
Had, having, and in quest to have, extreme;
A bliss in proof, and proved, a very woe;
Before, a joy proposed; behind, a dream.
All this the world well knows; yet none knows well
To shun the heaven that leads men to this hell.

WILLIAM SHAKESPEARE
ENGLISH (1564–1616)

I envy not in any moods

From *In Memoriam*

I envy not in any moods
   The captive void of noble rage,
   The linnet born within the cage,
That never knew the summer woods;

I envy not the beast that takes
   His license in the field of time,
   Unfetter'd by the sense of crime,
To whom a conscience never wakes;

Nor, what may count itself as blest,
   The heart that never plighted troth
   But stagnates in the weeds of sloth;
Nor any want-begotten rest.

I hold it true, whate'er befall;
   I feel it, when I sorrow most;
   'Tis better to have loved and lost
Than never to have loved at all.

ALFRED, LORD TENNYSON
ENGLISH (1809–1892)

Pity Me Not

Pity me not because the light of day
At close of day no longer walks the sky;
Pity me not for beauties passed away
From field and thicket as the year goes by;
Pity me not the waning of the moon,
Nor that the ebbing tide goes out to sea,
Nor that a man's desire is hushed so soon,
And you no longer look with love on me.

This have I known always: Love is no more
Than the wide blossom which the wind assails,
Than the great tide that treads the shifting shore,
Strewing fresh wreckage gathered in the gales;
Pity me that the heart is slow to learn
What the swift mind beholds at every turn.

EDNA ST. VINCENT MILLAY
AMERICAN (1892–1950)

the sonnet-ballad

Oh mother, mother, where is happiness?
They took my lover's tallness off to war.
Left me lamenting. Now I cannot guess
What I can use an empty heart-cup for.
He won't be coming back here any more.
Some day the war will end, but, oh, I knew
When he went walking grandly out that door
That my sweet love would have to be untrue.
Would have to be untrue. Would have to court
Coquettish death, whose impudent and strange
Possessive arms and beauty (of a sort)
Can make a hard man hesitate — and change.
And he will be the one to stammer, "Yes."
Oh mother, mother, where is happiness?

GWENDOLYN BROOKS
AMERICAN (1917–2000)

SEPARATIONS AND FAREWELLS

Slim-waisted friend

Slim-waisted friend,
look —
spreading its arch
over Love's
phantom city,
the faint crescent moon —
where the separate
gazes of lovers
parted to separate
countries meet.

RAJASEKHARA
INDIAN (FL. 880–920)
TRANSLATED BY ANDREW SCHELLING

Thoughts from the Women's Quarter

To the Tune "The Boat of Stars"

Year after year I have watched
My jade mirror. Now my rouge
And cream sicken me. It is one more
Year that he has not come back.
My flesh shakes when a letter
Comes from South of the river.
I cannot drink wine since he left,
But sorrow has drunk up all my tears.
I have lost my mind, far-off
In the jungle mists of the South.
The gates of Heaven are nearer
Than the body of my beloved.

LI CH'ING-CHAO
CHINESE (1084–C. 1151)
TRANSLATED BY KENNETH REXROTH

Western wind, when will thou blow

Western wind, when will thou blow,
The small rain down can rain?
Christ, if my love were in my arms
And I in my bed again!

ANONYMOUS
ENGLISH (16TH CENTURY)

Alas, departing is ground of woe

Alas, departing is ground of woe, —
    Other song can I not sing.
But why part I my lady fro,
    Sith love was cause of our meeting?
    The bitter tears of her weeping
        Mine heart hath pierced so mortally
    That to the death it will me bring
        But if I see her hastily.

ANONYMOUS
ENGLISH (15TH CENTURY)

Sith fortune favors not and all things backward go

Sith fortune favors not and all things backward go,
And sith your mind hath so decreed to make an end of woe,
Sith now is no redress, but hence I must away,
Farewell, I waste no vainer words, I hope for better day.

BARNABE GOOGE
ENGLISH (1540–1594)

And wilt thou leave me thus

And wilt thou leave me thus?
    Say nay, say nay, for shame,
    To save thee from the blame
    Of all my grief and grame.
And wilt thou leave me thus?
    Say nay, say nay.

And wilt thou leave me thus,
    That hath loved thee so long
    In wealth and woe among?
    And is thy heart so strong
As for to leave me thus?
    Say nay, say nay.

And wilt thou leave me thus,
    That hath given thee my heart,
    Never for to depart
    Neither for pain nor smart?
And wilt thou leave me thus?
    Say nay, say nay.

And wilt thou leave me thus,
    And have no more pity
    Of him that loveth thee?
    Alas! thy cruelty!
And wilt thou leave me thus?
    Say nay, say nay.

SIR THOMAS WYATT
ENGLISH (C. 1503–1542)

Oft have I mused, but now at length I find

Oft have I mused, but now at length I find,
Why those that die, men say they do depart.
'Depart!' — a word so gentle, to my mind,
Weakly did seem to paint death's ugly dart.
But now the stars, with their strange course, do bind
Me one to leave, with whom I leave my heart;
I hear a cry of spirits, faint and blind,
That, parting thus, my chiefest part I part.

Part of my life, the loathëd part to me,
Lives to impart my weary clay some breath;
But that good part, wherein all comforts be,
Now dead, doth show departure is a death —
Yea, worse than death: death parts both woe and joy:
From joy I part, still living in annoy.

SIR PHILIP SIDNEY
ENGLISH (1554–1586)

Farewell! thou art too dear for my possessing

Farewell! thou art too dear for my possessing,
And like enough thou know'st thy estimate:
The charter of thy worth gives thee releasing;
My bonds in thee are all determinate.
For how do I hold thee but by thy granting?
And for that riches where is my deserving?
The cause of this fair gift in me is wanting,
And so my patent back again is swerving.
Thyself thou gav'st, thy own worth then not knowing,
Or me, to whom thou gav'st it, else mistaking;
So thy great gift, upon misprision growing,
Comes home again, on better judgement making.
    Thus have I had thee as a dream doth flatter,
    In sleep, a king; but waking, no such matter.

WILLIAM SHAKESPEARE
ENGLISH (1564–1616)

How like a winter hath my absence been

How like a winter hath my absence been
From thee, the pleasure of the fleeting year!
What freezings have I felt, what dark days seen,
What old December's bareness everywhere!
And yet this time removed was summer's time;
The teeming autumn, big with rich increase,
Bearing the wanton burthen of the prime
Like widowed wombs after their lords' decease:

Yet this abundant issue seemed to me
But hope of orphans, and unfathered fruit;
For summer and his pleasures wait on thee,
And, thou away, the very birds are mute;
  Or if they sing, 'tis with so dull a cheer,
  That leaves look pale, dreading the winter's near.

WILLIAM SHAKESPEARE
ENGLISH (1564–1616)

Since there's no help, come let us kiss and part

Since there's no help, come let us kiss and part —
Nay, I have done: you get no more of me;
And I am glad, yea, glad with all my heart,
That thus so cleanly I myself can free.
Shake hands for ever, cancel all our vows,
And when we meet at any time again,
Be it not seen in either of our brows
That we one jot of former love retain.
Now at the last gasp of love's latest breath,
When, his pulse failing, Passion speechless lies,
When Faith is kneeling by his bed of death,
And Innocence is closing up his eyes, —
  Now, if thou wouldst, when all have given him over,
  From death to life thou might'st him yet recover.

MICHAEL DRAYTON
ENGLISH (1563–1631)

Sweetest love, I do not go

Sweetest love, I do not go,
  For weariness of thee,
Nor in hope the world can show
  A fitter love for me;
    But since that I
Must die at last, 'tis best
To use myself in jest
  Thus by feigned deaths to die.

Yesternight the sun went hence,
    And yet is here to-day;
He hath no desire nor sense,
    Nor half so short a way;
        Then fear not me,
But believe that I shall make
Speedier journeys, since I take
    More wings and spurs than he.

O how feeble is man's power,
    That if good fortune fall,
Cannot add another hour
    Nor a lost hour recall!
        But come bad chance,
And we join to it our strength,
And we teach it art and length,
    Itself o'er us to advance.

When thou sigh'st, thou sigh'st not wind,
    But sigh'st my soul away;
When thou weep'st, unkindly kind,
    My life's blood doth decay.
        It cannot be
That thou lov'st me, as thou say'st,
If in thine my life thou waste,
    That art the best of me.

Let not thy divining heart
    Forethink me any ill,
Destiny may take thy part,
    And may thy fears fulfil;
        But think that we
Are but turned aside to sleep;
They who one another keep
    Alive, ne'er parted be.

JOHN DONNE
ENGLISH (1572–1631)

A Valediction: Forbidding Mourning

As virtuous men pass mildly away,
   And whisper to their souls to go,
Whilst some of their sad friends do say
   The breath goes now, and some say, No;

So let us melt, and make no noise,
   No tear-floods, nor sigh-tempests move,
'Twere profanation of our joys
   To tell the laity our love.

Moving of th' earth brings harms and fears,
   Men reckon what it did and meant;
But trepidation of the spheres,
   Though greater far, is innocent.

Dull sublunary lovers' love
   (Whose soul is sense) cannot admit
Absence, because it doth remove
   Those things which elemented it.

But we, by a love so much refined
   That our selves know not what it is,
Inter-assurèd of the mind,
   Care less, eyes, lips, and hands to miss.

Our two souls therefore, which are one,
   Though I must go, endure not yet
A breach, but an expansion,
   Like gold to airy thinness beat.

If they be two, they are two so
   As stiff twin compasses are two;
Thy soul, the fixed foot, makes no show
   To move, but doth, if th' other do.

And though it in the center sit,
   Yet when the other far doth roam,

It leans and hearkens after it,
And grows erect, as that comes home.

Such wilt thou be to me, who must
Like th' other foot, obliquely run;
Thy firmness makes my circle just,
And makes me end where I begun.

JOHN DONNE
ENGLISH (1572–1631)

Why should a foolish marriage vow

Why should a foolish marriage vow
Which long ago was made
Oblige us to each other now,
When passion is decayed?
We loved, and we loved, as long as we could,
Till our love was loved out in us both;
But our marriage is dead when the pleasure is fled;
'Twas pleasure first made it an oath.

If I have pleasures for a friend
And further love in store,
What wrong has he whose joys did end,
And who could give no more?
'Tis a madness that he
Should be jealous of me,
Or that I should bar him of another;
For all we can gain is to give ourselves pain
When neither can hinder the other.

JOHN DRYDEN
ENGLISH (1631–1700)

To Lucasta, Going Beyond the Seas

If to be absent were to be
    Away from thee;
    Or that when I am gone
    You or I were alone;
Then, my Lucasta, might I crave
Pity from blustering wind or swallowing wave.

But I'll not sigh one blast or gale
    To swell my sail,
    Or pay a tear to 'suage
    The foaming blue god's rage;
For whether he will let me pass
Or no, I'm still as happy as I was.

Though seas and land betwixt us both,
    Our faith and troth,
    Like separated souls,
    All time and space controls:
Above the highest sphere we meet
Unseen, unknown; and greet as Angels greet.

So then we do anticipate
    Our after-fate,
    And are alive i' the skies,
    If thus our lips and eyes
Can speak like spirits unconfined
In Heaven, their earthy bodies left behind.

RICHARD LOVELACE
ENGLISH (1618–1658)

Farewell to Nancy

Ae fond kiss, and then we sever!
Ae fareweel, alas, for ever!
Deep in heart-wrung tears I'll pledge thee,
Warring sighs and groans I'll wage thee.
Who shall say that fortune grieves him
While the star of hope she leaves him?

Me, nae cheerfu' twinkle lights me,
Dark despair around benights me.

I'll ne'er blame my partial fancy,
Naething could resist my Nancy;
But to see her, was to love her;
Love but her, and love for ever.
Had we never lov'd sae kindly,
Had we never lov'd sae blindly,
Never met — or never parted,
We had ne'er been broken hearted.

Fare thee weel, thou first and fairest!
Fare thee weel, thou best and dearest!
Thine be ilka joy and treasure,
Peace, enjoyment, love, and pleasure.
Ae fond kiss, and then we sever;
Ae farewell, alas, for ever!
Deep in heart-wrung tears I pledge thee,
Warring sighs and groans I'll wage thee.

ROBERT BURNS
SCOTTISH (1759–1796)

When we two parted

When we two parted
   In silence and tears,
Half broken-hearted
   To sever for years,
Pale grew thy cheek and cold,
   Colder thy kiss;
Truly that hour foretold
   Sorrow to this.

The dew of the morning
   Sunk chill on my brow —
It felt like the warning
   Of what I feel now.

Thy vows are all broken,
   And light is thy fame;
I hear thy name spoken,
   And share in its shame.

They name thee before me,
   A knell to mine ear;
A shudder comes o'er me —
   Why wert thou so dear?
They know not I knew thee,
   Who knew thee too well: —
Long, long shall I rue thee,
   Too deeply to tell.

In secret we met —
   In silence I grieve,
That thy heart could forget,
   Thy spirit deceive.
If I should meet thee
   After long years,
How should I greet thee?
   With silence and tears.

GEORGE GORDON, LORD BYRON
ENGLISH (1788–1824)

My life closed twice before its close

My life closed twice before its close;
It yet remains to see
If Immortality unveil
A third event to me,

So huge, so hopeless to conceive
As these that twice befell.
Parting is all we know of heaven,
And all we need of hell.

EMILY DICKINSON
AMERICAN (1830–1886)

Ulysses

It little profits that an idle king,
By this still hearth, among these barren crags,
Matched with an aged wife, I mete and dole
Unequal laws unto a savage race,
That hoard, and sleep, and feed, and know not me.
I cannot rest from travel; I will drink
Life to the lees. All times I have enjoyed
Greatly, have suffered greatly, both with those
That loved me, and alone; on shore, and when
Through scudding drifts the rainy Hyades
Vext the dim sea. I am become a name;
For always roaming with a hungry heart
Much have I seen and known, — cities of men
And manners, climates, councils, governments,
Myself not least, but honoured of them all, —
And drunk delight of battle with my peers,
Far on the ringing plains of windy Troy.
I am a part of all that I have met;
Yet all experience is an arch wherethrough
Gleams that untravelled world whose margin fades
For ever and for ever when I move.
How dull it is to pause, to make an end,
To rust unburnished, not to shine in use!
As though to breathe were life! Life piled on life
Were all too little, and of one to me
Little remains; but every hour is saved
From that eternal silence, something more,
A bringer of new things; and vile it were
For some three suns to store and hoard myself,
And this gray spirit yearning in desire
To follow knowledge like a sinking star,
Beyond the utmost bound of human thought.

This is my son, mine own Telemachus,
To whom I leave the sceptre and the isle, —
Well-loved of me, discerning to fulfill
This labour, by slow prudence to make mild

A rugged people, and through soft degrees
Subdue them to the useful and the good.
Most blameless is he, centred in the sphere
Of common duties, decent not to fail
In offices of tenderness, and pay
Meet adoration to my household gods,
When I am gone. He works his work, I mine.
There lies the port; the vessel puffs her sail;
There gloom the dark, broad seas. My mariners,
Souls that have toiled and wrought, and thought with me, —
That ever with a frolic welcome took
The thunder and the sunshine, and opposed
Free hearts, free foreheads, — you and I are old;
Old age hath yet his honour and his toil.
Death closes all; but something ere the end,
Some work of noble note, may yet be done,
Not unbecoming men that strove with Gods.
The lights begin to twinkle from the rocks;
The long day wanes; the slow moon climbs; the deep
Moans round with many voices. Come, my friends,
'Tis not too late to seek a newer world.
Push off, and sitting well in order smite
The sounding furrows; for my purpose holds
To sail beyond the sunset, and the baths
Of all the western stars, until I die.
It may be that the gulfs will wash us down;
It may be we shall touch the Happy Isles,
And see the great Achilles, whom we knew.
Though much is taken, much abides; and though
We are not now that strength which in old days
Moved earth and heaven, that which we are, we are, —
One equal temper of heroic hearts,
Made weak by time and fate, but strong in will
To strive, to seek, to find, and not to yield.

ALFRED, LORD TENNYSON
ENGLISH (1809–1892)

Meeting at Night

The grey sea and the long black land;
And the yellow half-moon large and low;
And the startled little waves that leap
In fiery ringlets from their sleep,
As I gain the cove with pushing prow,
And quench its speed i' the slushy sand.

Then a mile of warm sea-scented beach;
Three fields to cross till a farm appears;
A tap at the pane, the quick sharp scratch
And blue spurt of a lighted match,
And a voice less loud, through its joys and fears,
Than the two hearts beating each to each!

ROBERT BROWNING
ENGLISH (1812–1889)

Dawn on the Night-Journey

Till dawn the wind drove round me. It is past
    And still, and leaves the air to lisp of bird,
    And to the quiet that is almost heard
Of the new-risen day, as yet bound fast
In the first warmth of sunrise. When the last
    Of the sun's hours to-day shall be fulfilled,
    There shall another breath of time be stilled
For me, which now is to my senses cast
As much beyond me as eternity,
    Unknown, kept secret. On the newborn air
The moth quivers in silence. It is vast,
Yes, even beyond the hills upon the sea,
    The day whose end shall give this hour as sheer
As chaos to the irrevocable Past.

DANTE GABRIEL ROSSETTI
ENGLISH (1828–1882)

Remember

Remember me when I am gone away,
Gone far away into the silent land;
When you can no more hold me by the hand,
Nor I half turn to go yet turning stay.
Remember me when no more day by day
You tell me of our future that you plann'd:
Only remember me; you understand
It will be late to counsel then or pray.
Yet if you should forget me for a while
And afterwards remember, do not grieve:
For if the darkness and corruption leave
A vestige of the thoughts that once I had,
Better by far you should forget and smile
Than that you should remember and be sad.

CHRISTINA ROSSETTI
ENGLISH (1830–1894)

Thus piteously Love closed what he begat

From *Modern Love*

Thus piteously Love closed what he begat:
The union of this ever-diverse pair!
These two were rapid falcons in a snare,
Condemned to do the flitting of the bat.
Lovers beneath the singing sky of May,
They wandered once; clear as the dew on flowers:
But they fed not on the advancing hours:
Their hearts held cravings for the buried day.
Then each applied to each that fatal knife,
Deep questioning, which probes to endless dole.
Ah, what a dusty answer gets the soul
When hot for certainties in this our life! —
In tragic hints here see what evermore
Moves dark as yonder midnight ocean's force,
Thundering like ramping hosts of warrior horse,
To throw that faint thin line upon the shore!

GEORGE MEREDITH
ENGLISH (1828–1909)

Departure

Seen enough. The vision was met with in every air.

Had enough. Sounds of cities, in the evening and in the sun and
  always.

Known enough. Life's halts. — O Sounds and Visions!

Departure in new affection and new noise.

ARTHUR RIMBAUD
FRENCH (1854–1891)
TRANSLATED BY LOUISE VARÈSE

Ithaka

As you set out for Ithaka
hope the voyage is a long one,
full of adventure, full of discovery.
Laistrygonians and Cyclops,
angry Poseidon — don't be afraid of them:
you'll never find things like that on your way
as long as you keep your thoughts raised high,
as long as a rare excitement
stirs your spirit and your body.
Laistrygonians and Cyclops,
wild Poseidon — you won't encounter them
unless you bring them along inside your soul,
unless your soul sets them up in front of you.

Hope the voyage is a long one.
May there be many a summer morning when,
with what pleasure, what joy,
you come into harbors seen for the first time;
may you stop at Phoenician trading stations
to buy fine things,
mother of pearl and coral, amber and ebony,
sensual perfume of every kind —
as many sensual perfumes as you can;
and may you visit many Egyptian cities
to gather stores of knowledge from their scholars.

Keep Ithaka always in your mind.
Arriving there is what you are destined for.
But do not hurry the journey at all.
Better if it lasts for years,
so you are old by the time you reach the island,
wealthy with all you have gained on the way,
not expecting Ithaka to make you rich.

Ithaka gave you the marvelous journey.
Without her you would not have set out.
She has nothing left to give you now.

And if you find her poor, Ithaka won't have fooled you.
Wise as you will have become, so full of experience,
you will have understood by then what these Ithakas mean.

C. P. CAVAFY
GREEK (1863–1933)
TRANSLATED BY EDMUND KEELEY
AND PHILIP SHERRARD

Passer Mortuus Est

Death devours all lovely things;
    Lesbia with her sparrow
Shares the darkness, — presently
    Every bed is narrow.

Unremembered as old rain
    Dries the sheer libation,
And the little petulant hand
    Is an annotation.

After all, my erstwhile dear,
    My no longer cherished,
Need we say it was not love,
    Now that love is perished?

EDNA ST. VINCENT MILLAY
AMERICAN (1892–1950)

Parting Gift

I cannot give you the Metropolitan Tower;
I cannot give you heaven;
Nor the nine Visigoth crowns in the Cluny Museum;
Nor happiness, even.
But I can give you a very small purse
Made out of field-mouse skin,
With a painted picture of the universe
And seven blue tears therein.

I cannot give you the island of Capri;
I cannot give you beauty;
Nor bake you marvellous crusty cherry pies
With love and duty.
But I can give you a very little locket
Made out of wildcat hide:
Put it into your left-hand pocket
And never look inside.

ELINOR WYLIE
AMERICAN (1885–1928)

Stop all the clocks, cut off the telephone

Stop all the clocks, cut off the telephone,
Prevent the dog from barking with a juicy bone,
Silence the pianos and with muffled drum
Bring out the coffin, let the mourners come.

Let aeroplanes circle moaning overhead
Scribbling on the sky the message He Is Dead,
Put crêpe bows round the white necks of the public doves,
Let the traffic policemen wear black cotton gloves.

He was my North, my South, my East and West,
My working week and my Sunday rest,

My noon, my midnight, my talk, my song;
I thought that love would last for ever: I was wrong.

The stars are not wanted now; put out every one:
Pack up the moon and dismantle the sun;
Pour away the ocean and sweep up the woods:
For nothing now can ever come to any good.

W. H. AUDEN
ENGLISH (1907–1973)

O the valley in the summer where I and my John

O the valley in the summer where I and my John
Beside the deep river would walk on and on
While the flowers at our feet and the birds up above
Argued so sweetly on reciprocal love,
And I leaned on his shoulder, "O Johnny, let's play":
But he frowned like thunder and he went away.

O that Friday near Christmas as I well recall
When we went to the Charity Matinee Ball,
The floor was so smooth and the band was so loud
And Johnny so handsome I felt so proud;
"Squeeze me tighter, dear Johnny, let's dance till it's day":
But he frowned like thunder and he went away.

Shall I ever forget at the Grand Opera
When music poured out of each wonderful star?
Diamonds and pearls they hung dazzling down
Over each silver or golden silk gown;
"O John I'm in heaven," I whispered to say:
But he frowned like thunder and he went away.

O but he was as fair as a garden in flower,
As slender and tall as the great Eiffel Tower,
When the waltz throbbed out on the long promenade
O his eyes and his smile they went straight to my heart;
"O marry me, Johnny, I'll love and obey":
But he frowned like thunder and he went away.

O last night I dreamed of you, Johnny, my lover,
You'd the sun on one arm and the moon on the other,
The sea it was blue and the grass it was green,
Every star rattled a round tambourine;
Ten thousand miles deep in a pit there I lay:
But you frowned like thunder and you went away.

W. H. AUDEN
ENGLISH (1907–1973)

Stone

Stone
and that hard
contact —
the human

On the mossed
massed quartz
on which spruce
grew dense

I met him
We were thick
We said good-bye
on The Passing Years
River

LORINE NIEDECKER
AMERICAN (1903–1970)

A Kind of Loss

Used together: seasons, books, a piece of music.
The keys, teacups, bread basket, sheets and a bed.
A hope chest of words, of gestures, brought back, used, used up.
A household order maintained. Said. Done. And always a hand
was there.

I've fallen in love with winter, with a Viennese septet, with
    summer.
With village maps, a mountain nest, a beach and a bed.
Kept a calendar cult, declared promises irrevocable,
bowed before something, was pious to a nothing

(— to a folded newspaper, cold ashes, the scribbled piece of
    paper),
fearless in religion, for our bed was the church.

From my lake view arose my inexhaustible painting.
From my balcony I greeted entire peoples, my neighbors.
By the chimney fire, in safety, my hair took on its deepest hue.
The ringing at the door was the alarm for my joy.

It's not you I've lost,
but the world.

INGEBORG BACHMANN
AUSTRIAN (1926–1973)
TRANSLATED BY MARK ANDERSON

SOLITUDE

Tonight I've watched

Tonight I've watched

The moon and then
the Pleiades
go down

The night is now
half-gone; youth
goes; I am

in bed alone

SAPPHO
GREEK (C. 612 B.C.)
TRANSLATED BY MARY BARNARD

Drinking Alone with the Moon

From a pot of wine among the flowers
I drank alone. There was no one with me —
Till, raising my cup, I asked the bright moon
To bring me my shadow and make us three.
Alas, the moon was unable to drink
And my shadow tagged me vacantly;
But still for a while I had these friends
To cheer me through the end of spring....
I sang. The moon encouraged me.
I danced. My shadow tumbled after.
As long as I knew, we were boon companions.
And then I was drunk, and we lost one another.
.... Shall goodwill ever be secure?
I watched the long road of the River of Stars.

LI PO
CHINESE (701–762)
TRANSLATED BY WITTER BYNNER

Dream Song of a Woman

Where the mountain crosses,
On top of the mountain,
   I do not myself know where.
I wandered where my mind and my heart
   seemed to be lost.
I wandered away.

FRANCES DENSMORE (FROM THE PAPAGO)
AMERICAN (1867–1957)

My Mind to Me a Kingdom Is

My mind to me a kingdom is,
   Such present joys therein I find,
That it excels all other bliss
   That earth affords or grows by kind.
Though much I want which most would have,
Yet still my mind forbids to crave.

No princely pomp, no wealthy store,
   No force to win the victory,
No wily wit to salve a sore,
   No shape to feed a loving eye;
To none of these I yield as thrall,
For why my mind doth serve for all.

I see how plenty suffers oft,
   And hasty climbers soon do fall;
I see that those which are aloft
   Mishap doth threaten most of all;
They get with toil, they keep with fear;
Such cares my mind could never bear.

Content I live, this is my stay —
   I seek no more than may suffice;
I press to bear no haughty sway;
   Look, what I lack my mind supplies:
Lo! thus I triumph like a king,
Content with that my mind doth bring.

Some have too much, yet still do crave;
   I little have, and seek no more.
They are but poor, though much they have,
   And I am rich with little store:
They poor, I rich; they beg, I give;
They lack, I leave; they pine, I live.

I laugh not at another's loss;
   I grudge not at another's gain;
No worldly waves my mind can toss;
   My state at one doth still remain:
I fear no foe, I fawn no friend;
I loathe not life, nor dread my end.

Some weigh their pleasure by their lust,
   Their wisdom by their rage of will;
Their treasure is their only trust,
   A cloakèd craft their store of skill:

But all the pleasure that I find
Is to maintain a quiet mind.

My wealth is health and perfect ease,
   My conscience clear, my choice defence;
I neither seek by bribes to please,
   Nor by deceit to breed offence:
Thus do I live; thus will I die;
Would all did so as well as I!

EDWARD DYER
ENGLISH (C. 1543–1607)

Verses Supposed to Be Written by Alexander Selkirk, During His Solitary Abode in the Island of Juan Fernandez

I am monarch of all I survey,
   My right there is none to dispute;
From the centre all round to the sea,
   I am lord of the fowl and the brute.
Oh, solitude! where are the charms
   That sages have seen in thy face?
Better dwell in the midst of alarms,
   Than reign in this horrible place.

I am out of humanity's reach,
   I must finish my journey alone,
Never hear the sweet music of speech;
   I start at the sound of my own.
The beasts, that roam over the plain,
   My form with indifference see;
They are so unacquainted with man,
   Their tameness is shocking to me.

Society, friendship, and love,
   Divinely bestow'd upon man,
Oh, had I the wings of a dove,
   How soon would I taste you again!
My sorrows I then might assuage
   In the ways of religion and truth,

Might learn from the wisdom of age,
  And be cheer'd by the sallies of youth.

Religion! what treasure untold
  Resides in that heavenly word!
More precious than silver and gold,
  Or all that this earth can afford.
But the sound of the church-going bell
  These vallies and rocks never heard,
Ne'er sigh'd at the sound of a knell,
  Or smil'd when a sabbath appear'd.

Ye winds, that have made me your sport,
  Convey to this desolate shore
Some cordial endearing report
  Of a land I shall visit no more.
My friends, do they now and then send
  A wish or a thought after me?
O tell me I yet have a friend,
  Though a friend I am never to see.

How fleet is a glance of the mind!
  Compar'd with the speed of its flight,
The tempest itself lags behind,
  And the swift wing'd arrows of light.
When I think of my own native land,
  In a moment I seem to be there;
But alas! recollection at hand
  Soon hurries me back to despair.

But the sea-fowl is gone to her nest,
  The beast is laid down in his lair,

Ev'n here is a season of rest,
　　And I to my cabin repair.
There is mercy in every place;
　　And mercy, encouraging thought!
Gives even affliction a grace,
　　And reconciles man to his lot.

WILLIAM COWPER
ENGLISH (1731–1800)

Ode to a Nightingale

My heart aches, and a drowsy numbness pains
　　My sense, as though of hemlock I had drunk,
Or emptied some dull opiate to the drains
　　One minute past, and Lethe-wards had sunk:
'Tis not through envy of thy happy lot,
　　But being too happy in thine happiness, —
　　　　That thou, light-winged Dryad of the trees
　　　　　　In some melodious plot
　　Of beechen green, and shadows numberless,
　　　　Singest of summer in full-throated ease.

O, for a draught of vintage! that hath been
　　Cool'd a long age in the deep-delved earth,
Tasting of Flora and the country green,
　　Dance, and Provençal song, and sunburnt mirth!
O for a beaker full of the warm South,
　　Full of the true, the blushful Hippocrene,
　　　　With beaded bubbles winking at the brim,
　　　　　　And purple-stained mouth;
　　That I might drink, and leave the world unseen,
　　　　And with thee fade away into the forest dim:

Fade far away, dissolve, and quite forget
　　What thou among the leaves hast never known,
The weariness, the fever, and the fret
　　Here, where men sit and hear each other groan;
Where palsy shakes a few, sad, last gray hairs,
　　Where youth grows pale, and spectre-thin, and dies;

Where but to think is to be full of sorrow
   And leaden-eyed despairs,
Where Beauty cannot keep her lustrous eyes,
   Or new Love pine at them beyond to-morrow.

Away! away! for I will fly to thee,
  Not charioted by Bacchus and his pards,
But on the viewless wings of Poesy,
  Though the dull brain perplexes and retards:
Already with thee! tender is the night,
  And haply the Queen-Moon is on her throne,
    Cluster'd around by all her starry Fays;
     But here there is no light,
  Save what from heaven is with the breezes blown
    Through verdurous glooms and winding mossy ways.

I cannot see what flowers are at my feet,
  Nor what soft incense hangs upon the boughs,
But, in embalmed darkness, guess each sweet
  Wherewith the seasonable month endows
The grass, the thicket, and the fruit-tree wild;
  White hawthorn, and the pastoral eglantine;
    And mid-May's eldest child,
  The coming musk-rose, full of dewy wine,
    The murmurous haunt of flies on summer eves.

Darkling I listen; and, for many a time
  I have been half in love with easeful Death,
Call'd him soft names in many a mused rhyme,
  To take into the air my quiet breath;
   Now more than ever seems it rich to die,
  To cease upon the midnight with no pain,
    While thou art pouring forth thy soul abroad
     In such an ecstasy!
  Still wouldst thou sing, and I have ears in vain —
    To thy high requiem become a sod.

Thou wast not born for death, immortal Bird!
  No hungry generations tread thee down;

The voice I hear this passing night was heard
   In ancient days by emperor and clown:
Perhaps the self-same song that found a path
   Through the sad heart of Ruth, when, sick for home,
     She stood in tears amid the alien corn;
      The same that oft-times hath
    Charm'd magic casements, opening on the foam
    Of perilous seas, in faery lands forlorn.

Forlorn! the very word is like a bell
   To toll me back from thee to my sole self!
Adieu! the fancy cannot cheat so well
   As she is fam'd to do, deceiving elf.
Adieu! adieu! thy plaintive anthem fades
   Past the near meadows, over the still stream,
    Up the hill-side; and now 'tis buried deep
     In the next valley-glades:
   Was it a vision, or a waking dream?
    Fled is that music: — Do I wake or sleep?

JOHN KEATS
ENGLISH (1795–1821)

Alone

From childhood's hour I have not been
As others were; I have not seen
As others saw; I could not bring
My passions from a common spring.
From the same source I have not taken
My sorrow; I could not awaken
My heart to joy at the same tone;
And all I loved, I loved alone.
Then — in my childhood, in the dawn
Of a most stormy life — was drawn
From every depth of good and ill
The mystery which binds me still:
From the torrent or the fountain,
From the red cliff of the mountain,
From the sun that round me rolled

In its autumn tint of gold,
From the lightning in the sky
As it passed me flying by,
From the thunder and the storm,
And the cloud that took the form
(When the rest of Heaven was blue)
Of a demon in my view.

EDGAR ALLAN POE
AMERICAN (1809–1849)

I'm happiest when most away

I'm happiest when most away
I can bear my soul from its home of clay
On a windy night when the moon is bright
And my eye can wander through worlds of light

When I am not and none beside
Nor earth nor sea nor cloudless sky
But only spirit wandering wide
Through infinite immensity

EMILY BRONTË
ENGLISH (1818–1848)

I Saw in Louisiana a Live-Oak Growing

I saw in Louisiana a live-oak growing,
All alone stood it and the moss hung down from the branches,
Without any companion it grew there uttering joyous leaves of
    dark green,
And its look, rude, unbending, lusty, made me think of myself,
But I wonder'd how it could utter joyous leaves standing alone
    there without its friend near, for I knew I could not,
And I broke off a twig with a certain number of leaves upon it,
    and twined around it a little moss,
And brought it away, and I have placed it in sight in my
    room,
It is not needed to remind me as of my own dear friends,
(For I believe lately I think of little else than of them,)

Yet it remains to me a curious token, it makes me think of manly
    love;
For all that, and though the live-oak glistens there in Louisiana
    solitary in a wide flat space,
Uttering joyous leaves all its life without a friend a lover near,
I know very well I could not.

WALT WHITMAN
AMERICAN (1819–1892)

The Soul selects her own Society

The Soul selects her own Society —
Then — shuts the Door —
To her divine Majority —
Present no more —

Unmoved — she notes the Chariots — pausing —
At her low Gate —
Unmoved — an Emperor be kneeling
Opon her Mat —

I've known her — from an ample nation —
Choose One —
Then — close the Valves of her attention —
Like Stone —

EMILY DICKINSON
AMERICAN (1830–1886)

Dank fens of cedar, hemlock branches gray

Dank fens of cedar, hemlock branches gray
With trees and trail of mosses, wringing-wet,
Beds of the black pitchpine in dead leaves set
Whose wasted red has wasted to white away,
Remnants of rain and droppings of decay,
Why hold ye so my heart, nor dimly let
Through your deep leaves the light of yesterday,
The faded glimmer of a sunshine set?

Is it that in your darkness, shut from strife,
The bread of tears becomes the bread of life?
Far from the roar of day, beneath your boughs
Fresh griefs beat tranquilly, and loves and vows
Grow green in your gray shadows, dearer far
Even than all lovely lights and roses are?

FREDERICK GODDARD TUCKERMAN
AMERICAN (1821–1873)

Sense of Something Coming

I am like a flag in the center of open space.
I sense ahead the wind which is coming, and must live it
   through,
While the creatures of the world beneath still do not move in
   their sleep:
The doors still close softly, and the chimneys are full of silence,
The windows do not rattle yet, and the dust still lies down.

I already know the storm, and I am as troubled as the sea,
And spread myself out, and fall into myself,
And throw myself out and am absolutely alone
In the great storm.

RAINER MARIA RILKE
GERMAN (1875–1926)
TRANSLATED BY ROBERT BLY

As Much As You Can

And if you can't shape your life the way you want,
at least try as much as you can
not to degrade it
by too much contact with the world,
by too much activity and talk.

Try not to degrade it by dragging it along,
taking it around and exposing it so often
to the daily silliness
of social events and parties,
until it comes to seem a boring hanger-on.

C. P. CAVAFY
GREEK (1863–1933)
TRANSLATED BY EDMUND KEELEY AND PHILIP SHERRARD

The New House

Now first, as I shut the door,
   I was alone
In the new house; and the wind
   Began to moan.

Old at once was the house,
   And I was old;
My ears were teased with the dread
   Of what was foretold,

Nights of storm, days of mist, without end;
   Sad days when the sun
Shone in vain: old griefs and griefs
   Not yet begun.

All was foretold me; naught
   Could I foresee;
But I learned how the wind would sound
   After these things should be.

EDWARD THOMAS
ENGLISH (1878–1917)

Solitaire

When night drifts along the streets of the city,
And sifts down between the uneven roofs,
My mind begins to peek and peer.
It plays at ball in old, blue Chinese gardens,
And shakes wrought dice-cups in Pagan temples,
Amid the broken flutings of white pillars.
It dances with purple and yellow crocuses in its hair,
And its feet shine as they flutter over drenched grasses.
How light and laughing my mind is,
When all the good folk have put out their bed-room candles,
And the city is still!

AMY LOWELL
AMERICAN (1874–1925)

Morning Song

A diamond of a morning
  Waked me an hour too soon;
Dawn had taken in the stars
  And left the faint white moon.

O white moon, you are lonely,
  It is the same with me,
But we have the world to roam over,
  Only the lonely are free.

SARA TEASDALE
AMERICAN (1884–1993)

The Lake Isle of Innisfree

I will arise and go now, and go to Innisfree,
And a small cabin build there, of clay and wattles made:
Nine bean-rows will I have there, a hive for the honey-bee,
And live alone in the bee-loud glade.

And I shall have some peace there, for peace comes dropping
  slow,
Dropping from the veils of the morning to where the cricket
  sings;

There midnight's all a glimmer, and noon a purple glow,
And evening full of the linnet's wings.

I will arise and go now, for always night and day
I hear lake water lapping with low sounds by the shore;
While I stand on the roadway, or on the pavements grey,
I hear it in the deep heart's core.

WILLIAM BUTLER YEATS
IRISH (1865–1939)

Acquainted with the Night

I have been one acquainted with the night.
I have walked out in rain — and back in rain.
I have outwalked the furthest city light.

I have looked down the saddest city lane.
I have passed by the watchman on his beat
And dropped my eyes, unwilling to explain.

I have stood still and stopped the sound of feet
When far away an interrupted cry
Came over houses from another street,

But not to call me back or say good-by;
And further still at an unearthly height,
One luminary clock against the sky

Proclaimed the time was neither wrong nor right.
I have been one acquainted with the night.

ROBERT FROST
AMERICAN (1874–1963)

He thought he kept the universe alone;
For all the voice in answer he could wake
Was but the mocking echo of his own
From some tree-hidden cliff across the lake.
Some morning from the boulder-broken beach
He would cry out on life, that what it wants
Is not its own love back in copy speech,
But counter-love, original response.
And nothing ever came of what he cried
Unless it was the embodiment that crashed
In the cliff's talus on the other side,
And then in the far distant water splashed,
But after a time allowed for it to swim,
Instead of proving human when it neared
And someone else additional to him,
As a great buck it powerfully appeared,
Pushing the crumpled water up ahead,
And landed pouring like a waterfall,
And stumbled through the rocks with horny tread,
And forced the underbrush — and that was all.

ROBERT FROST
AMERICAN (1874–1963)

Then up the ladder of the earth I climbed

From *The Heights of Machu Picchu*

Then up the ladder of the earth I climbed
through the barbed jungle's thickets
until I reached you Machu Picchu.

Tall city of stepped stone,
home at long last of whatever earth
had never hidden in her sleeping clothes.
In you two lineages that had run parallel
met where the cradle both of man and light
rocked in a wind of thorns.

Mother of stone and sperm of condors.

High reef of the human dawn.

Spade buried in primordial sand.

This was the habitation, this is the site:
here the fat grains of maize grew high
to fall again like red hail.

The fleece of the vicuña was carded here
to clothe men's loves in gold, their tombs and mothers,
the king, the prayers, the warriors.

Up here men's feet found rest at night
near eagles' talons in the high
meat-stuffed eyries. And in the dawn
with thunder steps they trod the thinning mists,
touching the earth and stones that they might recognize
that touch come night, come death.

I gaze at clothes and hands,
traces of water in the booming cistern,
a wall burnished by the touch of a face
that witnessed with my eyes the earth's carpet of tapers,
oiled with my hands the vanished wood:
for everything, apparel, skin, pots, words,
wine, loaves, has disappeared,
fallen to earth.

And the air came in with lemon blossom fingers
to touch those sleeping faces:
a thousand years of air, months, weeks of air,
blue wind and iron cordilleras —
these came with gentle footstep hurricanes
cleansing the lonely precinct of the stone.

PABLO NERUDA
CHILEAN (1904–1973)
TRANSLATED BY NATHANIEL TARN

In all the world, one man has been born, one man has died.

To insist otherwise is nothing more than statistics, an impossible
 extension.

No less impossible than bracketing the smell of rain with your
 dream of two nights ago.

That man is Ulysses, Abel, Cain, the first to make constellations
 of the stars, to build the first pyramid, the man who contrived
 the hexagrams of the Book of Changes, the smith who
 engraved runes on the sword of Hengist, Einar Tamberskelver
 the archer, Luis de León, the bookseller who fathered Samuel
 Johnson, Voltaire's gardener, Darwin aboard the *Beagle,* a Jew
 in the death chamber, and, in time, you and I.

One man alone has died at Troy, at Metaurus, at Hastings, at
 Austerlitz, at Trafalgar, at Gettysburg.

One man alone has died in hospitals, in boats, in painful
 solitude, in the rooms of habit and of love.

One man alone has looked on the enormity of dawn.

One man alone has felt on his tongue the fresh quenching of
 water, the flavor of fruit and of flesh.

I speak of the unique, the single man, he who is always alone.

JORGE LUIS BORGES
ARGENTINEAN (1899–1986)
TRANSLATED BY ALASTAIR REID

Soledad

(And I, I am no longer of that world)

Naked, he lies in the blinded room
chainsmoking, cradled by drugs, by jazz
as never by any lover's cradling flesh.

Miles Davis coolly blows for him:
O pena negra, sensual Flamenco blues;
the red clay foxfire voice of Lady Day

(lady of the pure black magnolias)
sobsings her sorrow and loss and fare you well,
dryweeps the pain his treacherous jailers

have released him from for awhile.
His fears and his unfinished self
await him down in the anywhere streets.

He hides on the dark side of the moon,
takes refuge in a stained-glass cell,
flies to a clockless country of crystal.

Only the ghost of Lady Day knows where
he is. Only the music. And he swings
oh swings: beyond complete immortal now.

ROBERT HAYDEN
AMERICAN (1913–1980)

Anxiety

I'm having a real day of it.
                    There was
something I had to do. But what?
There are no alternatives, just
the one something.
                    I have a drink,
it doesn't help — far from it!
                                    I
feel worse. I can't remember how
I felt, so perhaps I feel better.
No. Just a little darker.
                    If I could
get really dark, richly dark, like
being drunk, that's the best that's
open as a field. Not the best,

but the best except for the impossible
pure light, to be as if above a vast
prairie, rushing and pausing over
the tiny golden heads in deep grass.

But still now, familiar laughter low
from a dark face, affection human and often even —

motivational? the warm walking night

                        wandering

amusement of darkness, lips,

                    and

the light, always in wind. Perhaps
that's it: to clean something. A window?

FRANK O'HARA
AMERICAN (1926–1966)

Fauré's Second Piano Quartet

On a day like this the rain comes
down in fat and random drops among
the ailanthus leaves — "the tree
of Heaven" — the leaves that on moonlit nights shimmer black and blade-
shaped at this third-floor window.
And there are bunches of small green
knobs, buds, crowded together. The
rapid music fills in the spaces of
the leaves. And the piano comes in,
like an extra heartbeat, dangerous
and lovely. Slower now, less like
the leaves, more like the rain which
almost isn't rain, more like the thawed-
out hail. All this beauty in the
mess of this small apartment on
West 20th in Chelsea, New York.
Slowly the notes pour out, slowly,
more slowly still, fat rain falls.

JAMES SCHUYLER
AMERICAN (1923–1991)

Unknown

                        I am not that one
walking alone
there near the garden
hedges   watching
a bird turn back on the side of
this hill   turning
always at this point on the hill
as if wary
of what is below
                        I am not
that one   but someone else
who dances
over the sand toward
evening   and floats in the water
peacefully as it darkens
this time

To the watchers along the steps she seems
to be singing   but they cannot hear
what it is
nor to whom

HILDA MORLEY
AMERICAN (1919–1998)

SORROW AND COMFORT

Pain penetrates

Pain penetrates

Me drop
by drop

SAPPHO
GREEK (C. 612 B.C.)
TRANSLATED BY MARY BARNARD

The flowers withered

The flowers withered,
Their color faded away,
While meaninglessly
I spent my days in the world,
And the long rains were falling.

ONO NO KOMACHI
JAPANESE (FL. C. 833–857)
TRANSLATED BY DONALD KEENE

Care-charmer Sleep, son of the sable night

Care-charmer Sleep, son of the sable night,
Brother to death, in silent darkness born,
Relieve my languish, and restore the light;
With dark forgetting of my care return.
And let the day be time enough to mourn
The shipwreck of my ill-adventured youth:
Let waking eyes suffice to wail their scorn,
Without the torment of the night's untruth.
Cease, dreams, the images of day-desires,
To model forth the passions of the morrow;
Never let rising sun approve you liars,
To add more grief to aggravate my sorrow:
    Still let me sleep, embracing clouds in vain,
    And never wake to feel the day's disdain.

SAMUEL DANIEL
ENGLISH (1562–1619)

In night when colours all to black are cast

In night when colours all to black are cast,
Distinction lost, or gone down with the light;
The eye a watch to inward senses plac'd,
Not seeing, yet still having power of sight,

Gives vain alarums to the inward sense,
Where fear stirr'd up with witty tyranny,

Confounds all powers, and thorough self-offence,
Doth forge and raise impossibility:

Such as in thick depriving darknesses,
Proper reflections of the error be,
And images of self-confusednesses,
Which hurt imaginations only see;
　And from this nothing seen, tells news of devils,
　Which but expressions be of inward evils.

FULKE GREVILLE
ENGLISH (1554–1628)

My thoughts hold mortal strife

My thoughts hold mortal strife;
I do detest my life,
And with lamenting cries,
Peace to my soul to bring,
Oft call that prince which here doth monarchise;
But he, grim-grinning king,
Who caitives scorns, and doth the blessed surprise,
　Late having decked with beauty's rose his tomb,
　Disdains to crop a weed, and will not come.

WILLIAM DRUMMOND
SCOTTISH (1585–1649)

The Pains of Sleep

Ere on my bed my limbs I lay,
It hath not been my use to pray
With moving lips or bended knees;
But silently, by slow degrees,
My spirits I to Love compose,
In humble trust mine eye-lids close,
With reverential resignation,
No wish conceived, no thought expressed,
Only a sense of supplication;
A sense o'er all my soul impressed

That I am weak, yet not unblest,
Since in me, round me, everywhere
Eternal Strength and Wisdom are.

But yesternight I prayed aloud
In anguish and in agony,
Up-starting from the fiendish crowd
Of shapes and thoughts that tortured me:
A lurid light, a trampling throng,
Sense of intolerable wrong,
And whom I scorned, those only strong!
Thirst of revenge, the powerless will
Still baffled, and yet burning still!
Desire with loathing strangely mixed
On wild or hateful objects fixed.
Fantastic passions! maddening brawl!
And shame and terror over all!
Deeds to be hid which were not hid,
Which all confused I could not know
Whether I suffered, or I did:
For all seemed guilt, remorse or woe,
My own or others still the same
Life-stifling fear, soul-stifling shame.

So two nights passed: the night's dismay
Saddened and stunned the coming day.
Sleep, the wide blessing, seemed to me
Distemper's worst calamity.
The third night, when my own loud scream
Had waked me from the fiendish dream,
O'ercome with sufferings strange and wild,
I wept as I had been a child;
And having thus by tears subdued
My anguish to a milder mood,
Such punishments, I said, were due
To natures depliest stained with sin, —
For aye entempesting anew
The unfathomable hell within,

The horror of their deeds to view,
To know and loathe, yet wish and do!
Such griefs with such men well agree,
But wherefore, wherefore fall on me?
To be beloved is all I need,
And whom I love, I love indeed.

SAMUEL TAYLOR COLERIDGE
ENGLISH (1772–1834)

On Melancholy

No, no! go not to Lethe, neither twist
   Wolf's-bane, tight-rooted, for its poisonous wine;
Nor suffer thy pale forehead to be kissed
   By nightshade, ruby grape of Proserpine;
Make not your rosary of yew-berries,
   Nor let the beetle nor the death-moth be
     Your mournful Psyche, nor the downy owl
A partner in your sorrow's mysteries;
   For shade to shade will come too drowsily,
     And drown the wakeful anguish of the soul.

But when the melancholy fit shall fall
   Sudden from heaven like a weeping cloud,
That fosters the droop-headed flowers all,
   And hides the green hill in an April shroud;
Then glut thy sorrow on a morning rose,
   Or on the rainbow of the salt sand-wave,
     Or on the wealth of globéd peonies;
Or if thy mistress some rich anger shows,
   Emprison her soft hand, and let her rave,
     And feed deep, deep upon her peerless eyes.

She dwells with Beauty — Beauty that must die;
   And Joy, whose hand is ever at his lips
Bidding adieu; and aching Pleasure nigh,
   Turning to poison while the bee-mouth sips:

Ay, in the very temple of Delight
   Veiled Melancholy has her sovran shrine,
      Though seen of none save him whose strenuous tongue
   Can burst Joy's grape against his palate fine:
His soul shall taste the sadness of her might,
   And be among her cloudy trophies hung.

JOHN KEATS
ENGLISH (1795–1821)

I Am

I am: yet what I am none cares or knows
   My friends forsake me like a memory lost;
I am the self-consumer of my woes —
   They rise and vanish in oblivious host,
Like shadows in love's frenzied stifled throes: —
And yet I am, and live — like vapours tost

Into the nothingness of scorn and noise,
   Into the living sea of waking dreams,
Where there is neither sense of life or joys,
   But the vast shipwreck of my life's esteems;
Even the dearest, that I love the best,
Are strange — nay, rather stranger than the rest.

I long for scenes where man hath never trod,
   A place where woman never smiled or wept —
There to abide with my Creator, God,
   And sleep as I in childhood sweetly slept,
Untroubling, and untroubled where I lie,
The grass below — above the vaulted sky.

JOHN CLARE
ENGLISH (1793–1864)

The Rainy Day

The day is cold, and dark, and dreary;
It rains, and the wind is never weary;
The vine still clings to the mouldering wall,
But at every gust the dead leaves fall,
  And the day is dark and dreary.

My life is cold, and dark, and dreary;
It rains, and the wind is never weary;
My thoughts still cling to the mouldering Past,
But the hopes of youth fall thick in the blast,
  And the days are dark and dreary.

Be still, sad heart! and cease repining;
Behind the clouds is the sun still shining;
Thy fate is the common fate of all,
Into each life some rain must fall,
  Some days must be dark and dreary.

HENRY WADSWORTH LONGFELLOW
AMERICAN (1807–1882)

Fall, leaves, fall; die, flowers, away

Fall, leaves, fall; die, flowers, away;
Lengthen night and shorten day;
Every leaf speaks bliss to me
Fluttering from the autumn tree.
I shall smile when wreaths of snow
Blossom where the rose should grow;
I shall sing when night's decay
Ushers in a drearier day.

EMILY BRONTË
ENGLISH (1818–1848)

There's a certain Slant of light

There's a certain Slant of light,
Winter Afternoons —
That oppresses, like the Heft
Of Cathedral Tunes —

Heavenly Hurt, it gives us —
We can find no scar,
But internal difference —
Where the Meanings, are —

None may teach it — Any —
'Tis the Seal Despair —
An imperial affliction
Sent us of the Air —

When it comes, the Landscape listens —
Shadows — hold their breath —
When it goes, 'tis like the Distance
On the look of Death —

EMILY DICKINSON
AMERICAN (1830–1886)

Tears, idle tears, I know not what they mean

Tears, idle tears, I know not what they mean,
Tears from the depth of some divine despair
Rise in the heart, and gather to the eyes,
In looking on the happy autumn-fields,
And thinking of the days that are no more.

Fresh as the first beam glittering on a sail,
That brings our friends up from the underworld,
Sad as the last which reddens over one
That sinks with all we love below the verge;
So sad, so fresh, the days that are no more.

Ah, sad and strange, as in dark summer dawns
The earliest pipe of half-awaken'd birds
To dying ears, when unto dying eyes
The casement slowly grows a glimmering square;
So sad, so strange, the days that are no more.

Dear as remember'd kisses after death,
And sweet as those by hopeless fancy feign'd
On lips that are for others; deep as love,
Deep as first love, and wild with all regret;
O Death in Life, the days that are no more!

ALFRED, LORD TENNYSON
ENGLISH (1809–1892)

Dregs

The fire is out, and spent the warmth thereof,
(This is the end of every song man sings!)
The golden wine is drunk, the dregs remain,
Bitter as wormwood and as salt as pain;
And health and hope have gone the way of love
Into the drear oblivion of lost things.
Ghosts go along with us until the end;
This was a mistress, this, perhaps, a friend.
With pale, indifferent eyes, we sit and wait
For the dropt curtain and the closing gate:
This is the end of all the songs man sings.

ERNEST DOWSON
ENGLISH (1867–1900)

No worst, there is none. Pitched past pitch of grief

No worst, there is none. Pitched past pitch of grief,
More pangs will, schooled at forepangs, wilder wring.
Comforter, where, where is your comforting?
Mary, mother of us, where is your relief?
My cries heave, herds-long; huddle in a main, a chief
Woe, world-sorrow; on an age-old anvil wince and sing —

Then lull, then leave off. Fury had shrieked 'No lingering! Let me be fell: force I must be brief'.

   O the mind, mind has mountains; cliffs of fall
Frightful, sheer, no-man-fathomed. Hold them cheap
May who ne'er hung there. Nor does long our small
Durance deal with that steep or deep. Here! creep,
Wretch, under a comfort serves in a whirlwind: all
Life death does end and each day dies with sleep.

GERARD MANLEY HOPKINS
ENGLISH (1844–1889)

I wake and feel the fell of dark, not day

   I wake and feel the fell of dark, not day.
What hours, O what black hoürs we have spent
This night! what sights you, heart, saw; ways you went!
And more must, in yet longer light's delay.

   With witness I speak this. But where I say
Hours I mean years, mean life. And my lament
Is cries countless, cries like dead letters sent
To dearest him that lives alas! away.

   I am gall, I am heartburn. God's most deep decree
Bitter would have me taste: my taste was me;
Bones built in me, flesh filled, blood brimmed the curse.

   Selfyeast of spirit a dull dough sours. I see
The lost are like this, and their scourge to be
As I am mine, their sweating selves; but worse.

GERARD MANLEY HOPKINS
ENGLISH (1844–1889)

Spring and Fall

to a young child

Márgarét, áre you gríeving
Over Goldengrove unleaving?
Leáves, líke the things of man, you
With your fresh thoughts care for, can you?
Áh! ás the heart grows older
It will come to such sights colder
By and by, nor spare a sigh
Though worlds of wanwood leafmeal lie;
And yet you wíll weep and know why.
Now no matter, child, the name:
Sórrow's spríngs áre the same.
Nor mouth had, no nor mind, expressed
What heart heard of, ghost guessed:
It ís the blight man was born for,
It is Margaret you mourn for.

GERARD MANLEY HOPKINS
ENGLISH (1844–1889)

In the desert

In the desert
I saw a creature, naked, bestial,
Who, squatting upon the ground,
Held his heart in his hands,
And ate of it.
I said, "Is it good, friend?"
"It is bitter — bitter," he answered;
"But I like it
"Because it is bitter,
"And because it is my heart."

STEPHEN CRANE
AMERICAN (1871–1900)

These

are the desolate, dark weeks
when nature in its barrenness
equals the stupidity of man.

The year plunges into night
and the heart plunges
lower than night

to an empty, windswept place
without sun, stars or moon
but a peculiar light as of thought

that spins a dark fire —
whirling upon itself until,
in the cold, it kindles

to make a man aware of nothing
that he knows, not loneliness
itself — Not a ghost but

would be embraced — emptiness,
despair — (They
whine and whistle) among

the flashes and booms of war;
houses of whose rooms
the cold is greater than can be thought,

the people gone that we loved,
the beds lying empty, the couches
damp, the chairs unused —

Hide it away somewhere
out of the mind, let it get roots
and grow, unrelated to jealous

ears and eyes — for itself.
In this mine they come to dig — all.
Is this the counterfoil to sweetest

music? The source of poetry that
seeing the clock stopped, says,
The clock has stopped

that ticked yesterday so well?
and hears the sound of lakewater
splashing — that is now stone.

WILLIAM CARLOS WILLIAMS
AMERICAN (1883–1963)

Résumé

Razors pain you;
Rivers are damp;
Acids stain you;
And drugs cause cramp.
Guns aren't lawful;
Nooses give;
Gas smells awful;
You might as well live.

DOROTHY PARKER
AMERICAN (1893–1967)

Away, Melancholy

Away, melancholy,
Away with it, let it go.

Are not the trees green,
The earth as green?
Does not the wind blow,
Fire leap and the rivers flow?
Away melancholy.

The ant is busy
He carrieth his meat,
All things hurry
To be eaten or eat.
Away, melancholy.

Man, too, hurries,
Eats, couples, buries,
He is an animal also
With a hey ho melancholy,
Away with it, let it go.

Man of all creatures
Is superlative
(Away melancholy)
He of all creatures alone
Raiseth a stone
(Away melancholy)
Into the stone, the god
Pours what he knows of good
Calling, good, God.
Away melancholy, let it go.

Speak not to me of tears,
Tyranny, pox, wars,
Saying, Can God
Stone of man's thought, be good?

Say rather it is enough
That the stuffed
Stone of man's good, growing,
By man's called God.
Away, melancholy, let it go.

Man aspires
To good,
To love
Sighs;

Beaten, corrupted, dying
In his own blood lying
Yet heaves up an eye above
Cries, Love, love.
It is his virtue needs explaining,
Not his failing.

Away, melancholy,
Away with it, let it go.

STEVIE SMITH
ENGLISH (1902–1971)

ENDURANCE, RESISTANCE, AND SURVIVAL

*To Toussaint L'Ouverture,
Leader of the African Slaves of San Domingo,
Imprisoned by Napoleon*

Toussaint, the most unhappy man of men!
  Whether the whistling rustic tend his plough
  Within thy hearing, or thy head be now
Pillowed in some deep dungeon's earless den; —
O miserable Chieftain! where and when
  Wilt thou find patience! Yet die not; do thou
  Wear rather in thy bonds a cheerful brow:
Though fallen thyself, never to rise again,
Live, and take comfort. Thou hast left behind
  Powers that will work for thee; air, earth, and skies;
There's not a breathing of the common wind
  That will forget thee; thou hast great allies;
  Thy friends are exultations, agonies,
And love, and man's unconquerable mind.

WILLIAM WORDSWORTH
ENGLISH (1770–1850)

No coward soul is mine

No coward soul is mine,
No trembler in the world's storm-troubled sphere:
  I see Heaven's glories shine,
And Faith shines equal, arming me from Fear.

  O God within my breast,
Almighty, ever-present Deity!
  Life, that in me hast rest
As I, undying Life, have power in Thee!

  Vain are the thousand creeds
That move men's hearts: unutterably vain;
  Worthless as withered weeds,
Or idlest froth amid the boundless main,

  To waken doubt in one
Holding so fast by Thy infinity,
  So surely anchored on
The steadfast rock of Immortality.

  With wide-embracing love
Thy Spirit animates eternal years,
  Pervades and broods above,
Changes, sustains, dissolves, creates, and rears.

  Though earth and moon were gone,
And suns and universes ceased to be,
  And Thou wert left alone,
Every existence would exist in Thee.

  There is not room for Death,
Nor atom that his might could render void:
  Since Thou art Being and Breath
And what Thou art may never be destroyed.

EMILY BRONTË
ENGLISH (1818–1848)

No Rack can torture me

No Rack can torture me —
My Soul — at Liberty —
Behind this mortal Bone
There knits a bolder One —

You cannot prick with Saw —
Nor pierce with Cimitar —
Two Bodies — therefore be —
Bind One — The Other fly —

The Eagle of his Nest
No easier divest —
And gain the Sky
Than mayest Thou —

Except Thyself may be
Thine Enemy —
Captivity is Consciousness —
So's Liberty —

EMILY DICKINSON
AMERICAN (1830–1886)

The Tuft of Kelp

All dripping in tangles green,
    Cast up by a lonely sea,
If purer for that, O Weed,
    Bitterer, too, are ye?

HERMAN MELVILLE
AMERICAN (1819–1891)

Say Not the Struggle Nought Availeth

Say not the struggle nought availeth,
   The labour and the wounds are vain,
The enemy faints not, nor faileth,
   And as things have been they remain.

If hopes were dupes, fears may be liars;
   It may be, in yon smoke concealed,
Your comrades chase e'en now the fliers,
   And, but for you, possess the field.

For while the tired waves, vainly breaking,
   Seem here no painful inch to gain,
Far back, through creeks and inlets making,
   Comes silent, flooding in, the main.

And not by eastern windows only,
   When daylight comes, comes in the light,
In front, the sun climbs slow, how slowly,
   But westward, look, the land is bright.

                 ARTHUR HUGH CLOUGH
                 ENGLISH (1819–1861)

Sympathy

I know what the caged bird feels, alas!
   When the sun is bright on the upland slopes;
When the wind stirs soft through the springing grass,
And the river flows like a stream of glass;
   When the first bird sings and the first bud opes,
And the faint perfume from its chalice steals —
I know what the caged bird feels!

I know why the caged bird beats his wing
   Till its blood is red on the cruel bars;
For he must fly back to his perch and cling
When he fain would be on the bough a-swing;
   And a pain still throbs in the old, old scars

And they pulse again with a keener sting —
I know why he beats his wing!

I know why the caged bird sings, ah me,
   When his wing is bruised and his bosom sore, —
When he beats his bars and he would be free;
It is not a carol of joy or glee,
   But a prayer that he sends from his heart's deep core,
But a plea, that upward to Heaven he flings —
I know why the caged bird sings!

PAUL LAURENCE DUNBAR
AMERICAN (1872–1906)

We Wear the Mask

We wear the mask that grins and lies,
It hides our cheeks and shades our eyes —
This debt we pay to human guile;
With torn and bleeding hearts we smile
And mouth with myriad subtleties,

Why should the world be over-wise,
In counting all our tears and sighs?
Nay, let them only see us, while
   We wear the mask.

We smile, but oh great Christ, our cries
To Thee from tortured souls arise.
We sing, but oh the clay is vile
Beneath our feet, and long the mile,
But let the world dream otherwise,
   We wear the mask!

PAUL LAURENCE DUNBAR
AMERICAN (1872–1906)

If We Must Die

If we must die, let it not be like hogs
Hunted and penned in an inglorious spot,
While round us bark the mad and hungry dogs,
Making their mock at our accursed lot.
If we must die, O let us nobly die,
So that our precious blood may not be shed
In vain; then even the monsters we defy
Shall be constrained to honor us though dead!
O kinsmen! we must meet the common foe!
Though far outnumbered let us show us brave,
And for their thousand blows deal one deathblow!
What though before us lies the open grave?
Like men we'll face the murderous, cowardly pack,
Pressed to the wall, dying, but fighting back!

CLAUDE MCKAY
AMERICAN (1890–1948)

Musée des Beaux Arts

About suffering they were never wrong,
The Old Masters: how well they understood
Its human position; how it takes place
While someone else is eating or opening a window or just
                                        walking dully along;
How, when the aged are reverently, passionately waiting
For the miraculous birth, there always must be
Children who did not specially want it to happen, skating
On a pond at the edge of the wood:
They never forgot
That even the dreadful martyrdom must run its course
Anyhow in a corner, some untidy spot
Where the dogs go on with their doggy
                                life and the torturer's horse
Scratches its innocent behind on a tree.
In Brueghel's *Icarus,* for instance: how everything turns away
Quite leisurely from the disaster; the ploughman may

Have heard the splash, the forsaken cry,
But for him it was not an important failure; the sun shone
As it had to on the white legs disappearing into the green
Water; and the expensive delicate ship that must have seen
Something amazing, a boy falling out of the sky,
Had somewhere to get to and sailed calmly on.

W. H. AUDEN
ENGLISH (1907–1973)

Spiritual Awakening

The Flower

How fresh, O Lord, how sweet and clean
Are thy returns! even as the flowers in spring,
   To which, besides their own demean,
The late-past frosts tributes of pleasure bring,
         Grief melts away
         Like snow in May,
As if there were no such cold thing.

Who would have thought my shrivelled heart
Could have recovered greenness? It was gone
   Quite underground; as flowers depart
To see their mother-root, when they have blown;
         Where they together
         All the hard weather,
Dead to the world, keep house unknown.

These are thy wonders, Lord of power,
Killing and quickening, bringing down to hell
   And up to heaven in an hour;
Making a chiming of a passing-bell.
         We say amiss,
         This or that is.
Thy word is all, if we could spell.

O that I once past changing were,
Fast in thy Paradise, where no flower can wither!
Many a spring I shoot up fair,
Offering at heaven, growing and groaning thither:
Nor doth my flower
Want a spring shower,
My sins and I joining together.

But while I grow in a straight line,
Still upwards bent, as if heaven were mine own,
Thy anger comes and I decline:
What frost to that? what pole is not the zone,
Where all things burn,
When thou dost turn,
And the least frown of thine is shown?

And now in age I bud again,
After so many deaths I live and write;
I once more smell the dew and rain,
And relish versing: O my only light,
It cannot be
That I am he
On whom thy tempests fell all night.

These are thy wonders, Lord of love,
To make us see we are but flowers that glide;
Which when we once can find and prove,
Thou hast a garden for us, where to bide.
Who would be more,
Swelling through store,
Forfeit their Paradise by their pride.

GEORGE HERBERT
ENGLISH (1593–1633)

Love

Love bade me welcome; yet my soul drew back,
    Guilty of dust and sin.
But quick-eyed Love, observing me grow slack
    From my first entrance in,
Drew nearer to me, sweetly questioning
    If I lack'd anything.

'A guest,' I answer'd, 'worthy to be here:'
    Love said, 'You shall be he.'
'I, the unkind, ungrateful? Ah, my dear,
    I cannot look on Thee.'
Love took my hand and smiling did reply,
    'Who made the eyes but I?'

'Truth, Lord; but I have marr'd them: let my shame
    Go where it doth deserve.'
'And know you not,' says Love, 'Who bore the blame?'
    'My dear, then I will serve.'
'You must sit down,' says Love, 'and taste my meat.'
    So I did sit and eat.

GEORGE HERBERT
ENGLISH (1593–1633)

And did those feet in ancient time

And did those feet in ancient time
Walk upon England's mountains green?
And was the holy Lamb of God
On England's pleasant pastures seen?

And did the Countenance Divine
Shine forth upon our clouded hills?
And was Jerusalem builded here
Among these dark Satanic Mills?

Bring me my Bow of burning gold!
Bring me my Arrows of desire!

Bring me my Spear! O clouds unfold!
Bring me my Chariot of fire!

I will not cease from Mental Fight,
Nor shall my Sword sleep in my hand,
Till we have built Jerusalem
In England's green and pleasant Land.

WILLIAM BLAKE
ENGLISH (1757–1827)

Simple Gifts

'Tis the gift to be simple, 'tis the gift to be free,
'Tis the gift to come down where we ought to be,
And when we find ourselves in the place just right,
'Twill be in the valley of love and delight.
When true simplicity is gain'd,
To bow and to bend we shan't be asham'd,
To turn, turn will be our delight
'Till by turning, turning we come round right.

ANONYMOUS (SHAKER HYMN)
AMERICAN (C. 1848)

Sursum Corda

Seek not the spirit, if it hide
Inexorable to thy zeal:
Baby, do not whine and chide:
Art thou not also real?
Why shouldst thou stoop to poor excuse?
Turn on the accuser roundly; say,
"Here am I, here will I remain
For ever to myself soothfast;
Go thou, sweet Heaven, or at thy pleasure stay!"
Already Heaven with thee its lot has cast,
For only it can absolutely deal.

RALPH WALDO EMERSON
AMERICAN (1803–1882)

A Noiseless Patient Spider

A noiseless patient spider,
I mark'd where on a little promontory it stood isolated,
Mark'd how to explore the vacant vast surrounding,
It launch'd forth filament, filament, filament, out of itself,
Ever unreeling them, ever tirelessly speeding them.

And you O my soul where you stand,
Surrounded, detached, in measureless oceans of space,
Ceaselessly musing, venturing, throwing, seeking the spheres to
    connect them,
Till the bridge you will need be form'd, till the ductile anchor
    hold,
Till the gossamer thread you fling catch somewhere, O my soul.

WALT WHITMAN
AMERICAN (1819–1892)

The Thread of Life

1

The irresponsive silence of the land,
    The irresponsive sounding of the sea,
    Speak both one message of one sense to me: —
Aloof, aloof, we stand aloof, so stand
Thou too aloof bound with the flawless band
    Of inner solitude; we bind not thee;
    But who from thy self-chain shall set thee free?
What heart shall touch thy heart? what hand thy hand? —
And I am sometimes proud and sometimes meek,
    And sometimes I remember days of old
When fellowship seemed not so far to seek
    And all the world and I seemed much less cold,
    And at the rainbow's foot lay surely gold,
And hope felt strong and life itself not weak.

2

Thus am I mine own prison. Everything
    Around me free and sunny and at ease:
    Or if in shadow, in a shade of trees
Which the sun kisses, where the gay birds sing

And where all winds make various murmuring;
   Where bees are found, with honey for the bees;
   Where sounds are music, and where silences
Are music of an unlike fashioning.
Then gaze I at the merrymaking crew,
   And smile a moment and a moment sigh
Thinking: Why can I not rejoice with you?
   But soon I put the foolish fancy by:
I am not what I have nor what I do;
   But what I was I am, I am even I.

3

Therefore myself is that one only thing
   I hold to use or waste, to keep or give;
   My sole possession every day I live,
And still mine own despite Time's winnowing.
Ever mine own, while moons and seasons bring
   From crudeness ripeness mellow and sanative;
   Ever mine own, till Death shall ply his sieve;
And still mine own, when saints break grave and sing.
And this myself as king unto my King
   I give, to Him Who gave Himself for me;
Who gives Himself to me, and bids me sing
   A sweet new song of His redeemed set free;
He bids me sing: O death, where is thy sting?
   And sing: O grave, where is thy victory?

CHRISTINA ROSSETTI
ENGLISH (1830–1894)

Archaic Torso of Apollo

We never knew his head and all the light
that ripened in his fabled eyes. But
his torso still glows like a candelabra,
in which his gazing, turned down low,

holds fast and shines. Otherwise the surge
of the breast could not blind you, nor a smile
run through the slight twist of the loins
toward that center where procreation thrived.

Otherwise this stone would stand deformed and curt
under the shoulders' invisible plunge
and not glisten just like wild beasts' fur;

and not burst forth from all its contours
like a star: for there is no place
that does not see you. You must change your life.

> RAINER MARIA RILKE
> GERMAN (1875–1926)
> TRANSLATED BY EDWARD SNOW

On a terribly clear day

On a terribly clear day,
A day that made you wish you'd worked very hard
So you'd not work at all that day,
I caught a glimpse, like a road through the trees,
Of what might after all be the Big Secret,
That Great Mystery crooked poets talk about.

I saw that there is no Nature,
That Nature does not exist,
That there are mountains, valleys, plains,
That there are trees, flowers, grasses,
That there are rivers and stones,
But that there's no one great All these things belong to,
That any really authentic unity
Is a sickness of all our ideas.

Nature is simply parts, nothing whole.
Maybe this is the mystery they talk about.

And this, without stopping, without thinking,
Is just what I hit on as being the truth
That everyone goes around looking for in vain,
And that only I, because I wasn't looking for it, found.

> FERNANDO PESSOA (WRITING AS ALBERTO CAEIRO)
> PORTUGUESE (1888–1935)
> TRANSLATED BY EDWIN HONIG AND SUSAN M. BROWN

Gratitude to the Unknown Instructors

What they undertook to do
They brought to pass;
All things hang like a drop of dew
Upon a blade of grass.

WILLIAM BUTLER YEATS
IRISH (1865–1939)

Phoenix

Are you willing to be sponged out, erased, cancelled,
made nothing?
Are you willing to be made nothing?
dipped into oblivion?

If not, you will never really change.

The phoenix renews her youth
only when she is burnt, burnt alive, burnt down
to hot and flocculent ash.
Then the small stirring of a new small bub in the nest
with strands of down like floating ash
shows that she is renewing her youth like the eagle,
immortal bird.

D. H. LAWRENCE
ENGLISH (1885–1930)

Sunflower Sutra

I walked on the banks of the tincan banana dock and sat down
    under the huge shade of a Southern Pacific locomotive to look
    at the sunset over the box house hills and cry.
Jack Kerouac sat beside me on a busted rusty iron pole,
    companion, we thought the same thoughts of the soul, bleak
    and blue and sad-eyed, surrounded by the gnarled steel roots
    of trees of machinery.
The oily water on the river mirrored by the red sky, sun sank on
    top of final Frisco peaks, no fish in that stream, no hermit in

those mounts, just ourselves rheumy-eyed and hungover like
old bums on the riverbank, tired and wily.

Look at the Sunflower, he said, there was a dead gray shadow
against the sky, big as a man, sitting dry on top of a pile of
ancient sawdust —

— I rushed up enchanted — it was my first sunflower, memories
of Blake — my visions — Harlem

and Hells of the Eastern rivers, bridges clanking, Joes Greasy
Sandwiches, dead baby carriages, black treadless tires forgotten
and unretreaded, the poem of the riverbank, condoms & pots,
steel knives, nothing stainless, only the dank muck and the
razor sharp artifacts passing into the past —

and the gray Sunflower poised against the sunset, crackly bleak
and dusty with the smut and smog and smoke of olden
locomotives in its eye —

corolla of bleary spikes pushed down and broken like a battered
crown, seeds fallen out of its face, soon-to-be-toothless mouth
of sunny air, sunrays obliterated on its hairy head like a dried
wire spiderweb,

leaves stuck out like arms out of the stem, gestures from the
sawdust root, broke pieces of plaster fallen out of the black
twigs, a dead fly in its ear,

Unholy battered old thing you were, my sunflower O my soul, I
loved you then!

The grime was no man's grime but death and human
locomotives,

all that dress of dust, that veil of darkened railroad skin, that
smog of cheek, that eyelid of black mis'ry, that sooty hand or
phallus or protuberance of artificial worse-than-dirt —
industrial — modern — all that civilization spotting your crazy
golden crown —

and those blear thoughts of death and dusty loveless eyes and
ends and withered roots below, in the home-pile of sand and
sawdust, rubber dollar bills, skin of machinery, the guts and
innards of the weeping coughing car, the empty lonely tincans
with their rusty tongues alack, what more could I name, the
smoked ashes of some cock cigar, the cunts of wheelbarrows
and the milky breasts of cars, wornout asses out of chairs &
sphincters of dynamos — all these

entangled in your mummied roots — and you there standing
  before me in the sunset, all your glory in your form!
A perfect beauty of a sunflower! a perfect excellent lovely
  sunflower existence! a sweet natural eye to the new hip moon,
  woke up alive and excited grasping in the sunset shadow
  sunrise golden monthly breeze!
How many flies buzzed round you innocent of your grime, while
  you cursed the heavens of the railroad and your flower soul?
Poor dead flower? when did you forget you were a flower? when
  did you look at your skin and decide you were an impotent
  dirty old locomotive? the ghost of a locomotive? the specter
  and shade of a once powerful mad American locomotive?
You were never no locomotive, Sunflower, you were a sunflower!
And you Locomotive, you are a locomotive, forget me not!
So I grabbed up the skeleton thick sunflower and stuck it at my
  side like a scepter,
and deliver my sermon to my soul, and Jack's soul too, and
  anyone who'll listen,
— We're not our skin of grime, we're not our dread bleak dusty
  imageless locomotive, we're all beautiful golden sunflowers
  inside, we're blessed by our own seed & golden hairy naked
  accomplishment-bodies growing into mad black formal
  sunflowers in the sunset, spied on by our eyes under the
  shadow of the mad locomotive riverbank sunset Frisco hilly
  tincan evening sitdown vision.

ALLEN GINSBERG
AMERICAN (1926–1997)

In a Dark Time

In a dark time, the eye begins to see,
I meet my shadow in the deepening shade;
I hear my echo in the echoing wood —
A lord of nature weeping to a tree.
I live between the heron and the wren,
Beasts of the hill and serpents of the den.

What's madness but nobility of soul
At odds with circumstance? The day's on fire!

I know the purity of pure despair,
My shadow pinned against a sweating wall.
That place among the rocks — is it a cave,
Or winding path? The edge is what I have.

A steady storm of correspondences!
A night flowing with birds, a ragged moon,
And in broad day the midnight come again!
A man goes far to find out what he is —
Death of the self in a long, tearless night,
All natural shapes blazing unnatural light.

Dark, dark my light, and darker my desire.
My soul, like some heat-maddened summer fly,
Keeps buzzing at the sill. Which I is *I*?
A fallen man, I climb out of my fear.
The mind enters itself, and God the mind,
And one is One, free in the tearing wind.

THEODORE ROETHKE
AMERICAN (1908–1963)

Public Moments and Ultimate Matters

THIS SECTION EXPLORES WAYS IN WHICH POETS OF DIFFERENT ERAS HAVE GRAPPLED WITH THE ABIDING THEMES OF COMMUNAL LIFE, HUMAN CONFLICT, AND THE ULTIMATE riddle of existence. From wars, upheavals, and every manner of public crisis, public triumph, public disaster, all the way to Wallace Stevens's "palm at the end of the mind," these poems chart a continual concern with mapping the world, the universe — and the unknowable that might lie in or beyond that universe — within which the poet is speaking. It is never a question of how large or how small is the subject under examination — a sudden, scarcely audible intake of breath or a panoramic view of the night sky, rainfall on a battlefield or a death scene glimpsed in an old painting — but only of the relation of parts within the whole.

Poets tend to offer not answers but questions, questions so vividly and completely inhabited that they no longer seem to require an answer. It is rare that one can speak of "happy" or "sad" poems, of "optimistic" or "pessimistic" readings of the world. What can be glibly summed up in a slogan or a tagline will not get close to the heart of the poetic matter.

THE FATES OF NATIONS AND EMPIRES

Spring Prospect

The nation shattered, hills and streams remain.
The city in spring, grass and trees deep:
feeling the times, flowers draw tears;
hating separation, birds alarm the heart.
Beacon fires three months running,
a letter from home worth ten thousand in gold —
white hairs, fewer for the scratching,
soon too few to hold a hairpin up.

TU FU
CHINESE (712–770)
TRANSLATED BY BURTON WATSON

When I have seen by Time's fell hand defac'd

When I have seen by Time's fell hand defac'd
The rich-proud cost of outworn buried age;
When sometime lofty towers I see down-razed,
And brass eternal slave to mortal rage;
When I have seen the hungry ocean gain
Advantage on the kingdom of the shore,
And the firm soil win of the watery main,
Increasing store with loss, and loss with store;
When I have seen such interchange of state,
Or state itself confounded to decay;
Ruin hath taught me thus to ruminate —
That Time will come and take my love away.
This thought is as a death, which cannot choose
But weep to have that which it fears to lose.

WILLIAM SHAKESPEARE
ENGLISH (1564–1616)

PUBLIC
MOMENTS
AND
ULTIMATE
MATTERS
414

On the Extinction of the Venetian Republic

Once did She hold the gorgeous east in fee;
And was the safeguard of the west: the worth
Of Venice did not fall below her birth,
Venice, the eldest Child of Liberty.
She was a maiden City, bright and free;
No guile seduced, no force could violate;
And, when she took unto herself a Mate,
She must espouse the everlasting Sea.
And what if she had seen those glories fade,
Those titles vanish, and that strength decay;
Yet shall some tribute of regret be paid
When her long life hath reached its final day:
Men are we, and must grieve when even the Shade
Of that which once was great is passed away.

WILLIAM WORDSWORTH
ENGLISH (1770–1850)

Ozymandias

I met a traveller from an antique land
Who said: Two vast and trunkless legs of stone
Stand in the desert . . . Near them, on the sand,
Half sunk, a shattered visage lies, whose frown,
And wrinkled lip, and sneer of cold command,
Tell that its sculptor well those passions read
Which yet survive, stamped on these lifeless things,
The hand that mocked them, and the heart that fed:
And on the pedestal these words appear:
'My name is Ozymandias, king of kings:
Look on my works, ye Mighty, and despair!'
Nothing beside remains. Round the decay
Of that colossal wreck, boundless and bare
The lone and level sands stretch far away.

PERCY BYSSHE SHELLEY
ENGLISH (1792–1822)

Love among the Ruins

Where the quiet-coloured end of evening smiles,
  Miles and miles
On the solitary pastures where our sheep
  Half-asleep
Tinkle homeward through the twilight, stray or stop
  As they crop —
Was the site once of a city great and gay,
  (So they say)
Of our country's very capital, its prince
  Ages since
Held his court in, gathered councils, wielding far
  Peace or war.

Now, — the country does not even boast a tree,
  As you see,
To distinguish slopes of verdure, certain rills
  From the hills
Intersect and give a name to, (else they run
  Into one)
Where the domed and daring palace shot its spires
  Up like fires
O'er the hundred-gated circuit of a wall
  Bounding all,
Made of marble, men might march on nor be pressed,
  Twelve abreast.

And such plenty and perfection, see, of grass
  Never was!
Such a carpet as, this summer time, o'erspreads
  And embeds
Every vestige of the city, guessed alone,
  Stock or stone —
Where a multitude of men breathed joy and woe
  Long ago;
Lust of glory pricked their hearts up, dread of shame
  Struck them tame;
And that glory and that shame alike, the gold
  Bought and sold.

PUBLIC
MOMENTS
AND
ULTIMATE
MATTERS
416 |

Now, — the single little turret that remains
    On the plains,
By the caper overrooted, by the gourd
    Overscored,
While the patching houseleek's head of blossom winks
    Through the chinks —
Marks the basement whence a tower in ancient time
    Sprang sublime,
And a burning ring, all round, the chariots traced
    As they raced,
And the monarch and his minions and his dames
    Viewed the games.

And I know, while thus the quiet-coloured eve
    Smiles to leave
To their folding, all our many-tinkling fleece
    In such peace,
And the slopes and rills in undistinguished grey
    Melt away —
That a girl with eager eyes and yellow hair
    Waits me there
In the turret whence the charioteers caught soul
    For the goal,
When the king looked, where she looks now, breathless, dumb
    Till I come.

But he looked upon the city, every side,
    Far and wide,
All the mountains topped with temples, all the glades'
    Colonnades,
All the causeys, bridges, aqueducts, — and then,
    All the men!
When I do come, she will speak not, she will stand,
    Either hand
On my shoulder, give her eyes the first embrace
    Of my face,
Ere we rush, ere we extinguish sight and speech
    Each on each.

In one year they sent a million fighters forth
    South and North,
And they built their gods a brazen pillar high
    As the sky,
Yet reserved a thousand chariots in full force —
    Gold, of course.
Oh heart! oh blood that freezes, blood that burns!
    Earth's returns
For whole centuries of folly, noise and sin!
    Shut them in,
With their triumphs and their glories and the rest!
    Love is best!

ROBERT BROWNING
ENGLISH (1812–1889)

In Time of "The Breaking of Nations"

I

Only a man harrowing clods
    In a slow silent walk
With an old horse that stumbles and nods
    Half asleep as they stalk.

II

Only thin smoke without flame
    From the heaps of couch-grass;
Yet this will go onward the same
    Though Dynasties pass.

III

Yonder a maid and her wight
    Come whispering by:
War's annals will cloud into night
    Ere their story die.

THOMAS HARDY
ENGLISH (1840–1928)

PUBLIC
MOMENTS
AND
ULTIMATE
MATTERS
418

Recessional

God of our fathers, known of old,
   Lord of our far-flung battle-line,
Beneath whose awful Hand we hold
   Dominion over palm and pine —
Lord God of Hosts, be with us yet,
Lest we forget — lest we forget!

The tumult and the shouting dies;
   The Captains and the Kings depart:
Still stands Thine ancient sacrifice,
   An humble and a contrite heart.
Lord God of Hosts, be with us yet,
Lest we forget — lest we forget!

Far-called, our navies melt away;
   On dune and headland sinks the fire:
Lo, all our pomp of yesterday
   Is one with Nineveh and Tyre!
Judge of the Nations, spare us yet,
Lest we forget — lest we forget!

If, drunk with sight of power, we loose
   Wild tongues that have not Thee in awe,
Such boastings as the Gentiles use,
   Or lesser breeds without the Law —
Lord God of Hosts, be with us yet,
Lest we forget — lest we forget!

For heathen heart that puts her trust
   In reeking tube and iron shard,
All valiant dust that builds on dust,
   And guarding, calls not Thee to guard,
For frantic boast and foolish word —
Thy mercy on Thy People, Lord!

RUDYARD KIPLING
ENGLISH (1865–1936)

Cities and Thrones and Powers

Cities and Thrones and Powers
　Stand in Time's eye,
Almost as long as flowers,
　Which daily die:
But, as new buds put forth
　To glad new men,
Out of the spent and unconsidered Earth
　The Cities rise again.

This season's Daffodil
　She never hears
What change, what chance, what chill,
　Cut down last year's;
But with bold countenance,
　And knowledge small,
Esteems her seven days' continuance
　To be perpetual.

So Time that is o'erkind
　To all that be,
Ordains us e'en as blind,
　As bold as she:
That in our very death,
　And burial sure,
Shadow to shadow, well persuaded, saith,
　'See how our works endure!'

RUDYARD KIPLING
ENGLISH (1865–1936)

Things Ended

Possessed by fear and suspicion,
mind agitated, eyes alarmed,
we desperately invent ways out,
plan how to avoid the inevitable
danger that threatens us so terribly.
Yet we're mistaken, that's not the danger ahead:

PUBLIC
MOMENTS
AND
ULTIMATE
MATTERS
420

the information was false
(or we didn't hear it, or didn't get it right).
Another disaster, one we never imagined,
suddenly, violently, descends upon us,
and finding us unprepared — there's no time left —
sweeps us away.

C. P. CAVAFY
GREEK (1863–1933)
TRANSLATED BY EDMUND KEELEY AND PHILIP SHERRARD

In Time of War

Thermopylae

Go tell the Spartans, thou that passest by,
That here, obedient to their laws, we lie.

SIMONIDES
GREEK (C. 556–C. 468 B.C.)
TRANSLATED BY WILLIAM LISLE BOWLES

The glories of our blood and state

The glories of our blood and state
   Are shadows, not substantial things;
There is no armour against Fate;
   Death lays his icy hand on kings:
      Sceptre and crown
      Must tumble down,
And in the dust by equal made
With the poor crooked scythe and spade.

Some men with swords may reap the field,
   And plant fresh laurels where they kill;
But their strong nerves at last must yield;
   They tame but one another still:
      Early or late,
      They stoop to fate,

And must give up their murmurming breath,
When they, pale captives, creep to death.

The garlands wither on your brow,
  Then boast no more your mighty deeds;
Upon Death's purple altar now
  See where the victor-victim bleeds:
      Your heads must come
      To the cold tomb;
Only the actions of the just
Smell sweet and blossom in the dust.

JAMES SHIRLEY
ENGLISH (1596–1666)

I hate that drum's discordant sound

  I hate that drum's discordant sound,
  Parading round, and round, and round:
  To thoughtless youth it pleasure yields,
  And lures from cities and from fields,
  To sell their liberty for charms
  Of tawdry lace, and glittering arms;
  And when Ambition's voice commands,
To march, and fight, and fall, in foreign lands.

  I hate that drum's discordant sound,
  Parading round, and round, and round:
  To me it talks of ravaged plains,
  And burning towns, and ruined swains,
  And mangled limbs, and dying groans,
  And widows' tears, and orphans' moans;
  And all that Misery's hand bestows.
To fill the catalogue of human woes.

JOHN SCOTT OF AMWELL
SCOTTISH (1730–1783)

PUBLIC
MOMENTS
AND
ULTIMATE
MATTERS
422

How sleep the brave, who sink to rest

How sleep the brave, who sink to rest
By all their country's wishes blessed!
When Spring with dewy fingers cold
Returns to deck their hallowed mould,
She there shall dress a sweeter sod
Than Fancy's feet have ever trod.

By fairy hands their knell is rung;
By forms unseen their dirge is sung;
There Honour comes, a pilgrim gray,
To bless the turf that wraps their clay;
And Freedom shall awhile repair,
To dwell a weeping hermit there.

WILLIAM COLLINS
ENGLISH (1721–1759)

Breathes there the man with soul so dead

Breathes there the man with soul so dead
Who never to himself hath said,
This is my own, my native land!
Whose heart hath ne'er within him burned,
As home his footsteps he hath turned
From wandering on a foreign strand?
If such there breathe, go, mark him well;
For him no minstrel raptures swell;
High though his titles, proud his name,
Boundless his wealth as wish can claim,
Despite those titles, power, and pelf,
The wretch, concentred all in self,
Living, shall forfeit fair renown,
And, doubly dying, shall go down
To the vile dust from whence he sprung,
Unwept, unhonored, and unsung.

SIR WALTER SCOTT
SCOTTISH (1771–1832)

The Battle of Blenheim

It was a summer evening,
　　Old Kaspar's work was done,
And he before his cottage door
　　Was sitting in the sun;
And by him sported on the green
His little grandchild Wilhelmine.

She saw her brother Peterkin
　　Roll something large and round,
Which he beside the rivulet
　　In playing there had found:
He came to ask what he had found,
That was so large, and smooth, and round.

Old Kaspar took it from the boy,
　　Who stood expectant by;
And then the old man shook his head,
　　And, with a natural sigh,
"'Tis some poor fellow's skull," said he,
"Who fell in the great victory!

"I find them in the garden,
　　For there's many here about;
And often when I go to plough,
　　The ploughshare turns them out;
For many thousand men," said he,
"Were slain in that great victory!"

"Now, tell us what 'twas all about,"
　　Young Peterkin he cries;
And little Wilhelmine looks up
　　With wonder-waiting eyes;
"Now tell us all about the war,
And what they fought each other for."

"It was the English," Kaspar cried,
　　"Who put the French to rout;

PUBLIC
MOMENTS
AND
ULTIMATE
MATTERS
424 |

But what they fought each other for
   I could not well make out.
But everybody said," quoth he,
   "That 'twas a famous victory!

"My father lived at Blenheim then,
   Yon little stream hard by;
They burn'd his dwelling to the ground,
   And he was forced to fly:
So with his wife and child he fled,
Nor had he where to rest his head.

"With fire and sword the country round
   Was wasted far and wide:
And many a childing mother then
   And new-born baby died.
But things like that, you know, must be
At every famous victory.

"They say it was a shocking sight
   After the field was won;
For many thousand bodies here
   Lay rotting in the sun.
But things like that, you know, must be
After a famous victory.

"Great praise the Duke of Marlb'ro' won,
   And our good Prince Eugene."
"Why, 'twas a very wicked thing!"
   Said little Wilhelmine.
"Nay, nay, my little girl," quoth he,
"It was a famous victory!

"And everybody praised the Duke
  Who such a fight did win."
"But what good came of it at last?"
  Quoth little Peterkin.
"Why, that I cannot tell," said he,
"But 'twas a famous victory!"

ROBERT SOUTHEY
ENGLISH (1774–1843)

The Charge of the Light Brigade

Half a league, half a league,
  Half a league onward,
All in the valley of Death
  Rode the six hundred.
"Forward the Light Brigade!
Charge the guns!" he said:
Into the valley of Death
  Rode the six hundred.

"Forward the Light Brigade!"
Was there a man dismay'd?
Not tho' the soldier knew
  Some one had blunder'd:
Theirs not to make reply,
Theirs not to reason why,
Theirs but to do and die:
Into the valley of Death
  Rode the six hundred.

Cannon to right of them,
Cannon to left of them,
Cannon in front of them
  Volley'd and thunder'd;
Storm'd at with shot and shell,
Boldly they rode and well,
Into the jaws of Death,
Into the mouth of Hell,
  Rode the six hundred.

PUBLIC
MOMENTS
AND
ULTIMATE
MATTERS
426

Flash'd all their sabres bare,
Flash'd as they turn'd in air,
Sabring the gunners there,
Charging an army, while
   All the world wonder'd:
Plunged in the battery-smoke
Right thro' the line they broke;
Cossack and Russian
Reel'd from the sabre-stroke
   Shatter'd and sunder'd.
Then they rode back, but not,
   Not the six hundred.

Cannon to right of them,
Cannon to left of them,
Cannon behind them
   Volley'd and thunder'd;
Storm'd at with shot and shell,
While horse and hero fell,
They that had fought so well
Came thro' the jaws of Death,
Back from the mouth of Hell,
All that was left of them,
   Left of six hundred.

When can their glory fade?
O the wild charge they made!
   All the world wonder'd.
Honour the charge they made!
Honour the Light Brigade,
   Noble six hundred!

ALFRED, LORD TENNYSON
ENGLISH (1809–1892)

War Is Kind

Do not weep, maiden, for war is kind.
Because your lover threw wild hands toward the sky
And the affrighted steed ran on alone,
Do not weep.
War is kind.

Hoarse, booming drums of regiment,
Little souls who thirst for fight,
These men were born to drill and die.
The unexplained glory flies above them,
Great is the battle-god, great, and his kingdom —
A field where a thousand corpses lie.

Do not weep, babe, for war is kind.
Because your father tumbled in the yellow trenches,
Raged at his breast, gulped and died,
Do not weep.
War is kind.

Swift blazing flag of the regiment,
Eagle with crest of red and gold,
These men were born to drill and die.
Point for them the virtue of slaughter,
Make plain to them the excellence of killing
And a field where a thousand corpses lie.

Mother whose heart hung humble as a button
On the bright splendid shroud of your son,
Do not weep.
War is kind.

STEPHEN CRANE
AMERICAN (1871–1900)

PUBLIC
MOMENTS
AND
ULTIMATE
MATTERS
428

Tommy

I went into a public-'ouse to get a pint o' beer,
The publican 'e up an' sez, "We serve no red-coats here."
The girls be'ind the bar they laughed an' giggled fit to die,
I outs into the street again an' to myself sez I:
O it's Tommy this, an' Tommy that, an' "Tommy, go away";
But it's "Thank you, Mister Atkins", when the band begins to
    play,
The band begins to play, my boys, the band begins to play,
O it's "Thank you, Mister Atkins", when the band begins to play.

I went into a theatre as sober as could be,
They gave a drunk civilian room, but 'adn't none for me;
They sent me to the gallery or round the music-'alls,
But when it comes to fightin', Lord! they'll shove me in the stalls!
For it's Tommy this, an' Tommy that, an' "Tommy, wait outside";
But it's "Special train for Atkins" when the trooper's on the tide,
The troopship's on the tide, my boys, the troopship's on the tide,
O it's "Special train for Atkins" when the trooper's on the tide.

Yes, makin' mock o' uniforms that guard you while you sleep
Is cheaper than them uniforms, an' they're starvation cheap;
An' hustlin' drunken soldiers when they're goin' large a bit
Is five times better business than paradin' in full kit.
Then it's Tommy this, an' Tommy that, an' "Tommy, 'ow's yer
    soul?"
But it's "Thin red line of 'eroes" when the drums begin to roll,
The drums begin to roll, my boys, the drums begin to roll,
O it's "Thin red line of 'eroes" when the drums begin to roll.

We aren't no thin red 'eroes, nor we aren't no blackguards too,
But single men in barricks, most remarkable like you;
An' if sometimes our conduck isn't all your fancy paints,
Why, single men in barricks don't grow into plaster saints;
While it's Tommy this, an' Tommy that, an' "Tommy, fall be'ind",
But it's "Please to walk in front, sir", when there's trouble in the
    wind,
There's trouble in the wind, my boys, there's trouble in the wind,

O it's "Please to walk in front, sir", when there's trouble in the
  wind.

You talk o' better food for us, an' schools, an' fires, an' all:
We'll wait for extry rations if you treat us rational.
Don't mess about the cook-room slops, but prove it to our face
The Widow's Uniform is not the soldier-man's disgrace.
For it's Tommy this, an' Tommy that, an' "Chuck him out, the
  brute!"
But it's "Savior of 'is country" when the guns begin to shoot;
An it's Tommy this, an' Tommy that, an' anything you please;
An' Tommy ain't a bloomin' fool — you bet that Tommy sees!

RUDYARD KIPLING
ENGLISH (1865–1936)

A Dead Statesman

I could not dig: I dared not rob:
Therefore I lied to please the mob.
Now all my lies are proved untrue
And I must face the men I slew.
What tale shall serve me here among
Mine angry and defrauded young?

RUDYARD KIPLING
ENGLISH (1865–1936)

Channel Firing

That night your great guns, unawares,
Shook all our coffins as we lay,
And broke the chancel window-squares,
We thought it was the Judgment-day

And sat upright. While drearisome
Arose the howl of wakened hounds:
The mouse let fall the altar-crumb,
The worms drew back into the mounds,

PUBLIC
MOMENTS
AND
ULTIMATE
MATTERS
430

The glebe cow drooled. Till God called, 'No;
It's gunnery practice out at sea
Just as before you went below;
The world is as it used to be:

'All nations striving strong to make
Red war yet redder. Mad as hatters
They do no more for Christès sake
Than you who are helpless in such matters.

'That this is not the judgment-hour
For some of them's a blessed thing,
For if it were they'd have to scour
Hell's floor for so much threatening . . .

'Ha, ha. It will be warmer when
I blow the trumpet (if indeed
I ever do; for you are men,
And rest eternal sorely need).'

So down we lay again. 'I wonder,
Will the world ever saner be,'
Said one, 'than when He sent us under
In our indifferent century!'

And many a skeleton shook his head.
'Instead of preaching forty year,'
My neighbour Parson Thirdly said,
'I wish I had stuck to pipes and beer.'

Again the guns disturbed the hour,
Roaring their readiness to avenge,
As far inland as Stourton Tower,
And Camelot, and starlit Stonehenge.

THOMAS HARDY
ENGLISH (1840–1928)

In Flanders Fields

In Flanders fields the poppies blow
Between the crosses, row on row,
    That mark our place; and in the sky
    The larks, still bravely singing, fly
Scarce heard amid the guns below.

We are the Dead. Short days ago
We lived, felt dawn, saw sunset glow,
    Loved and were loved, and now we lie
        In Flanders fields.

Take up our quarrel with the foe:
To you from failing hands we throw
    The torch; be yours to hold it high.
    If ye break faith with us who die
We shall not sleep, though poppies grow
        In Flanders fields.

JOHN McCRAE
CANADIAN (1872–1918)

Rain

Rain, midnight rain, nothing but the wild rain
On this bleak hut, and solitude, and me
Remembering again that I shall die
And neither hear the rain nor give it thanks
For washing me cleaner than I have been
Since I was born into this solitude.
Blessed are the dead that rain rains upon:
But here I pray that none whom once I loved
Is dying to-night or lying still awake
Solitary, listening to the rain,
Either in pain or thus in sympathy
Helpless among the living and the dead,

PUBLIC
MOMENTS
AND
ULTIMATE
MATTERS
432

Like a cold water among broken reeds,
Myriads of broken reeds all still and stiff,
Like me who have no love which this wild rain
Has not dissolved except the love of death,
If love it be for what is perfect and
Cannot, the tempest tells me, disappoint.

EDWARD THOMAS
ENGLISH (1878–1917)

An Irish Airman Foresees His Death

I know that I shall meet my fate
Somewhere among the clouds above;
Those that I fight I do not hate,
Those that I guard I do not love;
My country is Kiltartan Cross,
My countrymen Kiltartan's poor,
No likely end could bring them loss
Or leave them happier than before.
Nor law, nor duty bade me fight,
Nor public men, nor cheering crowds,
A lonely impulse of delight
Drove to this tumult in the clouds;
I balanced all, brought all to mind,
The years to come seemed waste of breath,
A waste of breath the years behind
In balance with this life, this death.

WILLIAM BUTLER YEATS
IRISH (1865–1939)

Strange Meeting

It seemed that out of battle I escaped
Down some profound dull tunnel, long since scooped
Through granites which titanic wars had groined.

Yet also there encumbered sleepers groaned,
Too fast in thought or death to be bestirred.
Then, as I probed them, one sprang up, and stared

With piteous recognition in fixed eyes,
Lifting distressful hands, as if to bless.
And by his smile, I knew that sullen hall, —
By his dead smile I knew we stood in Hell.
With a thousand pains that vision's face was grained;
Yet no blood reached there from the upper ground,
And no guns thumped, or down the flues made moan.
"Strange friend," I said, "here is no cause to mourn."
"None," said the other, "save the undone years,
The hopelessness. Whatever hope is yours,
Was my life also; I went hunting wild
After the wildest beauty in the world,
Which lies not calm in eyes, or braided hair,
But mocks the steady running of the hour,
And if it grieves, grieves richlier than here.
For by my glee might many men have laughed,
And of my weeping something had been left,
Which must die now. I mean the truth untold,
The pity of war, the pity war distilled.
Now men will go content with what we spoiled,
Or, discontent, boil bloody, and be spilled.
They will be swift with swiftness of the tigress.
None will break ranks, though nations trek from progress.
Courage was mine, and I had mystery,
Wisdom was mine, and I had mastery:
To miss the march of this retreating world
Into vain citadels that are not walled.
Then, when much blood had clogged their chariot-wheels,
I would go up and wash them from sweet wells,
Even with truths that lie too deep for taint.
I would have poured my spirit without stint

PUBLIC
MOMENTS
AND
ULTIMATE
MATTERS
434

But not through wounds; not on the cess of war.
Foreheads of men have bled where no wounds were.

"I am the enemy you killed, my friend.
I knew you in this dark: for so you frowned
Yesterday through me as you jabbed and killed.
I parried; but my hands were loath and cold.
Let us sleep now . . ."

WILFRED OWEN
ENGLISH (1893–1918)

There died a myriad

There died a myriad,
And of the best, among them,
For an old bitch gone in the teeth,
For a botched civilization,

Charm, smiling at the good mouth,
Quick eyes gone under earth's lid,

For two gross of broken statues,
For a few thousand battered books.

EZRA POUND
AMERICAN (1885–1972)

There Will Come Soft Rains

(War Time)

There will come soft rains and the smell of the ground,
And swallows circling with their shimmering sound;

And frogs in the pools singing at night,
And wild plum-trees in tremulous white;

Robins will wear their feathery fire
Whistling their whims on a low fence-wire;

And not one will know of the war, not one
Will care at last when it is done.

Not one would mind, neither bird nor tree
If mankind perished utterly;

And Spring herself, when she woke at dawn,
Would scarcely know that we were gone.

SARA TEASDALE
AMERICAN (1884–1933)

plato told

> plato told
>
> him:he couldn't
> believe it(jesus
>
> told him;he
> wouldn't believe
> it)lao
>
> tsze
> certainly told
> him,and general
> (yes
>
> mam)
> sherman;
> and even
> (believe it
> or
>
> not)you
> told him:i told
> him;we told him
> (he didn't believe it,no

PUBLIC
MOMENTS
AND
ULTIMATE
MATTERS
436

sir)it took
a nipponized bit of
the old sixth

avenue
el;in the top of his head:to tell

him

E. E. CUMMINGS
AMERICAN (1894–1962)

What Did I Learn in the Wars

What did I learn in the wars:
To march in time to swinging arms and legs
Like pumps pumping an empty well.

To march in a row and be alone in the middle,
To dig into pillows, featherbeds, the body of a beloved woman,
And to yell "Mama," when she cannot hear,
And to yell "God," when I don't believe in Him,
And even if I did believe in Him
I wouldn't have told Him about the war
As you don't tell a child about grown-ups' horrors.

What else did I learn. I learned to reserve a path for retreat.
In foreign lands I rent a room in a hotel
Near the airport or railroad station.
And even in wedding halls
Always to watch the little door
With the "Exit" sign in red letters.

A battle too begins
Like rhythmical drums for dancing and ends
With a "retreat at dawn." Forbidden love
And battle, the two of them sometimes end like this.

But above all I learned the wisdom of camouflage,
Not to stand out, not to be recognized,

Not to be apart from what's around me,
Even not from my beloved.

Let them think I am a bush or a lamb,
A tree, a shadow of a tree,
A doubt, a shadow of a doubt,
A living hedge, a dead stone,
A house, a corner of a house.

If I were a prophet I would have dimmed the glow of the vision
And darkened my faith with black paper
And covered the magic with nets.

And when my time comes, I shall don the camouflage garb of
  my end:
The white of clouds and a lot of sky blue
And stars that have no end.

YEHUDA AMICHAI
HEBREW (1924–2000)
TRANSLATED BY BENJAMIN HARSHAV AND BARBARA HARSHAV

FROM THE AMERICAN STORY

On the Prospect of Planting Arts and Learning in America

The Muse, disgusted at an Age and Clime
     Barren of every glorious Theme,
In distant Lands now waits a better Time,
     Producing Subjects worthy Fame:

In happy Climes, where from the genial Sun
     And virgin Earth such Scenes ensue,
The Force of Art by Nature seems outdone,
     And fancied Beauties by the true:

In happy Climes the Seat of Innocence,
     Where Nature guides and Virtue rules,

PUBLIC
MOMENTS
AND
ULTIMATE
MATTERS
438

Where Men shall not impose for Truth and Sense
    The Pedantry of Courts and Schools:

There shall be sung another golden Age,
    The rise of Empire and of Arts,
The Good and Great inspiring epic Rage,
    The wisest Heads and noblest Hearts.

Not such as *Europe* breeds in her decay;
    Such as she bred when fresh and young,
When heav'nly Flame did animate her Clay,
    By future Poets shall be sung.

Westward the Course of Empire takes its Way;
    The four first Acts already past,
A fifth shall close the Drama with the Day;
    Time's noblest offspring is the last.

GEORGE BERKELEY
IRISH (1685–1753)

Paul Revere's Ride

Listen, my children, and you shall hear
Of the midnight ride of Paul Revere,
On the eighteenth of April, in Seventy-five;
Hardly a man is now alive
Who remembers that famous day and year.

He said to his friend, "If the British march
By land or sea from the town tonight,
Hang a lantern aloft in the belfry arch
Of the North Church tower as a signal light, —
One, if by land, and two, if by sea;
And I on the opposite shore will be,
Ready to ride and spread the alarm
Through every Middlesex village and farm,
For the country folk to be up and to arm."

Then he said, "Good night!" and with muffled oar
Silently rowed to the Charlestown shore,
Just as the moon rose over the bay,
Where swinging wide at her moorings lay
The *Somerset*, British man-of-war;
A phantom ship, with each mast and spar
Across the moon like a prison bar,
And a huge black hulk, that was magnified
By its own reflection in the tide.

Meanwhile, his friend through alley and street
Wanders and watches, with eager ears,
Till in the silence around him he hears
The muster of men at the barrack door,
The sound of arms, and the tramp of feet,
And the measured tread of the grenadiers,
Marching down to their boats on the shore.

Then he climbed the tower of the Old North Church,
By the wooden stairs, with stealthy tread,
To the belfry-chamber overhead,
And startled the pigeons from their perch
On the sombre rafters, that round him made
Masses and moving shapes of shade, —
By the trembling ladder, steep and tall,
To the highest window in the wall,
Where he paused to listen and look down
A moment on the roofs of the town
And the moonlight flowing over all.

Beneath, in the churchyard, lay the dead,
In their night-encampment on the hill,
Wrapped in silence so deep and still
That he could hear, like a sentinel's tread,
The watchful night-wind, as it went
Creeping along from tent to tent,
And seeming to whisper, "All is well!"
A moment only he feels the spell

PUBLIC
MOMENTS
AND
ULTIMATE
MATTERS
440

Of the place and the hour, and the secret dread
Of the lonely belfry and the dead;
For suddenly all his thoughts are bent
On a shadowy something far away,
Where the river widens to meet the bay, —
A line of black that bends and floats
On the rising tide, like a bridge of boats.

Meanwhile, impatient to mount and ride,
Booted and spurred, with a heavy stride
On the opposite shore walked Paul Revere.
Now he patted his horse's side,
Now gazed at the landscape far and near,
Then, impetuous, stamped the earth,
And turned and tightened his saddle girth;
But mostly he watched with eager search
The belfry's tower of the Old North Church,
As it rose above the graves on the hill,
Lonely and spectral and sombre and still.
And lo! as he looks, on the belfry height
A glimmer, and then a gleam of light!
He springs to the saddle, the bridle he turns,
But lingers and gazes, till full on his sight
A second lamp in the belfry burns!

A hurry of hoofs in a village street,
A shape in the moonlight, a bulk in the dark,
And beneath, from the pebbles, in passing, a spark
Struck out by a steed flying fearless and fleet;
That was all! And yet, through the gloom and the light,
The fate of a nation was riding that night;
And the spark struck out by that steed, in his flight,
Kindled the land into flame with its heat.
He has left the village and mounted the steep,
And beneath him, tranquil and broad and deep,
Is the Mystic, meeting the ocean tides;
And under the alders that skirt its edge,
Now soft on the sand, now loud on the ledge,
Is heard the tramp of his steed as he rides.

It was twelve by the village clock,
When he crossed the bridge into Medford town.
He heard the crowing of the cock,
And the barking of the farmer's dog,
And he felt the damp of the river fog,
That rises after the sun goes down.

It was one by the village clock,
When he galloped into Lexington.
He saw the gilded weathercock
Swim in the moonlight as he passed,
And the meeting-house windows, blank and bare,
Gaze at him with a spectral glare,
As if they already stood aghast
At the bloody work they would look upon.

It was two by the village clock,
When he came to the bridge in Concord town.
He heard the bleating of the flock,
And the twitter of birds among the trees,
And felt the breath of the morning breeze
Blowing over the meadows brown.

And one was safe and asleep in his bed
Who at the bridge would be first to fall,
Who that day would be lying dead,
Pierced by a British musket-ball.

You know the rest. In books you have read,
How the British Regulars fired and fled, —
How the farmers gave them ball for ball,
From behind each fence and farmyard wall,
Chasing the redcoats down the lane,
Then crossing the fields to emerge again
Under the trees at the turn of the road,
And only pausing to fire and load.
So through the night rode Paul Revere;
And so through the night went his cry of alarm
To every Middlesex village and farm, —

PUBLIC
MOMENTS
AND
ULTIMATE
MATTERS
442

A cry of defiance, and not of fear,
A voice in the darkness, a knock at the door,
And a word that shall echo for evermore!
For, borne on the night-wind of the Past,
Through all our history, to the last,
In the hour of darkness and peril and need,
The people will waken and listen to hear
The hurrying hoof-beats of that steed,
And the midnight message of Paul Revere.

HENRY WADSWORTH LONGFELLOW
AMERICAN (1807–1882)

Concord Hymn

Sung at the completion of the Battle Monument, 4 July 1837
By the rude bridge that arched the flood,
    Their flag to April's breeze unfurled,
Here once the embattled farmers stood
    And fired the shot heard round the world.

The foe long since in silence slept;
    Alike the conqueror silent sleeps;
And Time the ruined bridge has swept
    Down the dark stream which seaward creeps.

On this green bank, by this soft stream,
    We set today, a votive stone;
That memory may their deed redeem,
    When, like our sires, our sons are gone.

Spirit, that made those heroes dare
    To die, and leave their children free,
Bid Time and Nature gently spare
    The shaft we raise to them and thee.

RALPH WALDO EMERSON
AMERICAN (1803–1882)

Old Ironsides

Ay, tear her tattered ensign down!
Long has it waved on high,
And many an eye has danced to see
That banner in the sky;
Beneath it rung the battle shout,
And burst the cannon's roar; —
The meteor of the ocean air
Shall sweep the clouds no more!

Her deck, once red with heroes' blood
Where knelt the vanquished foe,
When winds were hurrying o'er the flood
And waves were white below,
No more shall feel the victor's tread,
Or know the conquered knee; —
The harpies of the shore shall pluck
The eagle of the sea!

O better that her shattered hulk
Should sink beneath the wave;
Her thunders shook the mighty deep,
And there should be her grave;
Nail to the mast her holy flag,
Set every thread-bare sail,
And give her to the god of storms, —
The lightning and the gale!

OLIVER WENDELL HOLMES
AMERICAN (1809–1894)

Once to every man and nation comes the moment to decide

Once to every man and nation comes the moment to decide,
In the strife of Truth with Falsehood, for the good or evil side;
Some great cause, God's new Messiah, offering each the bloom or
blight,
Parts the goats upon the left hand, and the sheep upon the right,
And the choice goes by for ever 'twixt that darkness and that
light.

PUBLIC
MOMENTS
AND
ULTIMATE
MATTERS
444 |

Hast thou chosen, O my people, on whose party thou shalt
    stand,
Ere the Doom from its worn sandals shakes the dust against our
    land?
Though the cause of Evil prosper, yet 't is Truth alone is strong,
And, albeit she wander outcast now, I see around her throng
Troops of beautiful, tall angels, to enshield her from all wrong.

Backward look across the ages and the beacon-moments see,
That, like peaks of some sunk continent, jut through Oblivion's
    sea;
Not an ear in court or market for the low foreboding cry
Of those Crises, God's stern winnowers, from whose feet earth's
    chaff must fly;
Never shows the choice momentous till the judgment hath
    passed by.

Careless seems the great Avenger; history's pages but record
One death-grapple in the darkness 'twixt old systems and the
    Word;
Truth for ever on the scaffold, Wrong for ever on the throne, —
Yet that scaffold sways the future, and, behind the dim unknown,
Standeth God within the shadow, keeping watch above his own.

We see dimly in the Present what is small and what is great,
Slow of faith how weak an arm may turn the iron helm of fate,
But the soul is still oracular; amid the market's din,
List the ominous stern whisper from the Delphic cave within, —
"They enslave their children's children who make compromise
    with sin."

JAMES RUSSELL LOWELL
AMERICAN (1819–1891)

Mine eyes have seen the glory of the coming of the Lord:
He is trampling out the vintage where the grapes of wrath are
    stored;
He hath loosed the fateful lightning of his terrible swift sword:
      His truth is marching on.

I have seen Him in the watch-fires of a hundred circling camps;
They have builded Him an altar in the evening dews and damps;
I can read his righteous sentence by the dim and flaring lamps.
      His day is marching on.

I have read a fiery gospel, writ in burnished rows of steel:
"As ye deal with my contemners, so with you my grace shall deal;
Let the Hero, born of woman, crush the serpent with his heel,
      Since God is marching on."

He has sounded forth the trumpet that shall never call retreat;
He is sifting out the hearts of men before his judgment-seat:
Oh! be swift, my soul, to answer Him! be jubilant, my feet!
      Our God is marching on.

In the beauty of the lilies Christ was born across the sea,
With a glory in his bosom that transfigures you and me:
As he died to make men holy, let us die to make men free,
      While God is marching on.

JULIA WARD HOWE
AMERICAN (1819–1910)

Shiloh

A Requiem (April, 1862)
    Skimming lightly, wheeling still,
      The swallows fly low
    Over the field in clouded days,
      The forest-field of Shiloh —
    Over the field where April rain
    Solaced the parched ones stretched in pain

PUBLIC
MOMENTS
AND
ULTIMATE
MATTERS
446

Through the pause of night
That followed the Sunday fight
    Around the church of Shiloh —
The church so lone, the log-built one,
That echoed to many a parting groan
    And natural prayer
    Of dying foemen mingled there —
Foemen at morn, but friends at eve —
    Fame or country least their care:
(What like a bullet can undeceive!)
    But now they lie low,
While over them the swallows skim,
    And all is hushed at Shiloh.

HERMAN MELVILLE
AMERICAN (1819–1891)

The House-top

A Night Piece (July, 1863)

No sleep. The sultriness pervades the air
And binds the brain — a dense oppression, such
As tawny tigers feel in matted shades,
Vexing their blood and making apt for ravage.
Beneath the stars the roofy desert spreads
Vacant as Libya. All is hushed near by.
Yet fitfully from far breaks a mixed surf
Of muffled sound, the Atheist roar of riot.
Yonder, where parching Sirius set in drought,
Balefully glares red Arson — there — and there.
The Town is taken by its rats — ship-rats
And rats of the wharves. All civil charms
And priestly spells which late held hearts in awe —
Fear-bound, subjected to a better sway
Than sway of self; these like a dream dissolve,
And man rebounds whole aeons back in nature.
Hail to the low dull rumble, dull and dead,
And ponderous drag that shakes the wall.
Wise Draco comes, deep in the midnight roll
Of black artillery; he comes, though late;

In code corroborating Calvin's creed
And cynic tyrannies of honest kings;
He comes, nor parlies; and the Town, redeemed,
Gives thanks devout; nor, being thankful, heeds
The grimy slur on the Republic's faith implied,
Which holds that Man is naturally good,
And — more — is Nature's Roman, never to be scourged.

HERMAN MELVILLE
AMERICAN (1819–1891)

The Colored Soldiers

If the muse were mine to tempt it
  And my feeble voice were strong,
If my tongue were trained to measures,
  I would sing a stirring song.
I would sing a song heroic
  Of those noble sons of Ham,
Of the gallant colored soldiers
  Who fought for Uncle Sam!

In the early days you scorned them,
  And with many a flip and flout
Said "These battles are the white man's,
  And the whites will fight them out."
Up the hills you fought and faltered,
  In the vales you strove and bled,
While your ears still heard the thunder
  Of the foes' advancing tread.

Then distress fell on the nation,
  And the flag was drooping low;
Should the dust pollute your banner?
  No! the nation shouted, No!
So when War, in savage triumph,
  Spread abroad his funeral pall —
Then you called the colored soldiers,
  And they answered to your call.

PUBLIC
MOMENTS
AND
ULTIMATE
MATTERS
448

And like hounds unleashed and eager
　For the life blood of the prey,
Sprung they forth and bore them bravely
　In the thickest of the fray.
And where'er the fight was hottest,
　Where the bullets fastest fell,
There they pressed unblanched and fearless
　At the very mouth of hell.

Ah, they rallied to the standard
　To uphold it by their might;
None were stronger in the labors,
　None were braver in the fight.
From the blazing breach of Wagner
　To the plains of Olustee,
They were foremost in the fight
　Of the battles of the free.

And at Pillow! God have mercy
　On the deeds committed there,
And the souls of those poor victims
　Sent to Thee without a prayer.
Let the fulness of Thy pity
　O'er the hot wrought spirits sway
Of the gallant colored soldiers
　Who fell fighting on that day!

Yes, the Blacks enjoy their freedom,
　And they won it dearly, too;
For the life blood of their thousands
　Did the southern fields bedew.
In the darkness of their bondage,
　In the depths of slavery's night,
Their muskets flashed the dawning,
　And they fought their way to light.

They were comrades then and brothers,
　Are they more or less to-day?
They were good to stop a bullet

And to front the fearful fray.
They were citizens and soldiers,
  When rebellion raised its head;
And the traits that made them worthy, —
  Ah! those virtues are not dead.

They have shared your nightly vigils,
  They have shared your daily toil;
And their blood with yours commingling
  Has enriched the Southern soil.
They have slept and marched and suffered
  'Neath the same dark skies as you,
They have met as fierce a foeman,
  And have been as brave and true.

And their deeds shall find a record
  In the registry of Fame;
For their blood has cleansed completely
  Every blot of Slavery's shame.
So all honor and all glory
  To those noble sons of Ham —
The gallant colored soldiers
  Who fought for Uncle Sam!

PAUL LAURENCE DUNBAR
AMERICAN (1872–1906)

Barbara Frietchie

Up from the meadows rich with corn,
Clear in the cool September morn,

The clustered spires of Frederick stand
Green-walled by the hills of Maryland.

Round about them orchards sweep,
Apple and peach tree fruited deep,

Fair as the garden of the Lord
To the eyes of the famished rebel horde,

PUBLIC
MOMENTS
AND
ULTIMATE
MATTERS
450

On that pleasant morn of the early fall
When Lee marched over the mountain-wall;

Over the mountains winding down,
Horse and foot, into Frederick town.

Forty flags with their silver stars,
Forty flags with their crimson bars,

Flapped in the morning wind: the sun
Of noon looked down, and saw not one.

Up rose old Barbara Frietchie then,
Bowed with her fourscore years and ten;

Bravest of all in Frederick town,
She took up the flag the men hauled down;

In her attic window the staff she set,
To show that one heart was loyal yet.

Up the street came the rebel tread,
Stonewall Jackson riding ahead.

Under his slouched hat left and right
He glanced; the old flag met his sight.

"Halt!" — the dust-brown ranks stood fast.
"Fire!" — out blazed the rifle-blast.

It shivered the window, pane and sash;
It rent the banner with seam and gash.

Quick as it fell, from the broken staff
Dame Barbara snatched the silken scarf.

She leaned far out on the window-sill,
And shook it forth with a royal will.

"Shoot, if you must, this old gray head,
But spare your country's flag," she said.

A shade of sadness, a blush of shame,
Over the face of the leader came;

The nobler nature within him stirred
To life at that woman's deed and word;

"Who touches a hair of yon gray head
Dies like a dog! March on!" he said.

All day long through Frederick street
Sounded the tread of marching feet:

All day long that free flag tossed
Over the heads of the rebel host.

Ever its torn folds rose and fell
On the loyal winds that loved it well;

And through the hill-gaps sunset light
Shone over it with a warm good-night.

Barbara Frietchie's work is o'er,
And the Rebel rides on his raids no more.

Honor to her! and let a tear
Fall, for her sake, on Stonewall's bier.

Over Barbara Frietchie's grave,
Flag of Freedom and Union, wave!

Peace and order and beauty draw
Round thy symbol of light and law;

And ever the stars above look down
On thy stars below in Frederick town!

JOHN GREENLEAF WHITTIER
AMERICAN (1807–1892)

PUBLIC
MOMENTS
AND
ULTIMATE
MATTERS

452

Vigil Strange I Kept on the Field One Night

Vigil strange I kept on the field one night;

When you my son and my comrade dropt at my side that day,

One look I but gave which your dear eyes return'd with a look I
  shall never forget,

One touch of your hand to mine O boy, reach'd up as you lay on
  the ground,

Then onward I sped in the battle, the even-contested battle,

Till late in the night reliev'd to the place at last again I made my
  way,

Found you in death so cold dear comrade, found your body son
  of responding kisses, (never again on earth responding,)

Bared your face in the starlight, curious the scene, cool blew the
  moderate night-wind,

Long there and then in vigil I stood, dimly around me the battlefield spreading,

Vigil wondrous and vigil sweet there in the fragrant silent night,

But not a tear fell, not even a long-drawn sigh, long, long I gazed,

Then on the earth partially reclining sat by your side leaning my
  chin in my hands,

Passing sweet hours, immortal and mystic hours with you dearest
  comrade — not a tear, not a word,

Vigil of silence, love and death, vigil for you my son and my
  soldier,

As onward silently stars aloft, eastward new ones upward stole,

Vigil final for you brave boy, (I could not save you, swift was
  your death,

I faithfully loved you and cared for you living, I think we shall
  surely meet again,)

Till at latest lingering of the night, indeed just as the dawn
  appear'd,

My comrade I wrapt in his blanket, envelop'd well his form,

Folded the blanket well, tucking it carefully over head and
  carefully under feet,

And there and then and bathed by the rising sun, my son in his
  grave, in his rude-dug grave I deposited,

Ending my vigil strange with that, vigil of night and battlefield
  dim,

Vigil for boy of responding kisses, (never again on earth
    responding,)
Vigil for comrade swiftly slain, vigil I never forget, how as day
    brighten'd,
I rose from the chill ground and folded my soldier well in his
    blanket,
And buried him where he fell.

WALT WHITMAN
AMERICAN (1819–1892)

Reconciliation

Word over all, beautiful as the sky,
Beautiful that war and all its deeds of carnage must in time be
    utterly lost,
That the hands of the sisters Death and Night incessantly softly
    wash again, and ever again, this soil'd world;
For my enemy is dead, a man divine as myself is dead,
I look where he lies white-faced and still in the coffin — I draw
    near,
Bend down and touch lightly with my lips the white face in
    the coffin.

WALT WHITMAN
AMERICAN (1819–1892)

Many Thousand Gone

No more auction block for me,
No more, no more;
No more auction block for me,
Many thousand gone.

No more peck o' corn for me,
No more, no more;
No more peck o' corn for me,
Many thousand gone,

No more driver's lash for me,
No more, no more;

PUBLIC
MOMENTS
AND
ULTIMATE
MATTERS
454

No more driver's lash for me,
Many thousand gone.

No more pint o' salt for me,
No more, no more;
No more pint o' salt for me,
Many thousand gone.

No more hundred lash for me,
No more, no more;
No more hundred lash for me,
Many thousand gone.

No more mistress' call for me,
No more, no more;
No more mistress' call for me,
Many thousand gone.

ANONYMOUS SPIRITUAL
AMERICAN

The Blue and the Gray

By the flow of the inland river,
 Whence the fleets of iron have fled,
Where the blades of the grave-grass quiver,
 Asleep are the ranks of the dead:
  Under the sod and the dew,
   Waiting the Judgment Day:
  Under the one, the Blue,
   Under the other, the Gray.

These in the robings of glory,
 Those in the gloom of defeat,
All with the battle-blood gory,
 In the dusk of eternity meet:
  Under the sod and the dew,
   Waiting the Judgment Day:
  Under the laurel, the Blue,
   Under the willow, the Gray.

From the silence of sorrowful hours
   The desolate mourners go,
Lovingly laden with flowers
   Alike for the friend and the foe:
      Under the sod and the dew,
         Waiting the Judgment Day:
      Under the roses, the Blue,
         Under the lilies, the Gray.

So with an equal splendor,
   The morning sunrays fall,
With a touch impartially tender,
   On the blossoms blooming for all:
      Under the sod and the dew,
         Waiting the Judgment Day:
      Broidered with gold, the Blue,
         Mellowed with gold, the Gray.

So, when the summer calleth,
   On forest and field of grain,
With an equal murmur falleth
   The cooling drip of the rain:
      Under the sod and the dew,
         Waiting the Judgment Day:
      Wet with the rain, the Blue.
         Wet with the rain, the Gray.

Sadly, but not with upbraiding,
   The generous deed was done,
In the storm of the years that are fading
   No braver battle was won:
      Under the sod and the dew,
         Waiting the Judgment Day:
      Under the blossoms, the Blue,
         Under the garlands, the Gray.

No more shall the war-cry sever,
   Or the winding rivers be red;

PUBLIC
MOMENTS
AND
ULTIMATE
MATTERS
456

They banish our anger forever
   When they laurel the graves of our dead!
    Under the sod and the dew,
      Waiting the Judgment Day:
   Love and tears for the Blue,
     Tears and love for the Gray.

FRANCIS MILES FINCH
AMERICAN (1827–1907)

The Fury of Aerial Bombardment

You would think the fury of aerial bombardment
Would rouse God to relent; the infinite spaces
Are still silent. He looks on shock-pried faces.
History, even, does not know what is meant.

You would feel that after so many centuries
God would give man to repent; yet he can kill
As Cain could, but with multitudinous will,
No farther advanced than in his ancient furies.

Was man made stupid to see his own stupidity?
Is God by definition indifferent, beyond us all?
Is the eternal truth man's fighting soul
Wherein the Beast ravens in its own avidity?

Of Van Wettering I speak, and Averill,
Names on a list, whose faces I do not recall
But they are gone to early death, who late in school
Distinguished the belt feed lever from the belt holding pawl.

RICHARD EBERHART
AMERICAN (B. 1904)

A Box Comes Home

I remember the United States of America
As a flag-draped box with Arthur in it
And six marines to bear it on their shoulders.

I wonder how someone once came to remember
The Empire of the East and the Empire of the West.
As an urn maybe delivered by chariot.

You could bring Germany back on a shield once
And France in a plume. England, I suppose,
Kept coming back a long time as a letter.

Once I saw Arthur dressed as the United States
Of America. Now I see the United States
Of America as Arthur in a flag-sealed domino.

And I would pray more good of Arthur
Than I can wholly believe. I would pray
An agreement with the United States of America

To equal Arthur's living as it equals his dying
At the red-taped grave in Woodmere
By the rain and oakleaves on the domino.

JOHN CIARDI
AMERICAN (1916–1986)

GOD

Each inmost piece in me is thine

From *Psalm 139*

Each inmost piece in me is thine:
    While yet I in my mother dwelt
      All that me clad
      From thee I had.
    Thou in my frame hast strangely dealt:
Needs in my praise thy works must shine
    So inly them my thoughts have felt.

PUBLIC
MOMENTS
AND
ULTIMATE
MATTERS
458 |

Thou, how my back was beam-wise laid,
  And raftering of my ribs, dost know:
    Know'st every point
    Of bone and joint,
  How to this whole these parts did grow,
In brave embroid'ry fair arrayed,
  Though wrought in shop both dark and low.

Nay fashionless, ere form I took,
  Thy all and more beholding eye
    My shapeless shape
    Could not escape:
  All these time framed successively
Ere one had being, in the book
  Of thy foresight enrolled did lie.

My God, how I these studies prize,
  That do thy hidden workings show!
    Whose sum is such,
    No sum so much:
  Nay summ'd as sand they sumless grow.
I lie to sleep, from sleep I rise,
  Yet still in thought with thee I go.

MARY HERBERT, COUNTESS OF PEMBROKE
ENGLISH (1561–1621)

I Look for You

I look for you early,
my rock and my refuge,
        offering you worship
    morning and night;
before your vastness
I come confused
      and afraid for you to see
  the thoughts of my heart.

What could the heart
and tongue compose,

or spirit's strength
within me to suit you?
But song soothes you
and so I'll give praise
to your being as long
as your breath-in-me moves.

SOLOMON IBN GABIROL
HEBREW/SPANISH (C. 1022–C. 1070)
TRANSLATED BY PETER COLE

Song of the Soul That Is Glad to Know God by Faith

How well I know that fountain's rushing flow
Although by night

Its deathless spring is hidden. Even so
Full well I guess from whence its sources flow
Though it be night.

Its origin (since it has none) none knows:
But that all origin from it arose
Although by night.

I know there is no other thing so fair
And earth and heaven drink refreshment there
Although by night.

Full well I know its depth no man can sound
And that no ford to cross it can be found
Though it be night.

Its clarity unclouded still shall be:
Out of it comes the light by which we see
Though it be night.

Flush with its banks the stream so proudly swells;
I know it waters nations, heavens, and hells
Though it be night.

PUBLIC
MOMENTS
AND
ULTIMATE
MATTERS
460

The current that is nourished by this source
I know to be omnipotent in force
Although by night.

From source and current a new current swells
Which neither of the other twain excels
Though it be night.

The eternal source hides in the Living Bread
That we with life eternal may be fed
Though it be night.

Here to all creatures it is crying, hark!
That they should drink their fill though in the dark,
For it is night.

This living fount which is to me so dear
Within the bread of life I see it clear
Though it be night.

ST. JOHN OF THE CROSS
SPANISH (1542–1591)
TRANSLATED BY ROY CAMPBELL

Hail holy light, ofspring of Heav'n first-born

From *Paradise Lost*

Hail holy light, ofspring of Heav'n first-born,
Or of th' Eternal Coeternal beam
May I express thee unblam'd? since God is light,
And never but in unapproachèd light
Dwelt from Eternitie, dwelt then in thee,
Bright effluence of bright essence increate.
Or hear'st thou rather pure Ethereal stream,
Whose Fountain who shall tell? before the Sun,
Before the Heavens thou wert, and at the voice
Of God, as with a Mantle didst invest
The rising world of waters dark and deep,
Won from the void and formless infinite.
Thee I re-visit now with bolder wing,

Escap't the Stygian Pool, though long detain'd
In that obscure sojourn, while in my flight
Through utter and through middle darkness borne
With other notes then to th' Orphean Lyre
I sung of Chaos and Eternal Night,
Taught by the heav'nly Muse to venture down
The dark descent, and up to reascend,
Though hard and rare: thee I revisit safe,
And feel thy sovran vital Lamp; but thou
Revisit'st not these eyes, that rowle in vain
To find thy piercing ray, and find no dawn;
So thick a drop serene hath quencht thir Orbs,
Or dim suffusion veild. Yet not the more
Cease I to wander where the Muses haunt
Cleer Spring, or shadie Grove, or Sunnie Hill,
Smit with the love of sacred song; but chief
Thee *Sion* and the flowrie Brooks beneath
That wash thy hallowd feet, and warbling flow,
Nightly I visit: nor somtimes forget
Those other two equal'd with me in Fate,
So were I equal'd with them in renown.
Blind Thamyris and blind Mæonides,
And Tiresias and Phineus Prophets old.
Then feed on thoughts, that voluntarie move
Harmonious numbers; as the wakeful Bird
Sings darkling, and in shadiest Covert hid
Tunes her nocturnal Note. Thus with the Year
Seasons return, but not to me returns
Day, or the sweet approach of Ev'n or Morn,
Or sight of vernal bloom, or Summers Rose,
Or flocks, or herds, or human face divine;
But cloud in stead, and ever-during dark
Surrounds me, from the chearful waies of men
Cut off, and for the Book of knowledg fair
Presented with a Universal blanc
Of Natures works to mee expung'd and ras'd,

PUBLIC
MOMENTS
AND
ULTIMATE
MATTERS
462

And wisdome at one entrance quite shut out.
So much the rather thou Celestial light
Shine inward, and the mind through all her powers
Irradiate, there plant eyes, all mist from thence
Purge and disperse, that I may see and tell
Of things invisible to mortal sight.

JOHN MILTON
ENGLISH (1608–1674)

The World

I saw Eternity the other night
Like a great *Ring* of pure and endless light,
   All calm, as it was bright,
And round beneath it, Time in hours, days, years
    Driv'n by the spheres
Like a vast shadow mov'd, in which the world
   And all her train were hurl'd;
The doting lover in his quaintest strain
    Did there complain,
Near him his lute, his fancy, and his flights,
    Wit's sour delights,
With gloves and knots, the silly snares of pleasure;
    Yet his dear treasure
All scattered lay, while he his eyes did pore
    Upon a flower.

The darksome statesman, hung with weights and woe,
Like a thick midnight-fog moved there so slow
   He did not stay, nor go;
Condemning thoughts (like sad eclipses) scowl
    Upon his soul,
And clouds of crying witnesses without
   Pursued him with one shout.
Yet digged the mole, and lest his ways be found
    Worked underground,
Where he did clutch his prey, but one did see
    That policy;

Churches and altars fed him, perjuries
    Were gnats and flies,
It rained about him blood and tears, but he
    Drank them as free.

The fearful miser on a heap of rust
Sat pining all his life there, did scarce trust
   His own hands with the dust,
Yet would not place one piece above, but lives
    In fear of thieves.
Thousand there were as frantic as himself
   And hugged each one his pelf,
The downright Epicure placed heaven in sense
    And scorned pretence
While others, slipped into a wide excess,
    Said little less;
The weaker sort slight, trivial wares enslave
    Who think them brave,
And poor, despisèd Truth sat counting by
    Their victory.

Yet some, who all this while did weep and sing,
And sing, and weep, soared up into the *Ring*,
   But most would use no wing.
'O fools' (said I) 'thus to prefer dark night
    Before true light,
To live in grots, and caves, and hate the day
   Because it shows the way,
The way which from this dead and dark abode
    Leads up to God,
A way where you might tread the sun, and be
    More bright than he.'
But as I did their madness so discuss
    One whispered thus:
'This Ring the Bridegroom did for none provide
    But for his bride.'

HENRY VAUGHAN
ENGLISH (1622–1695)

PUBLIC
MOMENTS
AND
ULTIMATE
MATTERS
464

Our God, Our Help in Ages Past

Our God, our help in ages past,
Our hope for years to come,
Our shelter from the stormy blast,
And our eternal home.

Under the shadow of thy throne
Thy saints have dwelt secure,
Sufficient is thine arm alone,
And our defense is sure.

Before the hills in order stood
Or earth received her frame,
From everlasting thou art God,
To endless years the same.

Thy word commands our flesh to dust,
"Return ye sons of men":
All nations rose from earth at first
And turn to earth again.

A thousand ages in thy sight
Are like an evening gone,
Short as the watch that ends the night
Before the rising sun.

The busy tribes of flesh and blood
With all their lives and cares
Are carried downwards by thy flood
And lost in following years.

Time like an ever-rolling stream
Bears all its sons away,
They fly forgotten as a dream
Dies at the op'ning day.

Like flow'ry fields the nations stand
Pleased with the morning light,

The flow'rs beneath the mower's hand
Lie withering ere 'tis night.

Our God our help in ages past,
Our hope for years to come,
Be thou our guard while troubles last,
And our eternal home.

ISAAC WATTS
ENGLISH (1674–1748)

Light Shining out of Darkness

God moves in a mysterious way
   His wonders to perform;
He plants His footsteps in the sea,
   And rides upon the storm.

Deep in unfathomable mines
   Of never failing skill
He treasures up His bright designs,
   And works His sovereign will.

Ye fearful saints, fresh courage take:
   The clouds ye so much dread
Are big with mercy, and shall break
   In blessings on your head.

Judge not the Lord by feeble sense,
   But trust Him for His grace;
Behind a frowning providence
   He hides a smiling face.

His purposes will ripen fast,
   Unfolding ev'ry hour;

PUBLIC
MOMENTS
AND
ULTIMATE
MATTERS
466

The bud may have a bitter taste,
But sweet will be the flow'r.

Blind unbelief is sure to err,
And scan His work in vain;
God is His own interpreter,
And He will make it plain.

WILLIAM COWPER
ENGLISH (1731–1800)

First-Day Thoughts

In calm and cool and silence, once again
I find my old accustomed place among
My brethren, where, perchance, no
human tongue
Shall utter words; where never hymn
is sung,
Nor deep-toned organ blown, nor censer
swung,
Nor dim light falling through the pictured
pane!
There, syllabled by silence, let me hear
The still small voice which reached the
prophet's ear;
Read in my heart a still diviner law
Than Israel's leader on his tables saw!
There let me strive with each besetting sin,
Recall my wandering fancies, and
restrain
The sore disquiet of a restless brain;
And, as the path of duty is made plain,
May grace be given that I may walk
therein,
Not like the hireling, for his selfish gain,
With backward glances and reluctant tread,
Making a merit of his coward dread,

But cheerful, in the light around me
    thrown,
Walking as one to pleasant service led;
   Doing God's will as if it were my own,
Yet trusting not in mine, but in His
    strength alone!

JOHN GREENLEAF WHITTIER
AMERICAN (1807–1892)

Lead, Kindly Light

Lead, kindly light, amid the encircling gloom,
    Lead thou me on;
The night is dark, and I am far from home;
    Lead thou me on.
Keep thou my feet; I do not ask to see
The distant scene: one step enough for me.

I was not ever thus, nor prayed that thou
    Shouldst lead me on;
I loved to choose and see my path; but now
    Lead thou me on.
I loved the garish day, and, spite of fears,
Pride ruled my will: remember not past years.

So long thy power hath blest me, sure it still
    Will lead me on
O'er moor and fen, o'er crag and torrent, till
    The night is gone,
And with the morn those angel faces smile
Which I have loved long since, and lost awhile.

JOHN HENRY NEWMAN
ENGLISH (1801–1890)

PUBLIC
MOMENTS
AND
ULTIMATE
MATTERS
468

Abide with Me

Abide with me; fast falls the eventide;
The darkness deepens; Lord, with me abide,
When other helpers fail, and comforts flee,
Help of the helpless, O abide with me.

Swift to its close ebbs out life's little day;
Earth's joys grow dim, its glories pass away;
Change and decay in all around I see:
O Thou who changest not, abide with me!

I need Thy presence every passing hour;
What but Thy grace can foil the tempter's power?
Who like Thyself my guide and stay can be?
Through cloud and sunshine, O abide with me.

I fear no foe, with Thee at hand to bless;
Ills have no weight, and tears no bitterness;
Where is death's sting? where, grave, thy victory?
I triumph still, if Thou abide with me.

Hold Thou Thy Cross before my closing eyes,
Shine through the gloom, and point me to the skies;
Heaven's morning breaks, and earth's vain shadows flee:
In life, in death, O Lord, abide with me!

HENRY FRANCIS LYTE
SCOTTISH (1793–1847)

God's Grandeur

The world is charged with the grandeur of God.
    It will flame out, like shining from shook foil;
    It gathers to a greatness, like the ooze of oil
Crushed. Why do men then now not reck his rod?
Generations have trod, have trod, have trod;
    And all is seared with trade; bleared, smeared with toil;
    And wears man's smudge and shares man's smell: the soil
Is bare now, nor can foot feel, being shod.

And for all this, nature is never spent;
    There lives the dearest freshness deep down things;
And though the last lights off the black West went
    Oh, morning, at the brown brink eastward, springs —
Because the Holy Ghost over the bent
    World broods with warm breast and with ah! bright
      wings.

GERARD MANLEY HOPKINS
ENGLISH (1844–1889)

The Creation

    And God stepped out on space,
    And he looked around and said:
    I'm lonely —
    I'll make me a world.

    And far as the eye of God could see
    Darkness covered everything,
    Blacker than a hundred midnights
    Down in a cypress swamp.

    Then God smiled,
    And the light broke,
    And the darkness rolled up on one side,
    And the light stood shining on the other,
    And God said: That's good!

    Then God reached out and took the light in his hands,
    And God rolled the light around in his hands
    Until he made the sun;
    And he set that sun a-blazing in the heavens.
    And the light that was left from making the sun
    God gathered it up in a shining ball
    And flung it against the darkness,
    Spangling the night with the moon and stars.
    Then down between
    The darkness and the light

PUBLIC
MOMENTS
AND
ULTIMATE
MATTERS
470 |

He hurled the world;
And God said: That's good!

Then God himself stepped down —
And the sun was on his right hand,
And the moon was on his left;
The stars were clustered about his head,
And the earth was under his feet.
And God walked, and where he trod
His footsteps hollowed the valleys out
And bulged the mountains up.

Then he stopped and looked and saw
That the earth was hot and barren.
So God stepped over to the edge of the world
And he spat out the seven seas —
He batted his eyes, and the lightnings flashed —
He clapped his hands, and the thunders rolled —
And the waters above the earth came down,
The cooling waters came down.

Then the green grass sprouted,
And the little red flowers blossomed,
The pine tree pointed his finger to the sky,
And the oak spread out his arms,
The lakes cuddled down in the hollows of the ground,
And the rivers ran down to the sea;
And God smiled again,
And the rainbow appeared,
And curled itself around his shoulder.

Then God raised his arm and he waved his hand
Over the sea and over the land,
And he said: Bring forth! Bring forth!
And quicker than God could drop his hand,
Fishes and fowls
And beasts and birds
Swam the rivers and the seas,
Roamed the forests and the woods,

And split the air with their wings.
And God said: That's good!

Then God walked around,
And God looked around
On all that he had made.
He looked at his sun,
And he looked at his moon,
And he looked at his little stars;
He looked on his world
With all its living things,
And God said: I'm lonely still.

Then God sat down —
On the side of a hill where he could think;
By a deep, wide river he sat down;
With his head in his hands,
God thought and thought,
Till he thought: I'll make me a man!

Up from the bed of the river
God scooped the clay;
And by the bank of the river
He kneeled him down,
And there the great God Almighty
Who lit the sun and fixed it in the sky,
Who flung the stars to the most far corner of the night,
Who rounded the earth in the middle of his hand;
This Great God,
Like a mammy bending over her baby,
Kneeled down in the dust
Toiling over a lump of clay
Till he shaped it in his own image;

Then into it he blew the breath of life,
And man became a living soul.
Amen.   Amen.

JAMES WELDON JOHNSON
AMERICAN (1871–1938)

PUBLIC
MOMENTS
AND
ULTIMATE
MATTERS

472

THE UNKNOWN AND THE UNKNOWABLE

To what shall I compare

To what shall I compare
This world?
To the white wake behind
A ship that has rowed away
At dawn!

THE PRIEST MANSEI
JAPANESE (C. 720)
TRANSLATED BY ARTHUR WALEY

Gazing Through the Night

Gazing through the
            night and its stars,

    or the grass and its bugs,

I know in my heart these swarms
are the craft of surpassing wisdom.

    Think: the skies
            resemble a tent,
        stretched taut by loops
and hooks;

and the moon with its stars,
    a shepherdess,
        on a meadow
            grazing her flock;

and the crescent hull in the looser clouds

    looks like a ship being tossed;

a whiter cloud, a girl
   in her garden
      tending her shrubs;

and the dew coming down is her sister
     shaking water
     from her hair onto the path;

as we
   settle in our lives,

like beasts in their ample stalls —

fleeing our terror of death,
  like a dove
    its hawk in flight —

though we'll lie in the end like a plate,
   hammered into dust and shards.

SHMUEL HA NAGID
HEBREW/SPANISH (993–1056)
TRANSLATED BY PETER COLE

Written at the Ise Shrine

Although I do not know
At all whether anything
Honorably deigns to be there,
Yet in extreme awe
My tears well forth.

SAIGYŌ
JAPANESE (1118–1190)
TRANSLATED BY ARTHUR WALEY

PUBLIC
MOMENTS
AND
ULTIMATE
MATTERS
474

The Rose

The rose has no "why," it blooms because it blooms.
It doesn't watch itself or wonder if anyone sees it.

ANGELUS SILESIUS
GERMAN (1624–1677)
TRANSLATED BY GEOFFREY O'BRIEN

The Fly

Little Fly,
Thy summers play
My thoughtless hand
Has brush'd away.

Am not I
A fly like thee?
Or art not thou
A man like me?

For I dance
And drink & sing:
Till some blind hand
Shall brush my wing.

If thought is life
And strength & breath,
And the want
Of thought is death;

Then am I
A happy fly,
If I live,
Or if I die.

WILLIAM BLAKE
ENGLISH (1757–1827)

Silence

There is a silence where hath been no sound,
  There is a silence where no sound may be,
  In the cold grave — under the deep deep sea,
Or in wide desert where no life is found,
Which hath been mute, and still must sleep profound;
  No voice is hush'd — no life treads silently,
  But clouds and cloudy shadows wander free,
That never spoke, over the idle ground:
But in green ruins, in the desolate walls
  Of antique palaces, where Man hath been,
Though the dun fox, or wild hyena, calls,
  And owls, that flit continually between,
Shriek to the echo, and the low winds moan,
There the true Silence is, self-conscious and alone.

THOMAS HOOD
ENGLISH (1799–1845)

Enosis

Thought is deeper than all speech,
  Feeling deeper than all thought;
Souls to souls can never teach
  What unto themselves was taught.

We are spirits clad in veils;
  Man by man was never seen;
All our deep communing fails
  To remove the shadowy screen.

Heart to heart was never known;
  Mind with mind did never meet;
We are columns left alone,
  Of a temple once complete.

Like the stars that gem the sky,
  Far apart, though seeming near,
In our light we scattered lie;
  All is thus but starlight here.

PUBLIC
MOMENTS
AND
ULTIMATE
MATTERS
476

What is social company
   But a babbling summer stream?
What our wise philosophy
   But the glancing of a dream?

Only when the sun of love
   Melts the scattered stars of thought;
Only when we live above
   What the dim-eyed world hath taught;

Only when our souls are fed
   By the Fount which gave them birth,
And by inspiration led,
   Which they never drew from earth,

We like parted drops of rain
   Swelling till they meet and run,
Shall be all absorbed again,
   Melting, flowing into one.

CHRISTOPHER CRANCH
AMERICAN (1813–1892)

Flower in the crannied wall

Flower in the crannied wall,
I pluck you out of the crannies,
I hold you here, root and all, in my hand,
Little flower — but if I could understand
What you are, root and all, and all in all,
I should know what God and man is.

ALFRED, LORD TENNYSON
ENGLISH (1809–1892)

When I Heard the Learn'd Astronomer

When I heard the learn'd astronomer,

When the proofs, the figures, were ranged in columns before me,

When I was shown the charts and diagrams, to add, divide, and
    measure them,

When I sitting heard the astronomer where he lectured with
    much applause in the lecture-room,

How soon unaccountable I became tired and sick,

Till rising and gliding out I wander'd off by myself,

In the mystical moist night-air, and from time to time,

Look'd up in perfect silence at the stars.

WALT WHITMAN
AMERICAN (1819–1892)

Four Trees — opon a solitary Acre

Four Trees — opon a solitary Acre —
Without Design
Or Order, or Apparent Action —
Maintain —

The Sun — opon a Morning meets them —
The Wind —
No nearer Neighbor — have they —
But God —

The Acre gives them — Place —
They — Him — Attention of Passer by —
Of Shadow, or of Squirrel, haply —
Or Boy —

What Deed is Their's unto the General Nature —
What Plan
They severally — retard — or further —
Unknown —

EMILY DICKINSON
AMERICAN (1830–1886)

PUBLIC
MOMENTS
AND
ULTIMATE
MATTERS
478

Magna Est Veritas

Here, in this little Bay,
Full of tumultuous life and great repose,
Where, twice a day,
The purposeless, glad ocean comes and goes,
Under high cliffs, and far from the huge town,
I sit me down.
For want of me the world's course will not fail:
When all its work is done, the lie shall rot;
The truth is great, and shall prevail,
When none cares whether it prevail or not.

COVENTRY PATMORE
ENGLISH (1823–1896)

A man said to the universe

A man said to the universe:
"Sir, I exist!"
"However," replied the universe,
"The fact has not created in me
"A sense of obligation."

STEPHEN CRANE
AMERICAN (1871–1900)

Buddha

As if he listened. Stillness: a distance . . .
We stop short and no longer hear it.
And he is a star. And other big stars,
that we don't see, are ranged about him.

Oh he is everything. Are we really waiting
for him to see us? Should he need to?

And even if we threw ourselves down before him
he would stay deep and hear himself like a dumb beast.

For what draws us to his feet
has been growing inside him for a million years.
He: who forgets what we experience
and experiences what is beyond us.

RAINER MARIA RILKE
GERMAN (1875–1926)
TRANSLATED BY GEOFFREY O'BRIEN

The Darkling Thrush

I leant upon a coppice gate
  When Frost was spectre-gray,
And Winter's dregs made desolate
  The weakening eye of day.
The tangled bine-stems scored the sky
  Like strings of broken lyres,
And all mankind that haunted nigh
  Had sought their household fires.

The land's sharp features seem'd to be
  The Century's corpse outleant,
His crypt the cloudy canopy,
  The wind his death-lament.
The ancient pulse of germ and birth
  Was shrunken hard and dry,
And every spirit upon earth
  Seem'd fervourless as I.

At once a voice arose among
  The bleak twigs overhead
In a full-hearted evensong
  Of joy illimited;
An aged thrush, frail, gaunt, and small,
  In blast-beruffled plume,
Had chosen thus to fling his soul
  Upon the growing gloom.

PUBLIC
MOMENTS
AND
ULTIMATE
MATTERS
480

So little cause for carollings
   Of such ecstatic sound
Was written on terrestrial things
   Afar or nigh around,
That I could think there trembled through
   His happy good-night air
Some blessèd Hope, whereof he knew
   And I was unaware.

THOMAS HARDY
ENGLISH (1840–1928)

The Unknown Bird

Three lovely notes he whistled, too soft to be heard
If others sang; but others never sang
In the great beech-wood all that May and June.
No one saw him: I alone could hear him
Though many listened. Was it but four years
Ago? or five? He never came again.

Oftenest when I heard him I was alone,
Nor could I ever make another hear.
La-la-la! he called, seeming far-off —
As if a cock crowed past the edge of the world,
As if the bird or I were in a dream.
Yet that he travelled through the trees and sometimes
Neared me, was plain, though somehow distant still
He sounded. All the proof is — I told men
What I had heard.

           I never knew a voice,
Man, beast, or bird, better than this. I told
The naturalists; but neither had they heard
Anything like the notes that did so haunt me
I had them clear by heart and have them still.
Four years, or five, have made no difference. Then
As now that La-la-la! was bodiless sweet:
Sad more than joyful it was, if I must say
That it was one or other, but if sad

'Twas sad only with joy too, too far off
For me to taste it. But I cannot tell
If truly never anything but fair
The days were when he sang, as now they seem.
This surely I know, that I who listened then,
Happy sometimes, sometimes suffering
A heavy body and a heavy heart,
Now straightway, if I think of it, become
Light as that bird wandering beyond my shore.

EDWARD THOMAS
ENGLISH (1878–1917)

Of Mere Being

The palm at the end of the mind,
Beyond the last thought, rises
In the bronze decor,

A gold-feathered bird
Sings in the palm, without human meaning,
Without human feeling, a foreign song.

You know then that it is not the reason
That makes us happy or unhappy.
The bird sings. Its feathers shine.

The palm stands on the edge of space.
The wind moves slowly in the branches.
The bird's fire-fangled feathers dangle down.

WALLACE STEVENS
AMERICAN (1879–1955)

Index

Title of poems are in *italics,* first lines in roman type. When the title and first line are the same, the poem is listed by first line.

Copyright Acknowledgments

About the Editor

Geoffrey O'Brien is a widely published poet, critic, editor, and cultural historian. He has been honored with a Whiting Award and fellowships from the Guggenheim Foundation and the New York Institute for the Humanities. A regular contributor to the *New York Review of Books,* he is the editor-in-chief of the Library of America. He lives in New York City.